Goals,

Priorities,

and Dollars

THE NEXT DECADE

Goals,

Priorities,

and

Dollars

THE NEXT DECADE

LEONARD A. LECHT
National Planning Association

THE FREE PRESS, *New York*
COLLIER-MACMILLAN LIMITED, *London*

Collier-Macmillan Canada, Ltd., Toronto, Ontario

Library of Congress Catalog Card Number 66-19798

ACKNOWLEDGMENTS

A study of so broad a scope is inevitably the product of the efforts of many persons. Many individuals in different organizations and agencies, private and public, have contributed ideas and source materials. The National Planning Association's *National Economic Projections Series,* in particular, has provided an important source for the general economic framework assumed in the study.

A research memorandum has been prepared for each goal by a consultant or a member of the Goals Project staff. The study has also benefited from the comments and suggestions of the persons who have acted as readers for the research memoranda. Their comments have contributed many ideas for improving the study. I have written the individual chapters drawing on the research memoranda and on other materials. Needless to say, the authors of the research memoranda are not responsible for the errors of omission and commission in the chapters.

The following individuals have participated in preparing the research memoranda or have served as readers:

Goal	Author of Research Memorandum	Reader
1. Consumer Expenditures and Savings	LEONARD A. LECHT Goals Project Staff	ELEANOR SNYDER Urban Medical Economics Research Project, New York City Department of Health
2. Private Plant and Equipment	LEONARD A. LECHT Goals Project Staff	GERHARD COLM Chief Economist, NPA
3. Urban Development	PETER WAGNER NPA	LEONARD FISCHMAN Economic Associates
4. Social Welfare	RAYMOND MUNTZ Social Security Department, AFL-CIO	SELMA MUSHKIN Council of State Governments
5. Health	HERBERT H. ROSENBERG Chief, Resources Analysis Branch, Office of Program Planning, National Institutes of Health	RASHI FEIN The Brookings Institution
6. Education	HAROLD WOLOZIN Department of Economics American University CHONG KEE PARK Goals Project Staff	ALICE RIVLIN The Brookings Institution
7. Transportation	LEONARD A. LECHT Goals Project Staff H. E. WEIHMILLER Consultant in Transportation and Aerospace Technology	WILFRED OWEN The Brookings Institution
8. National Defense	ELIOT S. ORTON Goals Project Staff	FRED MOORE The Rand Corporation
9. Housing	DAVID K. GILLOGLY Federal Housing Administration	JAY ATKINSON Assistant Chief, Current Business Section, Office of Business Economics, U.S. Department of Commerce

Goal	Author of Research Memorandum	Reader
10. Research and Development	MARSHALL HALL Department of Economics Washington University	SUMNER MYERS Director, R & D Utilization Project, NPA
11. Natural Resources	NEAL POTTER Resources for the Future	
12. International Aid	LEONARD A. LECHT Goals Project Staff RANBIR A. VARMA Department of Economics Long Island University	ROBERT E. ASHER The Brookings Institution
13. Space	H. E. WEIHMILLER Consultant in Transportation and Aerospace Technology	GEORGE L. SIMPSON Assistant Administrator, Policy Planning, NASA
14. Agriculture	ELIOT S. ORTON Goals Project Staff	ALVIN C. EGBERT, Head, Long Run Projections Section, Outlook and Projections, U.S. Department of Agriculture
15. Manpower Retraining	ELIOT S. ORTON Goals Project Staff	SAR LEVITAN Upjohn Institute
16. Area Redevelopment	ELIOT S. ORTON Goals Project Staff	SAR LEVITAN Upjohn Institute

Each of the chapters has been read by a member of the National Committee on America's Goals and Resources, the advisory committee for the Goals Project. The committee is composed of persons from business, labor, government, and academic life. They have served as a continuing advisory board from the initiation of the project to its conclusion. The encouragement and the ideas provided by the committee have played a major role in making it possible to undertake and to complete this project.

I am also indebted to the kindly and wise guidance of Gerhard Colm, Chief Economist of the National Planning Association, and to the generous support of John Miller, Assistant Chairman and Executive Secretary of the National Planning Association. Members of the Goals Project staff have contributed to this work in many ways. Eliot Orton drew on his experience in the NPA

Budget Study and in government service to prepare four of the research memoranda. Chong Kee Park supplied invaluable statistical competence and a familiarity with data and problems in education. Alaeddine S. Hreib has provided a high degree of competence as a research assistant. The work of typing the many drafts and memoranda has been ably performed by Mrs. Judith Mariassy and Miss Barbara Nash. And last, my wife deserves more than the usual gratitude for suffering through many a tedious evening while I labored in the throes of composition.

LEONARD A. LECHT

June, 1965

CONTENTS

TABLES AND CHARTS

On

Goals

Research

BY GERHARD COLM

We often hear the rhetorical question: Why should we go to the moon before conquering the common cold? Or we are asked: Why should vacuum cleaners for our homes be essential to our standard of living, but street cleaners an unfortunate expense? This is the way in which "the man (or woman) on the street"—or a Harvard professor—raises questions of national priorities.

The social sciences cannot give the final answer to these and similar questions. The answers emerge from the interplay of value judgments made by millions of people in the market place and through the political process. But research

can assist these millions of people in making better judgments by clarifying the issues and by providing information
about the likely consequences of the alternative decisions
that might be made. It is the task of goals research to clarify
such issues and to provide relevant information for people
in public and private life who must or wish to take a
position on such choices. The present book is a contribution of the National Planning Association to this field. It
is the purpose of this essay to place the subject of this book
in the broad perspective of goals research.

Thoughtful readers looking at a book on *Goals, Priorities,
and Dollars* may wonder how it is possible to deal objec-
tively with national goals. Are not attitudes toward national
goals very largely determined by the values and traditions
embedded in our culture? And, where a deliberate decision
has to be made in a pluralistic society, should not the choice
be left primarily to the judgment of individuals in accord-
ance with their interests and their consciences? A few decades
ago, I am sure, there would have been general doubt that
national goals could or should be a legitimate field for de-
tached research.

National goals could not become a subject of research before there had arisen a national goals consciousness and a
recognition that decision-makers needed help in the clarifica-
tion of goals and of the consequences of decisions to be made
concerning them.

EMERGENCE OF A NATIONAL GOALS CONSCIOUSNESS

In permissible simplification, we may distinguish four
phases in the evolution of a national goals consciousness.

1. In the first phase, national goals are not articulated as
such. Individuals try to find remunerative jobs; they strive
to better their standard of living; they grumble about mer-
chants who raise the prices of goods. Businessmen work to
make profits, improving their machinery and their methods

in order to gain in the competitive struggle. However, people interested in jobs, price stability, and business investments are not aware that they are pursuing national goals of full employment, price stability, and economic growth.

2. The second phase is characterized by a crisis. When the pursuit of individual and corporate interests becomes frustrated on a large scale, it becomes clear that more is involved than individual or corporate failure. Out of the experience of the Great Depression and the Second World War, full employment, price stability, economic growth, and international economic balance emerged as national goals. These were *performance goals* because they were related to the restoration of a desirable economic performance. The adoption of the Employment Act of 1946 can be regarded as the milestone symbolizing that the American people had become performance-goal conscious.

These goals are related to a satisfactory level and to the general character of economic activity; they are not concerned with the substance, the results of that activity.

3. In the third phase, we are concerned not only about whether our economic machinery is in smooth working condition, but also about what it produces. These concerns arose temporarily during the war emergency, when the question "guns or butter?" was asked. It was believed that, after the war, the concern for the type and quality of our production could safely revert to individual preferences expressed through demand in the market place and the conventional process of government policy formation. Again a crisis was necessary to make us aware of what may be called *achievement goals*. It had been taken for granted that, in a democratic society, not only economic performance but also education, research, and technological achievements were superior to achievements in any other type of society. This confidence was shaken by Soviet accomplishments, especially the orbiting of the Sputnik spacecraft in 1957. Competitive coexistence in this and other fields provided a challenge which compelled us to look critically at deficiencies in our

own achievements. Of course, there has been periodic dissatisfaction with the deficiencies in medical training and other aspects of education, and with poverty and especially with poor housing. But, for the first time, it was felt necessary to look at the achievement of Western society as a whole and at the allocation of resources as it is accomplished through the market and the political process.

4. In the second and third phases, it was the experience of failure and frustration which resulted in a reexamination of assumptions taken for granted, and in the birth of a new goals consciousness. The fourth phase is one in which, after controversy and debate, some general acceptance of these goals emerges and consensus is approached, at least to the extent of absence of significant opposition to the goals. In this phase, controversy centers more on the speed and the means with which to pursue the goals than on the goals themselves. It is also the phase in which the mutual relationship between performance goals, especially a desirable rate of growth, and achievement goals is recognized. I do not suggest that concern with education or health is something new. But what is characteristic of this phase of development is the recognition that the development of resources (economic growth) is desirable because it promotes achievement of the many goals we are pursuing. Equally characteristic of this phase is the recognition that pursuit of the goals, in such fields as education, research, industrial modernization, urban development, and so on, contributes to economic growth. At this phase it becomes urgent to study the mutual interrelationship between economic performance on the one side of the ledger, and the resources which are mobilized and utilized in pursuit of individual and collective goals on the other side. Various goals have a different impact on economic growth. Therefore, growth depends not only on the intensity of efforts in pursuit of goals but also on the combination of goals which is selected for pursuit through the public and private sectors of the economy.

In this phase, goals research becomes feasible because

some consensus is evolving about goals which are desired.
Goals research becomes required because choices need to be
made about priorities and combinations of goals and the
manner in which to pursue them. Here the need for scientific guidance arises. It is the phase which we have now
entered.

THE APPROACH TO
GOALS RESEARCH

Partly in response to the shock that the Soviet space
achievement brought to the American public, President
Eisenhower appointed a Commission on National Goals.
The report of that Commission, published in 1960, was significant in that a group of outstanding leaders from different
walks of life recognized the importance of a critical examination of our national goals, but no attempt was made to
evaluate what advances could and should be made with respect to these goals and what the costs would be either in
terms of dollars or of resources. Also, the compatibility of the
several goals and the relative priorities in pursuit of them
were not examined. Nonetheless, the work of the Eisenhower
Commission was very significant because it helped to articu-
late the rising concern for national goals. Many studies followed, concerned with individual goals, such as education,
health, research, and others. The National Planning Association recognized the need for providing information for
those concerned with the totality of, and the interrelation-
ships among, the national goals. It established a Center for
Priority Analysis in response to that need.

The present first study of the Center for Priority Analysis
deals with the economics of national goals. That means, it
deals with the resources utilized in the pursuit of the goals.
The economics of goals is only one of several aspects of goals
research, and even the economics of goals cannot be merely
economics. By their nature, goals are related to the basic
values of a society and in that respect reach beyond eco-

nomics. Economics is concerned with the development and use of resources and with the resources needed for accomplishing goals. This is, however, not the same as saying that we are concerned only with the means which serve given ends. For example, one of the resources involved is manpower. Manpower, however, is human beings, and work is a part of human life. Human beings and the quality of life are ends. Therefore, the manner in which human resources are used and the conditions under which managers and laborers work are means in one sense and ends in another.

We are dealing with the distribution of resources among various goals. But the manner by which the use of resources is determined (e.g., the freedom of individuals to choose among existing opportunities) is also a goal. Some functions must be determined and possibly performed by government, and some degree of compulsion and regulation is inevitable. These positive and negative values cannot be measured. When the economist in our culture speaks of the "dollar costs of national goals" he specifically assumes that he is working within the frame of a social system in which human self-determination is one of the major goals and in which some degree of compulsion is inevitable. He cannot measure to what extent the goal of human freedom and dignity is or is not accomplished. He also cannot measure to what extent respect for human freedom and dignity promotes or hinders achievements of other goals. But the fact that it cannot be measured does not mean that the goal of human freedom will be omitted from the economist's analysis. It enters as a restraint in the consideration of means to be selected in the pursuit of goals. In determining, for example, a feasible and desirable rate of growth, the degree of controls which will be needed should be considered.

Goals-consciousness does not mean that all deficiencies in goals will be or should be remedied by direct government action. The largest part of resources is allocated through the market mechanism by individuals—as consumers, as workers, as farmers, as managers of corporations, and so on. The result of the allocation of resources by the market and political processes can be and is observed and should be appraised. Achievements and deficiencies are noted. All over the country, groups of experts and citizens ask themselves such questions as: Does our educational system give us satisfactory results? Do we make necessary advances in physical and mental health? Do we provide the basic and applied research needed for technological progress? Are our homes and cities adequate by modern standards of living and transportation? Are we conquering poverty and eliminating race discrimination in our own country? Are we contributing adequately to the development of allied and friendly countries in other parts of the world? If there are serious deficiencies in achieving goals, how can the market mechanism be improved to remedy the deficiencies? What government action may be needed to remedy deficiencies in the market mechanism and to improve the performance in the public sector? These and similar questions regarding goals are raised and debated by many individuals and organizations throughout the United States. Goals research as conceived here would not provide the answers to these questions, but could contribute information for those seeking an answer.

SOME BASIC CONCEPTS

In the attempt to make goals amenable to research it is useful to introduce some distinguishing concepts. Of all performance goals, the most important is the rate of economic growth. Here we distinguish three interrelated sets of assumptions. First, it is possible to estimate the probable rate of growth that would result from continuation of *present policies* of Government and *present attitudes* of business, labor, and consumers. A present policy rate of growth might give us, for example, a rate of 3 per cent per annum or less for the United States. With continued increase in the labor force and productivity-raising technology (but present hours of work), this rate of growth would result in a rapid rise in the rate of unemployment and heavy cyclical fluctuations. A change in the attitudes of business and labor and in Government policies would certainly follow. To evaluate these changes, it is necessary to construct a second model of growth which would prevent a rise of unemployment, counteract recessions, make it possible to realize desirable objectives, but would not require drastic controls. This construction gives us the *target* rate of growth and a device for considering the change in policies and attitudes consistent with that target. Let us assume that we reach the conclusion that, considering all factors involved, a long-term rate of growth of 4-1/2 per cent should be the target. Now why is not the sky the limit for a target? Why 4-1/2 per cent, and not 6 or 8 per cent? The highest sustainable rate of growth compatible with other national objectives is believed to be 4-1/2 per cent. Aiming at a substantially higher rate of continuing growth would be likely to create conflicts between the goals of domestic growth and international balance of payments, or might necessitate Government controls not believed acceptable under peacetime conditions but deemed necessary in order to prevent bottlenecks and price rises. This is where the previously mentioned restraints become important.

The establishment of targets of economic performance is useful for a consideration of policies. The setting of targets, however, is not prediction. In order to make projections which may be needed as realistic benchmarks for the guidance of business decisions and many other purposes, we introduce as a third concept a *judgment* rate of growth. An estimate, in this case, is based on the assumption that policies and attitudes will change in the direction of the changes required by the targets. In reality, attitudes change only after some time has lapsed, and there will be slippages in the process of formulation, legislative adoption, and implementation of policy changes. To continue our numerical illustration we assume that the long-term judgment rate of growth in the United States will be somewhat above 4 per cent, which is less than the target rate but substantially more than the present-policy rate of growth.

We make similar distinctions with respect to achievement goals. The base estimate is again that of a continuation of the present condition, in this case the continuation of present standards in education, health, and so on, for determining the costs of goals. We assume, for example, that for each category of schools, costs per pupil remain the same. Corresponding estimates can be made for the other achievement goals. Total costs rise only because of increase in population, changes in the age and occupational distribution of the population, and movement of the population from rural to urban communities. Actually, a large part of the prospective increase in the production of goods and services is "preempted" by the need to provide for a growing and increasingly urbanized population.

Estimates of the *preempted* increase in production are significant because they are based on continuation of present political and individual preferences and take account mainly of the relatively predictable increase in population of various age groups, and of trends in geographic and occupational shifts in the population. The fact that a large part of the expected increase in the economic potential will be absorbed by rising use of resources for existing goals narrows the amount of resources which can be mobilized and utilized by future *discretionary* decisions about new goals or improved standards for existing goals.

The next step, also with respect to achievement goals, is the formulation of targets which reflect the need to provide for rising standards in addition to the rise and shift in population. The combination of the desired improvement in standards with the rise and changing distribution of population gives us the *aspiration goals*. These reflect what knowledgeable people regard as desirable achievement and what could be obtained if the specific goal under consideration were to have high priority. In other words, the estimate of aspiration goals does not allow for the fact that advocates of other goals may make claims for the same financial or real resources. These aspiration goals reflect the subjective judgment of knowledgeable people, but they are not arbitrary. They are regarded as realistic by people who are familiar with one particular field, but who do not consider the place a particular goal may have in the totality of goals.

A further step is needed to estimate *feasible priority combinations of goals*. This requires a reconciliation of the aspiration goals with projections of the judgment rate of growth. If the sum of aspiration goals exceeds the projected production total, priorities must be established. The decision-makers on priorities can best be served if they obtain information on alternative priority combinations which are internally consistent and consistent with the projected economic potential.

We have distinguished conceptually between performance and achievement goals as the two sides of an economic account (comparable to the distinction between sources and uses of funds). In this study we are directly concerned with the achievement goals. To repeat, what combination of achievement goals can be realized depends on the success in economic performance. Actually, there is a close interrelationship between the two kinds of goals. The economy will grow in a satisfactory manner only in the pursuit of national goals. Conversely, little progress in the direction of achieving our goals can be made if the economy fails to grow in a satisfactory manner.

The achievement goals include the goals of individuals and their families, the goals of businesses to modernize and expand their operations, the goals pursued through government programs at Federal, state, and local levels. Thereby it becomes possible to relate the resources in dollars or manpower required for each goal, and for all goals combined, to a total Economic Budget (total gross national product), or to a total manpower budget for the nation as a whole. This makes goals research operational.

QUALITY AND QUANTITY

The quantification of the costs of goals in a manner which makes them comparable with resource availabilities is essential for making goals research applicable. However, we cannot express qualities in quantities without losing something. While some such loss is unavoidable, the goals researcher and those using the findings of goals research must be fully aware of this limitation. I have already referred to the fact that ultimate goals such as human dignity and freedom enter quantitative goals research only as a restraint on policies (e.g., minimizing government regulation and controls). Goals research is not directly concerned with ultimate values but with the proximate values—such as national security, individual well-being, and cultural achievements—on which people can often agree who disagree on ultimate values.

There are goals in our civilization which have become goals only because we have to compensate for "costs" which are not measured in our usual cost accounting. Combating pollution of air and water, restoring scenic beauty, and providing for recreational facilities are activities that belong in this category. These are goals, costly goals in our society, even though of lesser need in less industrialized societies. The importance of these goals affects the comparability of costs of goals between countries of different culture.

Expressing the production of goods and services in terms of GNP also disregards certain qualities. With rising national income, consumers can buy more goods—this is reflected in GNP. But with rising ability to buy, the consumer also obtains a greater freedom of choice in the use of his income, which is a source of additional satisfaction (although sometimes also of a headache). On the other hand, our society compels the individual to spend money on socially prescribed clothing or on commuting, which may be items of not unqualified "enjoyment" and might better be treated as social costs rather than as fulfillment of goals. Nevertheless, in our system of national economic accounts (or national economic budgets), expenditures for these purposes are treated as consumption—and are thereby regarded as contributing to the achievement of goals.

Very important advances in quality of products or services escape statistical measurement. A substantial portion of the benefits of automation, for example, accrues to the consumer in terms not of lower costs, but of higher quality and of speedier service. It has been estimated that the improvement in the quality of goods and services corresponds to something like a 1 per cent hidden increase in the GNP per annum. Thus, when we refer to a 4 per cent per annum long-term increase (judgment model) in the measured supply of goods and services available for meeting our national goals, we may in reality refer to a yearly increase of 5 per cent in the ability to meet goals and in the costing of goals.

THE NATIONAL
PLANNING ASSOCIATION'S
COSTING OF GOALS

In the present study by Dr. Leonard Lecht for the Center for Priority Analysis, an estimate was prepared of the measurable dollar costs which would be involved in pursuing the aspirations for each of the achievement goals of the American economy. The aspiration goals were based on estimates prepared by experts for the various fields. Again, it should be emphasized that the study is not supposed to show the aspirations of these experts, nor those of the National Planning Association (NPA) advisory committee and staff, but what are, to the best of their judgment, the aspirations of "knowledgeable people" in the respective fields. After elimination of double counting, the costs for all these goals were summed up and compared with the total annual production of goods and services which could be expected to be available at that future time. Thereby, it became possible to compare these aspiration goals with resources expected to be available to meet them.

The result of this comparison supports two broad conclusions. First, substantial advances toward the achievement of these goals appear to be feasible. Second, not all aspirations for all goals can be met simultaneously within the given period of time.

The sum of all aspiration goals exceeds substantially what can be achieved even if a satisfactory performance of the economy is assumed. It follows that priority decisions need to be made for bringing aspirations and resources into balance. Does that mean that our experts are over-ambitious and should set their sights lower? I would not draw that conclusion at all. I believe that the experts should be ambitious for the fields with which they are concerned. They should set the sights too high rather than too low, but they should recognize that society has to reconcile goals and resources.

Every person with experience in government budget-making knows that devoted and imaginative bureau chiefs will always submit program proposals in excess of those which can be granted. This means, however, that a mechanism must exist for reconciling aspirations and resources. In Government proper, this function is performed by the Chief Executive, with the assistance of the Budget Bureau and the Cabinet, and by the Legislature.

Fifty years ago it became essential for a democracy such as the United States to develop a more meaningful budget system in order to enable the officials in the Executive and the Legislative branches of Government to base budget decisions on the best possible factual information and also to enable interested individuals to judge the wisdom of actions taken by the Government. This process of providing meaningful information for the decision-makers in Government is far advanced but by no means completed. We are today, with respect to decisions on national goals, where we were about fifty years ago in the development of government budgeting.

For national goals, the priority decisions are made by governmental processes and the market system. These actions involve every citizen, either as a decision-maker in public and private life or as a person who accepts these decisions or voices disagreement, thereby attempting to work toward changes in the future.

PERSPECTIVES IN GOALS RESEARCH

The estimates of the dollar costs of aspiration goals should be very useful for those who wish to form an opinion of the advances which can be made within the limits of available resources. We *can* go a good part of the way toward achieving the aspiration goals. However, these estimates also show the limits and the necessity for public and private decision-makers to adopt priorities in the pursuit of the goals. A necessary refinement consists in translating the dollar terms of the cost estimate into manpower requirements. This might show that, for certain goals, restraints from competing claims may become effective sooner than suggested by the dollar estimates. Work on estimating the manpower requirements for the various goals is in progress at the NPA Center for Priority Analysis.

In the present study, the costs of the goals have been added up, with adjustment only for overlapping and consequent double counting. However, the various goals are so related to each other that progress toward one goal facilitates the achievement of some of the others. In other cases, various goals compete for the same kind of manpower or other resources and, therefore, may conflict with each other. For example, up to a certain point, more adequate education and training of scientists or engineers would diminish the number of scientists and engineers immediately available for practical research work, because a longer period of education and training would be required, and a larger proportion of graduates would be absorbed by teaching rather than become available for practical work. Only in the longer run would more adequate education and training increase the quantity and quality of scientists and engineers available for research and development. Alternative combinations should therefore be presented both with a shorter and a longer time horizon. Priority analysis should aim at analyzing such relationships and presenting alternative, internally compatible packages of goals.

Thus, one function of goals research aims at trying out alternative priority combinations of goals that are compatible with each other and with the resources that can be activated in their pursuit. Another function of goals research is the study of the manner in which the forces in society are mobilized in pursuit of these goals. We said before that our society became goals-conscious through failure and frustration. However, a steady, less dramatic process seems to be evolving now in which goals are more rationally formulated and forces of society are mobilized for the realization of the goals. In our democratic society, which are the key positions for determination and realization of goals? What are the motivations of individuals in these key positions? To what extent are their actions based on relevant information, and to what extent on prejudice or obsolete knowledge? What kinds of information resulting from goals research should they have? These are some of the problems on which research has been initiated through other projects of the Center for Priority Analysis.

Considering these and many other questions it is clear that the present study is merely a first—though, I believe, significant—expedition into an uncharted territory. Some other studies have been initiated and will follow. Much more needs to be done. Even this first attempt at estimating the dollar costs of our aspiration goals should be regarded as the beginning of a continuing undertaking which will need to be redone and revised periodically. Our aspirations don't stand still. What is a gleam in the eye of some visionaries today may become a goal recognized by realistic and knowledgeable people tomorrow—and what is regarded as a goal today may become obsolete tomorrow. The establishment of the NPA Center for Priority Analysis and the publication of this book testify to the belief that goals research will have to play an important role in our dynamic democratic society.

CHAPTER 1

An Overall View

I.

Unprecedented prosperity for most Americans has gone hand in hand with a deep-seated concern that our resources are insufficient to support an expanding array of national objectives ranging from supplying schools and teachers for mushrooming enrollments to landing a man on the moon.

The core of the problem of matching resources and aspirations is the problem of priorities, of determining "what comes first." Priorities are the issue in President Johnson's recommendations that the Federal Government spend more than a billion dollars a year as a first step in eliminating poverty in the United States. They are the underlying problems in the decisions of private groups and business firms (e.g., in

Pittsburgh) to sponsor programs for rebuilding and revital-
izing the downtown core of their central cities. "What comes
first" is also the issue behind the statistic that almost a dozen
nations have lower infant mortality rates than the United
States.[1]

Where and how we assign priorities in a democracy is determined by political processes and by the decisions of firms,
unions, and consumers, rather than by experts or government
officials. Yet, research and analysis are essential if we are to
have the information which is necessary for intelligent
choices. Research can indicate what the attainment of our
objectives would probably cost if the individual goals were
considered separately, and what they would cost if they were
all pursued at the same time. Economic analysis can also
estimate whether our resources are likely to be adequate
for our aspirations. In the absence of such estimates, even
rough ones, we may attempt to pursue all the tasks which
appear desirable and overstrain our resources. Alternatively,
we may fail to utilize our resources for urgent tasks because
of fear that we cannot "afford" them.

These cost estimates and a discussion of their significance
provide the substance of this report. They are the result of
a two-year study of the cost of our nation's objectives by the
Goals Project of the National Planning Association's Center
for Priority Analysis. The materials incorporated in the study
generally reflect the information available before the last
part of 1964.

The overall findings of the report can be summed up as
follows:

1. Large increases in expenditures can be anticipated for
most of the individual goals in the 1970's. The largest dollar increases are listed for consumer expenditures, private
plant and equipment, urban development, social welfare,
health, and education.

2. The costs projected for full realization of all the goals

---

1. *Statistical Abstract*, 1963, pp. 910–911.

are estimated to exceed the gross national product anticipated in 1975 by approximately $150 billion, or 15 per cent of GNP.

3. The potential growth in GNP sets limits for the feasible targets for our goals. Within these limits, more vigorous pursuit of our objectives would raise the actual rate of GNP growth to a closer approximation to its potential.

II.

Concern with the high and rising cost of national objectives coexists with a widely held legend of economic omnipotence. The legend persists because it seemingly contains some truth. With 7 per cent of the world's land area, and 6 per cent of the globe's 3 billion inhabitants, our output accounts for about one third of the world's total industrial production.[2] A record of dramatically expanding production on short notice in two world wars, the absence of a major depression since the 1930's, plus the scientific advances symbolized by atomic energy, the computer, and space travel, make it appear credible that once we set our economic colossus to work, all our goals as a nation can be fulfilled. The impact of these beliefs is evident in the terms we sometimes use to describe ourselves, e.g., in phrases such as "the affluent society," or the "economy of abundance."

The weight of the evidence supporting the legend of omnipotence is offset by the pressures of unmet needs, and by new claimants for expenditure offering ample evidence of expanding their claims in the near future. With an anticipated seven tenths of the population concentrated in metropolitan areas by 1975, a recent study by the National Planning Association estimates the cost of transforming the nation's metropolitan centers into viable communities at some $2.1 trillion, representing both private and public ex-

---

2. Colm, G., and Geiger, T., *The Economy of the American People*, National Planning Association, 1961, p. 9.

penditures, spread over twenty years.[3] The social changes likely to result from the drive of the Negro population for equal rights indicate new perspectives in programs for education, slum clearance, social welfare, and retraining. The 1963 McGraw-Hill survey reported that one fifth of all the private industrial plant and equipment in the United States was outmoded. Slightly over half the productive capacity in the railroad industry was described as obsolete.[4] The primary cause for this obsolescence is massive spending for research and development, a new experience for America. With expenditures for the conduct of R & D tripling from $5 billion in 1953 to nearly $16 billion in 1962[5] (largely because of Federal expenditures for defense and the space effort), research and development has become, for the first time, a major claimant on the nation's resources.

In many other areas, the role of government in our economy has undergone a transformation in a single generation. The Federal Government's expenditures, measured by GNP, zoomed from 2.5 per cent in 1929 to over 19 per cent in 1963 and 1964. Less strikingly, expenditures by state and local governments rose from 7 per cent of GNP to nearly 11 per cent.[6]

Coupled with the apprehension over rising claims for expenditures are the doubts created by our inability to fully utilize our productive potential. The gap between actual output and the potential output the economy could have

3. Wagner, P., *The Cost and Financing of Urban Renewal and Development*, National Planning Association, 1963, p. 27.

4. McGraw-Hill Department of Economics, *16th Annual McGraw-Hill Survey, Business Plans for New Plant and Equipment*, McGraw-Hill Book Company, 1963, pp. 11, 12, Table X.

5. *Research Funds Used in the Nation's Scientific Endeavor, 1963*, National Science Foundation, May, 1965.

6. These estimates include some overlapping in expenditures by different levels of government. Eliminating this double counting, expenditures by all levels of government increased from over 9 per cent of GNP in 1929 to over 28 per cent in 1963 and 1964. *Annual Report of the Council of Economic Advisers*, January, 1965, p. 262.

produced with reasonably full use of manpower has been estimated at \$30 billion in 1962 and 1963 by the President's Council of Economic Advisers.[7] This sum is about equal to total expenditures for education or for housing in 1962.

The myth of omnipotence lingers on because we tend to focus our attention on individual goals which are considered as isolated instances. Many groups and agencies, public and private, are concerned with specific individual goals. Teachers' associations and government agencies publicize needs for expanding facilities and improving compensation in education. The Administration's "war on poverty" concentrates attention on the special needs of low-income or unemployed individuals. Daily contact with deteriorating or inadequate mass transit or highway congestion in our central cities thrusts the problems of urban development into a prominent place in our national consciousness. Similarly, the publicity surrounding achievements such as the GEMINI 4 "space walks" makes the nation aware of its commitment to a sustained space program.

Concentration on our society's objectives in terms of individual goals overlooks the fact that our objectives make up a system of competing claims on resources. We could well afford the cost of any single goal at levels reflecting current aspirations, and we could probably afford the full cost for any group of goals over the next decade. We could rebuild our cities, or abolish poverty, or replace all the obsolete plant and equipment in private industry, or we could begin to develop the hardware to get us to Mars and back before the year 2000. We can make substantial progress on many of the nation's goals, and very probably some progress on others, but we cannot accomplish all of our aspirations at the same time. Collectively, their costs would exceed the economy's capacity for supplying resources, and they are likely to exceed it by large amounts, estimated at \$150 billion, or 15 per cent of GNP by 1975. Confronted with the need to make

---

7. *Annual Report of the Council of Economic Advisers,* January, 1964, p. 37.

sense of this system of steadily expanding claims, we face the options of increasing our resources, utilizing them more fully, and setting feasible targets for our objectives. And, if we are to do more than muddle through in mobilizing our resources to realize the many improvements in our society's performance which can be achieved, we face the underlying problem of planning in a democracy—of devising more effective public and private techniques for balancing resources and aspirations.

III.

In their broadest sense, the goals refer to the ends which have shaped our national tradition. At this level the considerations are essentially qualitative, related to the values of American society. They include, among other things, preserving the democratic process, building a peaceful world, enhancing the dignity and welfare of the individual, enlarging the area of freedom and opportunity, and encouraging the pursuit of knowledge.

At an individually more operational level, our objectives stem from traits in American character that have been apparent to observers from other countries since De Tocqueville. Emphasis on the good life here and now, or at least for one's children, a rough and ready equalitarianism, and a unique degree of mobility are the typical attributes singled out as critical in forming our objectives. These attributes reflect the culture of a dynamic and pragmatic society firmly committed to the idea of progress.

No price can be set on freedom nor can the cost of the good life meaningfully be expressed in dollars. Economic activities become involved with the broad qualitative values as the means for their realization. These means, in turn, constitute goals whose costs can be measured. To enhance the dignity and welfare of individuals in the metropolitan complexes which increasingly characterize America requires large private and public expenditures for housing, social welfare, and transportation. Also implied in this activity are substantial expenditures for parks, libraries, theaters, and museums, if the vast stretches of suburbia are not to grow into human deserts. Building a secure and open international society in the mid-twentieth century commits us to massive spending for defense, and to lesser expenditures to support international organizations and to assist the newly industrializing countries. Moreover, the vision of the good life held by most Americans includes, as an essential ingredient, high and rising standards of consumption, and it excludes the existence of a large substratum of families transmitting the culture of poverty from one generation to its successors.

All of us are involved with our society's goals as citizens, businessmen, or employees, and all of us have notions, more or less specific, of what our goals and priorities as a nation ought to be. As citizens, we are called upon to assess priorities in education by voting for or against bond issues or tax increases, or for candidates for local school boards. We are said to be a nation of joiners, and a host of voluntary organizations publicize, educate, and lobby for more spending to preserve parks and wilderness areas, or for mental health, or for a variety of other causes. The markets and earnings prospects of our business firms are influenced, often decisively, by the manner in which changes in national priorities affect spending for defense or space, or for the construction of highways, schools, and hospitals. Changes in the tempo of these programs create prospective "shortages" or "surpluses" of scientists and engineers or of personnel in other occupations.[8] And, with all levels of government spending $168 billion in 1963 and $176 billion in 1964, public and private decisions have become intertwined in a manner lacking precedent in earlier peacetime American history. The rate of

8. For a discussion of the relationship of national priorities to "shortages" of scientists and engineers, see Colm, G., and Lecht, L., "Requirements for Scientific and Engineering Manpower in the 1970's," in *Toward Better Utilization of Scientific and Engineering Talent,* Committee on Utilization of Scientific and Engineering Manpower, National Academy of Sciences, 1964.

unemployment, the volume of business investment, expenditures for residential construction, or the state of the nation's health are different from what they would otherwise be because of national objectives leading to public expenditures.

Concern with the nation's objectives is, of course, nothing new. What is new is our society's degree of concern with its purposes and with the directions in which we are moving. While this concern was probably most dramatically underscored by the impact of Sputnik, it is also evident in the numerous public and private bodies set up to study needs and purposes in education, health, social welfare, urban mass transit, and other areas. The same concern is present in the recent legislation to establish a national foundation for the arts and the humanities similar to the National Science Foundation. What is also new is the development of techniques of national income accounting, enabling us to prepare a balance sheet indicating the nation's probable resources on one side of the ledger and the claims on resources our objectives are likely to represent on the other.

President Eisenhower's Commission on National Goals represents a historical landmark in articulating this concern. The Commission's 1960 report, *Goals for Americans,* identified and discussed goals in 15 areas affecting most aspects of American life.[9] The Goals Project has taken the fifteen areas considered by the Goals Commission as a point of departure in making the transition from the qualitative values of American society to specific standards reflecting the thinking of the early and mid-1960's. Space was added as an additional goal after the late President Kennedy proposed in 1961 that it become a national objective "to put men on the moon and bring them back." This we interpret to mean the goal of embarking on a sustained space program.

The sixteen areas for which the costs of goals have been estimated in this study are

---

9. *Goals for Americans, The Report of the President's Commission on National Goals,* Prentice-Hall, 1960.

1. Consumer Expenditures and Savings
2. Private Plant and Equipment
3. Urban Development
4. Social Welfare
5. Health
6. Education
7. Transportation
8. National Defense
9. Housing
10. Research and Development
11. Natural Resources
12. International Aid
13. Space
14. Agriculture
15. Manpower Retraining
16. Area Redevelopment

Each of the goals has been investigated to formulate a quantitative standard reflecting the current trend of informed opinion in the United States. Some of the sixteen goals, e.g., consumer expenditures or housing, are concerned with general individual well-being. Others, such as manpower retraining, are directed at removing the adverse effects of economic change on groups of individuals. Still others, as in private plant and equipment, make their contributions by increasing the productive capacity available to provide additional output needed to pursue the other goals.

Listing goals and standards and estimating their cost presupposes an overall national consensus regarding the desirability of the goals. In part, this consensus grows out of the sharing of a common culture with a common body of values, such as an emphasis on individual freedom. In part, a consensus is present because many goals emerge out of changes which affect society generally. The need to avoid unleashing the destructive potential of nuclear warfare is an obvious instance. While a consensus exists, it is also apparent that it exists alongside many contrary and dissenting tendencies. Not all Americans are agreed that economic aid to the developing countries improves the nation's security, or that increasing teachers' salaries is essential to improve education. The consensus concept merely serves to point out the existence of deeply rooted and broadly shared tendencies in spelling out the national interest in selecting our objectives.

In a decentralized, pluralistic society such as our own, the mechanisms by which goals are defined and implemented are frequently obscure. Goals in a totalitarian society—Soviet Russia serves as an illustration—are unambiguously defined by a national authority and this definition has the force of law. The targets in the Soviet Five Year Plans, for example, have an imperative character. In a society such as our own, many groups, private and public, participate officially and unofficially in determining objectives and in implementing them. In major segments of the economy, the role of public authority is minimal—e.g., consumers determine the manner in which they spend their incomes. In some areas, as in national defense, public authority alone determines the standard and makes the decisions controlling expenditures. In others, such as urban renewal or the aid to dependent children programs, the Federal Government makes use of its expenditures to encourage private firms and municipalities to rebuild their central cities or to assist state governments in developing more adequate public assistance programs.

Furthermore, broad agreement on goals in the United States often goes hand in hand with considerable differences in opinion as to the programs for achieving particular goals, the speed with which they should be achieved, or the priorities to be given specific goals in relation to others. Thus, individuals equally committed to the objective of a sustained space research program may differ markedly in their opinion of the desirability of landing a man on the moon before 1970.

The goals framework is concerned with the relationship between our expenditures and our aspirations rather than with ultimate values or with the manner in which we, as a nation, arrive at decisions. From the perspective of society, expenditures for health or housing by consumers, for research and development by government, non-profit organizations, and industry, or for plant and equipment by firms, become means for facilitating the attainment of national purposes. Research and analysis in national priorities attempts to make our notions about national goals more specific and quantitative, to see them as a system, to estimate their cost, and to draw out their implications for American society.

I V .

The cost estimates for the goals refer to the economic framework anticipated in 1970 and 1975. The limiting factor in realizing our objectives in the next decade is likely to be a level of output expected to increase to $1 trillion by 1975. This increase assumes a GNP growing at a rate of about 4 per cent a year from 1962 to 1975 (measured in constant prices from the full capacity level of output in 1962).[10] All dollar estimates pertaining to the 1970's are in 1962 dollars.

The GNP projected for the 1970's and the other basic ingredients in this economic framework are summarized in Table 1–1.

Table 1–1
Estimated GNP, Population, and Family Personal Income,
1962, 1970 and 1975
(in 1962 dollars)

| | | YEAR | |
| Item | Actual | Projected | |
	1962	1970	1975
1. GNP (in billions)	$ 556[a]	$ 787	$ 981
2. Population (in millions)	187	209	226
3. Civilian Labor Force (in millions)	72	83	91
4. GNP per Person	$2,970[a]	$3,770	$ 4,340
5. Average Family Personal Income[b]	$7,260	$8,850	$10,100

a. Revisions of the national income and product accounts published by the Department of Commerce after the research for this study was completed would increase this estimate by something less than 1 per cent. See *Survey of Current Business,* August, 1965, Table 1, p. 25.
b. This estimate of average family personal income refers to consumer units—to families and unattached individuals. See *Survey of Current Business,* July, 1964, Table 17, p. 18.

---

10. More precisely, this growth rate is 4.1 per cent. Calculated from the actual level of output in 1962, this is the equivalent of 4.5 per cent annually from 1962 to 1975. However, the growth rate calculated from the actual level of output in 1962 would include the effects of recovery from an initial situation of underutilization of capacity as well as the long-term growth.

A 4-per cent annual rate of increase in GNP exceeds the historical rate for the past generation, which has averaged approximately 3 per cent a year. However, a 4-per cent growth rate, or one slightly higher, according to the late President Kennedy, is "well within our capability."[11] It is also in line with the full-employment target rate considered by the United States in discussions with the Organization for Economic Cooperation and Development. On an economy-wide basis, the productivity increases corresponding to this pace of growth, using GNP per manhour as an indicator, are expected to average around 3 per cent a year between 1962 and 1975.[12] Taking into account the anticipated increases in the labor force and in productivity, the volume of employment required to produce the near-trillion GNP in 1975 is consistent with an unemployment rate of 4 per cent of the civilian labor force.[13]

Extending the historical growth rate of about 3 per cent forward to 1975 yields a GNP of $810 billion in that year, or $170 billion less than the amount projected for the 4-per cent rate. If this level of growth were to characterize the economic history of the next decade, unemployment, according to NPA's *National Economic Projections Series,* would probably rise to 10 per cent of the labor force or somewhat higher by 1975.[14] Since mass unemployment and

11. *Annual Report of the Council of Economic Advisers,* January, 1962, p. 114.

12. More precisely, the annual rate is 3.1 per cent. This projected rate of increase in productivity, like the 4 per cent GNP growth rate, has been calculated from the full capacity level of output in 1962. Translating this estimate into a rate based on the actual level of output in 1962 yields an annual increase in GNP per manhour in the 1962–1975 period of 3.3 per cent. This compares with the 2.5 per cent a year typical of the 1957–1962 period. See *National Economic Projections Series, 1963,* National Planning Association, p. I–9.

13. This assumes an annual increase in the labor force of slightly more than 1.5 per cent, and an annual decline in hours worked of about 1 per cent per manyear.

14. With slow growth, GNP per manhour is also projected to increase more slowly—by an annual average rate of 2.8 per cent. This rate is calculated

slow growth in output would frustrate the attainment of the nation's aspirations in virtually every area, the 4-per cent rate, rather than the long-term growth rate, furnishes the basis for the economic framework of this report.

Otherwise, the study assumes that the trends characterizing American economic development since the end of World War II will essentially continue through 1975. The concentration of population in urban centers is expected to accelerate, with the most rapid urbanization projected to take place in the Southwest and the Far West. The movement of the Negro population away from the rural South to urban centers is also very likely to continue. The Negro population of 19 million in 1960 is expected to rise to 26 million by 1975 with the proportion living in cities projected to grow from 73 to 85 per cent in this period.[15] The problems of job opportunities, housing, and education associated with civil rights, long considered a southern problem, will become a national problem as the percentage of Negroes living in the South diminishes from slightly less than half of the Negro population in 1960 to approximately three eighths by 1975.

As urbanization proceeds, expanding metropolitan centers will merge to form a new social and economic unit—the megalopolis. The 500-mile stretch from Alexandria, Virginia, to Portsmouth, New Hampshire, including some 64 metropolitan communities, will constitute a northeastern megalopolis whose main outlines are already discernible. Other megalopolitan centers will form in the Chicago-Indiana-Wisconsin area, in the Dallas-Fort Worth area, in San Francisco Bay, and elsewhere. Problems of transportation, land and water use, and of recreation and housing will be common to all parts of these units and they are likely to intensify. At present there are virtually no political units whose scope is equivalent to the scope of these problems.

---

from the actual level of output in 1962. *National Economic Projections to 1974*, National Planning Association, 1964, p. 28.

15. *Regional Projection to 1976*, National Planning Association, 1962, pp. 17–18.

Technological change in the next decade can be expected to continue to increase the demand for skilled and highly educated manpower in many occupations, to make other job skills obsolete, and to perpetuate the highest unemployment rates among the unskilled and the poorly educated. Rising personal incomes are likely to add to the shift in demand for manpower from the unskilled an semiskilled workers in the goods-producing industries to the more highly trained and the professional workers in the service industries.[16] Larger public and private expenditures for health, education, research and development, or space will probably expand employment opportunities for scientists and many categories of engineers, for physicians and nurses, and for teachers at all levels of education. The largest decreases in employment in any single economic sector are projected for agriculture.

The percentage of women in this labor force is expected to increase only slightly, from somewhat under to something over one third of the total. Similarly, the length of the workweek is projected to decline only moderately. The 40.5 hours worked in the average workweek in 1962 and 1963 are estimated to fall to 38 by 1970 and to about 37 by 1975.[17] Hours worked per manyear are expected to decline at a more rapid pace as longer annual vacations and "sabbaticals" become standard for much of the work force. If, as some observers anticipate, productivity increases significantly exceed the growth in GNP per manhour assumed in this study, the impact of rapidly rising productivity for employment could be

16. Between 1963 and 1964, there was a resurgence of employment in the goods-producing industries. This was in contrast to the 1957–1962 period when employment in these industries declined by an average of 100,000 a year. Employment in the goods-producing industries in 1964 was 2 per cent higher than in 1963. However, employment in the service industries increased at a more rapid rate, by 3 per cent. See *Manpower Report of the President*, 1965, p. 10.

17. *National Economic Projections Series*, 1963, p. 1–22. This estimate represents a judgment concerning what is likely to happen to hours of work rather than reflecting a goal concerned with leisure.

expected to set up pressures to reduce hours of work by considerably more than the modest decreases projected in our economic framework.

The balance of countervailing power in the triad of business, labor, and government is unlikely to be disturbed in the next decade. The greater weight of white collar occupations will complicate the tasks of unions in maintaining their membership base. The network of collectively bargained health and welfare benefits and job protections will very probably expand as the focus of collective bargaining progressively shifts to the problems of adapting to the changing labor market requirements created by the new technology and by other economic changes.

On the international level, our study generally assumes that the tensions between the great powers will not increase to proportions substantially different from what they are at present. One of the standards for the defense goal is based on the expectation of a relaxation of tensions sufficient to encourage substantial arms reduction.

V.

Pursuit of national goals refers to the future—to the 1970's in the framework of this study. The problems and the possibilities they raise relate to a future in which both expenditures and resources can be expected to increase. The magnitudes involved in pursuing our objectives can be spelled out by comparing the current expenditures for each goal with the expenditures corresponding to two concepts referring to costs in the next decade. They are the costs listed for the "preempted benchmarks" in 1970 and 1975, and the expenditures projected for the "aspiration standards" in the same years.

The base year for the study is 1962, the most recent year for which fairly complete information has been available. The current level of costs, accordingly, refers to the actual expenditures in that year. The $32 billion spent for health and the $29 billion spent for housing in 1962 serve as illustrations. The increases in spending beyond the current levels of cost for the preempted benchmarks are primarily due to population increase, and they assume no improvement in the quality of our society's performance. The larger expenditures for the aspiration standards include the additional costs of expanding our objectives in transportation, housing, or for other purposes.

Again, with reference to 1962 as the base year, the increase in potential production, conventionally measured by GNP in constant prices, is expected to amount to some $425 billion a year by 1975, a growth from $556 billion in 1962 to $981 billion in 1975. The increase of over $400 billion in GNP may appear to be so enormous as to suggest that as a nation we could do whatever we thought desirable in the next ten years. However, between 1962 and 1975 the population is expected to grow by 39 million. There will be an estimated 13.5 million more families and over 11 million more pupils enrolled in school. Nineteen million more persons are likely to be in the civilian labor force. Without allowing for any improvement in standards of living, or standards of health or education, part of the potential increase in production will be absorbed to support the larger number of workers, to provide medical care for the additional families, or education for more pupils. The greater input of resources, just to keep ourselves where we are in terms of standards for the larger population in the 1970's, makes up the "treadmill" part of the preempted yardstick for expenditures in the future.

In 1962, expenditures for the 45 million pupils enrolled in elementary and secondary schools, and the 4 million in colleges and universities, amounted to $30 billion. Population growth is expected to raise these totals to 54 million students in elementary and secondary schools by 1975, and to 6.5 million in higher education. Providing the same quality of education as in 1962, with teachers' salaries, class sizes, and facilities per student at their 1962 levels, would mean raising spending for education in 1975 to almost $40 billion. Without any change in our standards of education, expenditures would increase by almost $10 billion.

The $1-trillion GNP anticipated for 1975 would be greater by 75 per cent than in 1962. To produce this large a volume of output would require far more productive capacity than in the early 1960's. Another part of the nation's resources, therefore, must be set aside to create the additional capacity for producing the greater output projected for the 1970's. Private outlays for plant and equipment in 1962 were $49 billion.[18] Producing the larger output expected in 1975 would involve estimated annual private capital outlays growing to $102 billion in that year, or a doubling of the 1962 levels. Like the inputs to maintain the *status quo* for the larger population in the 1970's, the resources used to create this additional productive capacity are included in the preempted benchmarks because they are not at the nation's disposal for upgrading standards for the sixteen goals. All told, the larger expenditures indicated for the preempted benchmarks are expected to absorb about half of the $425-billion potential increase in GNP.

The aspiration standards, the second of the concepts, refer to the standards defining the improvements for each goal. Typical examples are the cost of eliminating the substandard housing in central cities, or the expenditures necessary to support the 77,000 health research workers the National Institutes of Health estimate will be needed by 1970.[19] Of the $425-billion potential increase in national product by 1975, only the surplus remaining after allowing for the resources absorbed by the preempted benchmarks would be available for the additional costs involved in realizing the changes in our society's performance included in the aspiration standards.

The aspiration standards for the sixteen goals are dis-

18. *Survey of Current Business,* July, 1964, Tables 35 and 65, pp. 25, 33.
19. *Resources for Medical Research,* National Institutes of Health, 1963, p. 14.

cussed in detail in the chapters dealing with each goal. The improvements considered in the standard for education have been translated into ratios of teachers per 1,000 students, changes in compensation of faculty, and into estimates of the number of additional classrooms and laboratories needed for the greater percentage of the eligible age groups assumed to be attending school in the education goal. In health, the improvements have been similarly transformed into ratios of hospital beds per million population, and into medical care costs per person in the 65-and-over and in the less-than-65 age group. In housing, the inadequate housing to be replaced or rehabilitated has been identified with the classification of substandard dwelling units listed in the *U.S. Census of Housing.* These quantitative relationships make up the basis for the cost estimates in the report.

To reflect the trend in the consensus of informed opinion, the standards have been derived, wherever possible, from legislative enactments, the findings of expert studies, or the hearings and recommendations of public bodies. Typical instances are the recommendations for natural resources and energy research of the Federal Council for Science and Technology, or the cost of community mental health facilities based on the objectives in the Mental Health Centers Act of 1963, or the report to the Secretary of Labor by manpower experts indicating that changing labor market requirements will make it desirable to retrain 1 per cent of the labor force a year. Where there are widespread differences in informed opinion, as in agriculture, defense, international aid, or space, alternative standards are presented. In space, one standard assumes the present objective of landing a man on the moon by 1970. The alternative assigns a slower pace to the space program; it presupposes that the scientific and informational gains obtained from instrumented probing will be sufficient to delay the manned landing to the mid-1970's.

The cost projections for the standards are tentative estimates reflecting the current state of knowledge and opinion. The aspiration standards are intended as reasonable representations of current informed opinion, rather than as scientific judgments, technological necessities, or subjective preferences. While the standards and the cost estimates can hardly be expected to yield definitive answers to the many problems arising out of the cost of a growing list of national objectives, they can supply a basis for exploring the implications of programs which are likely to receive widespread consideration in the coming decade.

VI.

The three cost estimates for each goal are presented in Table 1–2. The estimates are listed in the order of the expenditures projected for the aspiration standards in 1975. They range from $660 billion for consumer expenditures to less than $1 billion for area redevelopment. Where there are alternative standards for the same goal, the more costly standard is included in the table.

All told, the gross expenditures for the sixteen goals add up to $1.5 trillion in 1975. On an average, the expenditures for the preempted benchmarks add one third to the 1962 expenditures in 1975. The spending listed for the aspiration standards in 1975 is typically two times the 1962 level.

The standards for three of the goals involve expenditures exceeding $100 billion by 1975. They are consumer expenditures, private plant and equipment, and urban development. All three are areas in which private spending makes up the predominant element in total expenditures. Social welfare, education, and defense are the goals expected to create the largest claims in the public economy. Consumer expenditures are by far the largest single item in the projections. Maintaining the 1962 living standards for the larger population anticipated in 1975 would raise consumer spending by over $100 billion as compared with 1962.[20] Raising levels of con-

---

20. This estimate also allows for the additional consumer expenditures likely to be generated as personal incomes rise because of changes in the occupational distribution of the labor force.

Table 1-2
Gross Expenditures for the Individual Goals, 1962, 1970 and 1975
(in millions of 1962 dollars)

Goal	Actual Expenditures in 1962	PROJECTED EXPENDITURES IN 1970		PROJECTED EXPENDITURES IN 1975	
		For Preempted Benchmarks	For Aspiration Standards	For Preempted Benchmarks	For Aspiration Standards
1. Consumer Expenditures and Savings	$356,750	$425,700	$ 532,600	$472,600	$ 659,600
2. Private Plant and Equipment	48,900	81,800	116,400	102,300	151,600
3. Urban Development	64,200	75,100	109,000	83,300	129,700
4. Social Welfare	38,250	49,400	74,850	55,450	92,400
5. Health	32,300	36,200	68,100	39,100	85,400
6. Education	29,700	38,000	65,900	39,700	82,100
7. Transportation	35,150	47,500	57,850	56,150	74,900
8. National Defense	51,450	45,900	59,550	39,050	67,550
9. Housing	29,400	33,200	49,900	36,300	62,000
10. Research and Development	16,850	23,850	32,150	29,700	38,850
11. Natural Resources	5,850	6,550	14,450	7,100	16,650
12. International Aid	5,400	3,100	9,800	3,100	12,250
13. Space	3,300	5,300	8,200	5,700	9,350
14. Agriculture	7,200	5,200	8,300	5,200	9,150
15. Manpower Retraining	100	400	2,450	400	2,850
16. Area Redevelopment	350	400	950	450	950
TOTAL GROSS COST	$725,150	$877,600	$1,210,450	$975,600	$1,495,300

sumption along the lines considered in the aspiration standard for consumer expenditures would add an additional $200 billion.

The cost estimates for the aspiration standards suggest probable areas of change in the claims of the different goals on resources in the next decade. The major changes are likely to concern education, health, private plant and equipment, defense, and agriculture. In the size of its expenditure, health currently occupies seventh place among the sixteen goals, and education occupies eighth place. By 1975, the spending anticipated by the standards in health and education shifts these two goals to the fifth and sixth place on the list. Similarly, private outlays for plant and equipment are expected to increase from fourth to second place in order of expenditure. In 1962, spending for national defense was exceeded only by consumer expenditures and by spending for the different facets of urban development. Projecting a continued expansion of defense capabilities through the incorporation of technological changes in weapons systems and the updating of conventional forces (the basis for the standard in Table 1–2), reduces defense spending to the eighth largest claim in 1975. With partial disarmament (the basis for the alternative standard in defense), spending for defense would fall to the tenth place. Agriculture, currently eleventh in order of expenditures, falls to fourteenth in the projections for the standards in 1975.

The increases in spending for the aspiration standards are summarized in Table 1–3 (page 38). The table lists the increases in spending projected for each goal and it classifies the goals on the basis of their estimated percentage increase in expenditure from 1962 to 1975.

The largest percentage increases in Table 1–3 are listed for manpower retraining and private plant and equipment. The percentage increase in manpower retraining is large because it reflects the growth of a new program just beginning in 1962. Consequently, only a small amount, approximately $100 million, was spent for retraining in that year. The standards for six of the goals list expenditures in 1975 which are greater than their 1962 equivalents by $50 billion or more. They are consumer expenditures, private plant and equipment, urban development, social welfare, health, and education.

Civil rights has not been investigated as a separate goal. The problems it poses cut across many goals, including consumer expenditures, education, health, housing, manpower retraining, and social welfare. Almost half of the nonwhites in the early 1960's were poor, i.e., with family incomes of less than $3,000. Employed adult nonwhites have typically completed fewer years of schooling than employed whites—

Table 1–3
Projected Increases in Spending for
Aspiration Standards,
1962 to 1975*

In 1975 Spending Projected to:	Percentage Increase in Spending 1962-1975	Amount of Increase in Spending 1962-1975 (in millions of 1962 dollars)
1. Less than double 1962 levels		
Agriculture	27%	$ 1,950
National Defense	31	16,100
Consumer Expenditures	85	302,850
2. Double 1962 levels or more		
Urban Development	102	65,500
Housing	111	32,600
Transportation	113	39,750
International Aid	127	6,850
Research and Development	131	22,000
Social Welfare	142	54,150
Health	164	53,100
Area Redevelopment	171	600
Education	176	52,400
Space	183	6,050
Natural Resources	185	10,800
3. Triple 1962 levels or more		
Private Plant and Equipment	210	102,700
Manpower Retraining	2,750	2,750

* Increases refer to expenditures for aspiration standards listed in Table 1-2.

an average of 9-1/2 years compared to 12. Infant mortality rates for nonwhites were twice as high as for whites, and life expectancy for nonwhite males at age 20 was almost 5 years less. Their unemployment rate from 1954 through 1964 was double the white average. Over two fifths of .nonwhite families have been living in substandard dwelling units.[21] While the largest group in the nonwhite population is made up of Negroes, very similar problems face the Puerto Ricans living in large cities, the Spanish-speaking population in the Southwest, and the Indians living on reservations. Probably the most important bearing of this study on civil rights is that the issue of civil rights involves all the nation's goals concerned with human welfare and manpower development. Substantial progress in attaining these goals is a necessary condition for reducing the far more than proportionate concentration of poverty, and social and physical ills in the nonwhite population.

VII.

The expenditures for the aspiration standards listed in Table 1–2 amount to $1.5 trillion in 1975. This estimate overstates the cost of the goals. The gross total obtained by adding up the expenditures for the 16 individual goals needs to be reduced because it contains overlapping and other double counting.

Spending by consumers for health and education, to cite instances, represents a large part of the costs for the health and education goals. It is also reckoned as part of the total for the consumer expenditures goal. Expenditures by business firms for trucks, automobiles, and airplanes are included in the estimates for the transportation goal. These expenditures also make up part of the capital outlays listed for pri-

21. See *Our Nonwhite Population and Its Housing,* Housing and Home Finance Agency, 1963, pp. 76–77; *Manpower Report of the President,* 1965, p. 197; *Annual Report of the Council of Economic Advisers,* January, 1964, p. 74.

vate plant and equipment. Such overlaps must be eliminated or the cost estimates would be inflated by reckoning the same item in the total more than once.

Eliminating the double counting reduces the cost estimates for the aspiration standards by about $370 billion in 1975. It also reduces the amounts listed for the preempted benchmarks, but by lesser amounts. The net cost of the goals, their cost after the double counting has been removed, is summed up in Table 1–4.

Table 1–4
Estimated Net Cost of the Goals, 1970 and 1975
(in billions of 1962 dollars)

	IN 1970		IN 1975	
Derivation of Net Cost	Preempted Benchmarks	Aspiration Standards	Preempted Benchmarks	Aspiration Standards
1. Total Gross Cost (from Table 1–2)	$878	$1,211	$976	$1,495
2. Minus Double Counting	190	304	206	368
3. Total Net Cost	688	907	770	1,127

After deducting the double counting, it would cost an anticipated $1.1 trillion to realize the aspiration standards for the sixteen goals in 1975. By 1975 the expenditures for the preempted benchmarks would increase to $770 billion.

Since the extent to which the nation can better its performance in transportation, urban renewal, health, and other areas depends on the increase in resources over the next decade, the strategic consideration in estimating our capacity for realizing our purposes is the growth in GNP anticipated in this period. Chart 1–1 describes the increase in gross national product which would occur if the 4-per cent annual growth rate assumed in the economic framework of the study were to materialize over the next ten years.

The part of the larger GNP listed for the 1970's which would be available for the improvements represented by the 16 goals is the part remaining after allowing for the greater absorption of resources to maintain existing standards of living, health, or housing for a population expected to increase from 187 million in 1962 to 226 million by 1975. The remainder must be further reduced to allow for the additional productive capacity needed to produce the $1-trillion 1975 GNP. The disposable gross national product available after making these deductions is indicated in Chart 1–2.

After allowing for the deductions, only a little more than one fifth of the 1975 GNP—$211 billion—would be available for the increases in consumption, teaching, research, and construction considered in the standards for that year. This amount is less than the increases in expenditures required for the improvements represented by our objectives. The additional spending they would involve is estimated to total $357 billion a year by the mid-1970's. This is the amount by

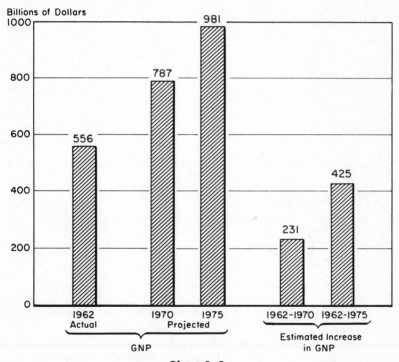

Chart 1–1
GNP, 1962, 1970 and 1975
(in 1962 dollars)

which the cost of the standards exceeds the expenditures listed for the preempted benchmarks—i.e., the amount by which the costs of the improvements add to the costs of extending the *status quo* in our society's performance for another decade, and of allowing for the additional productive capacity to produce the $1-trillion GNP. The net result is a deficit in gross national product of almost $150 billion in 1975. The corresponding deficit in 1970 is $120 billion. In both years, the deficit adds up to 15 per cent of GNP. The derivation of the estimates for the deficit is summarized in Chart 1–3.

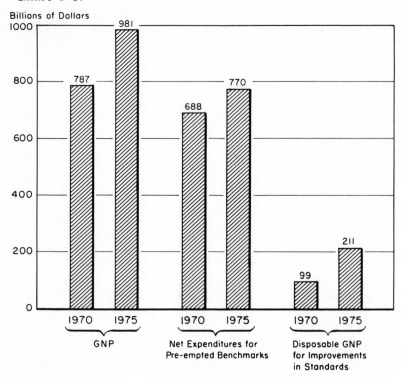

Chart 1–2
Estimated Disposable GNP for Standards, 1970 and 1975
(in 1962 dollars)

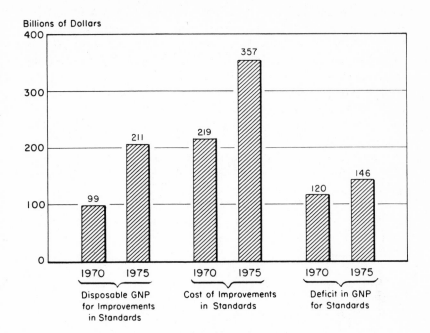

Chart 1–3
Estimated Deficit in GNP for Aspiration Standards,
1970 and 1975
(in 1962 dollars)

Creating sufficient output to realize the aspiration standards for the 16 goals would entail a GNP growth rate approaching 5.5 per cent a year between 1962 and 1975
(measured by GNP in constant prices from the full capacity
level of production in 1962). This compares with an increase in GNP averaging 3 per cent a year in the past generation and 3.5 per cent between 1948 and 1962. Sustaining
a 5.5 per cent annual growth rate for over a decade would
require technological changes leading to massive increases
in productivity, considerably beyond the 3-per cent growth
in GNP per manhour anticipated for the next 10 years.

Without a rapid acceleration in productivity, the alternatives for achieving "forced draft" growth to produce the additional output and the types of output needed to realize all sixteen goals could include a longer workweek, as well as price and wage controls to regulate the allocation of critical raw materials and manpower in "shortage" occupations. In the absence of major increases in productivity or far-reaching economic controls, the frustrations of inflation, balance of payments problems, and bottlenecks of critical resources would be the probable consequences of attempting to realize simultaneously all the aspirations which, considered by themselves, appear as reasonable or eminently desirable objectives. For these reasons, full achievement of the aspiration standards in the 1970's does not figure as a feasible alternative.[22]

The estimates of disposable resources and of the deficit for the goals illustrate the potentials and they underscore the problems inherent in the pursuit of our nation's objectives. In a growing economy these potentials are the greater prospects for serving human needs and national purposes. The disposable GNP of over $200 billion a year in the mid-1970's would enable our society to do far more than merely extend the *status quo* in education, in conserving our natural resources, in rebuilding our cities, and in other areas. The problems are when, how, and to what degree.

VIII.

What is the status of our estimates? They are, of necessity, frequently derived from rough projections. Since they relate to an unknown future, they are by their nature speculative. The trillion-dollar GNP, the $150-billion deficit for the

---

22. If all the increases in spending listed for the improvements in the aspiration standards were to materialize in 1975, they would set up successive rounds of spending which would increase GNP to more than the near-trillion dollars projected for that year. In the close-to-full employment economy assumed for the 1970's, the combined effect of these "multipliers" would result in a substantial price rise.

goals, or the assumed population growth and labor force figures are "best guesses" as to how the forces which have shaped our economy in the past decade are likely to continue to change in the next one. And, since the figures presented are the first estimates of the overall cost of the nation's goals, the check of similar estimates independently arrived at is largely lacking.

The introduction of different standards which are also reasonable could result in somewhat different cost magnitudes. Technical problems in developing the internal consistency of the parts which contribute to the total and for eliminating the double counting require time-consuming adjustments and basic data which have not always been available. Yet, after voicing these caveats, what the estimates fundamentally test is a hypothesis. The hypothesis is that the cost of the nation's objectives will exceed the anticipated GNP in 1970 and 1975. The findings are consistent with this hypothesis after allowing for a margin of error of 10 per cent in our estimates. It is unlikely that changes in the standards would affect the overall conclusions unless they included radical changes in standards of living or in the roles of government and business.

Estimating the deficit in GNP for the goals is only the beginning in an attempt to understand the factors to be considered in establishing the balanced priorities which are within our means. While the costs of the nation's objectives are discussed in this study in terms of dollar expenditures, the problems they raise pertain more essentially to resources. A billion dollars spent on space involves different manpower and raw materials requirements than a billion dollars spent on urban renewal or economic aid to the newly developing countries. The limiting factor in achieving some objectives—health research, for example—is more likely to be the barrier of insufficient trained manpower than of insufficient dollars.

Although the dollar estimates are a necessary first step for an analysis of the cost of goals, the dollar figures do not disclose the bottlenecks, the feedbacks, or the effects of changing the time relationships involved in the simultaneous pursuit of a large number of objectives. Expanding educational opportunities or access to medical care on a large scale, to cite instances, would reduce the resources potentially disposable for other purposes while the programs in health or education were being enlarged. Over longer periods of time, these relationships change, and the feedback effects of larger investments in education or health in increasing productivity would very probably add to the resources available for other objectives by considerably more than the cost of the resources involved in the improvements considered for the education or health goals.

Our study sheds little light on the sources of the funds necessary to achieve the goals. The aspiration standards are consistent with a variety of combinations of private and public expenditures. The goal of adequate medical care could be achieved by a national health service as in Great Britain. It could also be realized by a combination of public programs for the aged and the low-income groups, and for research and facilities, plus a sizeable expansion in the coverage and benefits offered in private health insurance plans. In the public sector, the study leaves undefined the respective roles of the Federal and the state-local levels of government and of the relatively new quasi-public bodies such as the Port of New York Authority. Which of the combinations of private-public or Federal-state action are likely to be more effective or desirable in any particular area is itself an important area for research. For the purposes of the present study, the cost magnitudes implied by the standards are generally assumed to remain the same whatever combinations are involved in the source of funds.

Similarly, the study does not take into account the complex problems of implementing the objectives considered in the report. Enlarging expenditures or resources will increase the means available for achieving our aspirations. It does not assure that the means will be effectively used. The near-tripling of expenditures for health could not lead to a corresponding expansion in medical care unless programs for expanding facilities in medical education were adopted well in advance to allow for the long lead times needed to train and educate professional manpower in the health professions. The $52-billion increase in spending listed for the education goal would be unlikely to achieve its purpose unless spending for more and better paid teachers were accompanied by widespread innovations to improve the training and utilization of teachers. The $33-billion increase in expenditures for the housing goal could be reduced, or objectives enlarged, through more intensive use of the knowledge already available in housing technology, such as mass production of housing components or use of synthetic building materials.

While this report is concerned with estimates of dollar costs, it make little attempt to balance these estimates with measures of dollar benefits. In some instances, e.g., in the selection of weapons systems or civil engineering projects, it is possible to compare the ratios of benefits to costs for each additional million or billion dollars to be spent for the different alternatives, and to select the system or project promising the greatest yield of benefits per dollar expended. In other fields, as in expenditures for consumer goods or business outlays for plant and equipment, the price system enables individuals to make their own cost-benefit comparisons and to guide their spending accordingly. In too many areas, such as space, health, education, or social welfare, the benefits are too diffuse, too scattered in time, and too heterogeneous a mixture of political and social values and economic elements to be reduced to a common dollar denominator.

IX.

The estimates of expenditures and deficits in this study refer to national objectives as they are currently conceived and defined. Some of the goals, such as the space program or manpower retraining, would have been absent from our list if this report had been prepared a decade ago. Many of the standards would very probably have been defined in a different manner. It is doubtful whether the large increases listed for the education goal, for example, would have provided a meaningful measure of the nation's aspirations in education before the arrival of Sputnik, the civil rights movement, and the "war on poverty."

With the passage of another decade, new problems and opportunities are likely to create new national objectives and to lead to reformulations of existing standards. Events which at present are largely unforeseeable may disrupt the historical continuities reflected by the projections, and transform old problems or create new ones. Scientific and engineering breakthroughs could significantly reduce the cost of power obtained from nuclear sources and these advances could substantially augment the energy resources available for industry, for domestic use, or for new uses, such as water desalination. Progress in water desalination or oceanography could increase strikingly the food available to support the mushrooming growth in population which has provided so formidable a barrier to the economic development of the non-industrialized nations. And, whether we land a man on the moon by 1970 or a few years later, the developments growing out of space exploration in the next generation could lead to exploitation of new raw materials and new techniques in industry or medicine, and to major changes in the technology of transportation, communications, and weather forecasting.

The conquest of heart disease and cancer, objectives figuring prominently in the projections for the health goal, would increase the share of the population in the over-65 age group to considerably more than the one tenth of the total anticipated for the 1970's. Along with the blessings of greater longevity, large masses of older job seekers or job holders would set up pressures to overhaul present hiring and retirement practices. The special needs of the aged for medical care, housing, recreational facilities, and meaningful participation would impinge on a society glorifying the stereotypes of youth.

Compounding the effects of the scientific and technological advances, social changes as striking as the increase in the aged population may alter the environment in which national objectives are defined in the next decade. Organized labor's drive to protect employment by a shorter workweek or workyear, the latter perhaps introduced in the form of widespread sabbatical leaves, may succeed well enough to modify present patterns of work and leisure. These changes, along with the expected growth in personal income and in overall educational attainment, could induce a flourishing of the arts or of handicrafts, as well as a greatly expanded volume of travel to other nations and continents, far beyond the increases projected in the aspiration standards. Mechanization of household tasks may proceed at a pace compelling recognition of the technological changes which have so profoundly affected the status of women. Reorganization of higher education to emphasize schooling for mature adults, refresher courses for professional persons, and acceptance of large-scale part-time participation in employment can be expected to figure more prominently in the nation's objectives in another decade than in the recent past.

President Johnson's Council of Economic Advisers has suggested a family money income of less than $3,000 as a rough measure of poverty in the economy of the early 1960's.[23] Economic growth, and new programs for increasing earning capacity and employment opportunities for low-income wage earners, are likely to reduce the number of families with incomes under $3,000 to significantly less than the fifth of the total they amounted to in 1962. And, as in the past, economic growth, translated into rising national levels of family income and higher living standards, can also be expected to raise the level of income regarded as con-

23. *Annual Report of the Council of Economic Advisers*, January, 1964, pp. 58–59.

stituting poverty. By 1975, with average family incomes expected to be in the neighborhood of $10,000 a year, the social deficit represented by an income of less than $3,000 would be considerably greater than it was when these same low incomes were compared with the 1962 average family income of about $7,300. With the same income in the 1970's as in the early 1960's, the poor would be relatively poorer in the next decade.

Progress along the lines indicated in the aspiration standards would itself be a major force in altering potentials and perspectives in the 1970's. Removing, or substantially reducing the barriers to equality of opportunity, and increasing the population of trained and educated citizenry, as proposed in the different goals concerned with manpower development, would raise productivity. The same result would follow from the greater expenditures for research. One student of economic growth, Edward Denison, attributes some 40 per cent of the increase in real national income between 1929 and 1957 to education and to advances in knowledge, or to programs reducing the time lapse in applying new knowledge.[24] The 4-per cent growth rate in GNP which appears to be a reasonably high rate in the mid-1960's could represent little more than a modest rate by 1975. If this optimistic version of the future were to become a reality, rapid growth in output would very probably also serve to create incentives for more ambitious standards. The leapfrogging of resources and aspirations could be expected to perpetuate the deficit in resources, although probably at a different level from the deficit discussed in the study.

X.

The overall finding of this report is that our nation's goals make up a complex of competing claims on resources. The costs of the entire complex are estimated to exceed the resources we are capable of generating without severe strains on our social and economic institutions. Yet it is characteristic of our nation's history to adopt objectives which exceed our reach, and these objectives, in turn, serve as incentives for taking steps to make greater progress than would have been considered possible with more modest aspirations.

Looking toward the future, eliminating the gap between our actual output and the potential output we are capable of producing is the least costly step in devising ways and means for transforming more of our aspirations into reality. The loss of output because the economy operates at less than its feasible maximum represents opportunities foregone in health, education, and in all the other goals. For the next decade, the difference in annual output if the economy grew at a rate of 4 per cent a year, rather than at the historic long-term rate of about 3 per cent, would amount to $170 billion by 1975. This is approximately the same amount as the costs projected for both the health and education goals in the 1970's.

As the reverse side of the growth process, a greater effort in pursuit of our objectives would raise the actual rate of GNP growth to a closer approximation to its potential. Over time, this pursuit would change the limits of the economy's potential for sustained growth. In addition, more vigorous pursuit of our goals, within the constraints of the available manpower and resources, would add to the effective demand encouraging industry to operate at close-to-capacity levels.

While there are limits to the possibilities of creating additional resources by stepping up the tempo of growth, the alternatives available in adapting our targets to the rates of growth we are able to achieve suggest a note of cautious optimism. We face no equivalent to the population explosion in the underdeveloped countries. Forecasts of exhaustion of strategic natural resources have failed to materialize with monotonous regularity. Measures such as the 1964–65 tax reductions or those included in the "war on poverty" indicate a broad consensus supporting policies for encouraging growth and coping with our society's unresolved problems. It has often been commented that the choice confronting the Nazi economy in the 1930's was "guns or butter," and the choice for the Soviet citizen has been "producer goods versus consumer goods" for the past generation. For the United States in the 1970's, there are likely to be no such stark alternatives. As a democratic, relatively wealthy nation, we shall very probably be pursuing all the goals on the list.

The relevant problem is not so much the question of which goals to pursue, but rather the questions of how much, in what quantitative combinations, and how soon. This leads to consideration of standards, available resources, and, consequently, of priorities. What kind of education will produce technologists who are also socially responsible, literate citizens, and what will it cost? Should urban land be used for more highways or for additional homesites and parks? Should fewer resources be devoted to developing a supersonic air transport plane and more to perfecting an intermediate-haul jet to encourage low-cost mass air travel? What is the cost of extending the affluence in our private consumption to a correspondingly generous provision for community facilities in our urban slums or in our mushrooming suburbs? To what extent are these genuine alternatives? And, how can a democratic, pluralistic society plan for all these objectives within the constraints imposed by the potentially available resources? It is questions such as these that emerge from this preliminary inquiry.

CHAPTER 2

Consumer
Expenditures
and Savings

I.

Our goal in consumer expenditures is to translate the economy's potential for growth into rising living standards for all Americans. The achievement of this objective in 1975 is estimated to increase consumer spending, in 1962 dollars, by $300 billion more than in 1962. Over half of the growth in expenditures for the improvements represented by the standards for all sixteen goals is accounted for by the rise in spending for private consumption.

Expectations of steadily rising living standards have become a built-in feature of our culture. They are part of our concept of progress. These expectations are cultivated by mass advertising, by the easy availability of consumer credit, and by the emphasis on "getting ahead" or at least "keeping up with the Joneses." As our incomes have grown, we have used most of the additional income to raise living standards rather than to add to personal savings. Between 1950 and 1962, personal income per capita after income taxes increased, after adjusting for price changes, by $350. Nine tenths of this increase was devoted to greater spending.[1]

The dollar totals for consumer goods and services omit one of the most important benefits consumers derive from technological advance and rising productivity—increased leisure. We have taken part of the gains arising from growth in output per manhour by working fewer hours. As a result, the length of the average workweek in the civilian economy has fallen from 60 hours in 1900 to 40.5 in 1962.[2] As productivity continues to rise in the next decade, the workweek is expected to fall to an average of about 37 hours by 1975. With annual vacations becoming widespread, and the sabbaticals (now offered to teachers and steelworkers) likely to gain broader acceptance, hours of work per year are projected to decline at a more rapid pace, by approximately 1 per cent a year.

Concern with raising living standards for the families at the bottom of the income structure has constituted an underlying theme in American history. The nation's interest in eliminating poverty was partially responsible for the development of public education and the Homestead Act in the nineteenth century. It figured in Henry Ford's introduction of the five-dollar daily wage shortly after World War I, in the organizing activities of trade unions, and in the social legislation enacted in the 1930's. This same concern is evident in the Government's current programs for increasing earning capacity and employment opportunities for individuals in the low-income groups.

---

1. *Annual Report of the Council of Economic Advisers,* January, 1963, p. 191.

2. *National Economic Projections Series,* 1963, National Planning Association, p. I–27.

The goods and services purchased by private consumers do not make up all of the good and services which contribute to higher living standards. Individuals also "consume" goods and services provided by the Government. While individuals purchase automobiles, the Government must build the highways on which they operate. The achievement of an appropriate balance between rising private consumption and spending for the public services that facilitate private consumption is responsible for a large share of the public expenditures listed for our goals in transportation, community development, and natural resources.

Attaining the higher living standards anticipated in the 1970's will involve many goals, since much of consumer spending is also included as part of the cost of other goals. Expenditures by private individuals make up a large part of the nation's spending for health and medical care, and, to a lesser extent, for education. Most of the 50-million increase in the country's stock of cars projected for 1975 represents automobiles to be purchased, including purchases of second cars, by individual families.[3] Considerations of standards of living must also take into account the fact that the feeling of security derived from a savings account or a life insurance policy can be as important for individual well-being as the alternative of consuming additional goods and services.

II.

Our projections for consumer expenditures take it for granted that the expectations of steadily rising living standards will characterize the next decade as they have in the past. Continuation of the steady growth in living standards will involve large increases in the demand for steel, aluminum, electricity, petroleum, and synthetic fibers. The ratio of physicians-to-population, nearly constant in the past generation, would probably rise with the increased ability of families to afford medical care and with the greater avail-

---

3. See Chapters 6, 7, and 8 for a discussion of these goals.

ability of comprehensive health insurance. Along with rising incomes, total consumer expenditures would increase, and the distribution of the total between the different types of goods and services would also change.

As income rises, a smaller share of family budgets would probably be allotted to nondurables such as food. Private spending for books, education, vacations, and personal care would be likely to rise by more than the overall average. Expenditures for auto repair and service and for parking, like those for automobile purchases, would loom larger in family outlays. Offsetting the increases in spending for services, families can be expected to continue replacing the purchase of outside services, such as laundry service, by the acquisition of items of durable equipment designed to serve the same purpose in home use. Spending for durables is projected to show the largest percentage increase in consumer expenditures, rising from 13 per cent of the total in 1962 to 15 per cent or somewhat more of the larger volume of consumer spending in the 1970's. As average family incomes rise to an anticipated $10,000 a year, there will be an increase in the funds set aside for private arrangements to protect economic security. Annual premiums for life insurance, for example, are expected to increase by over two thirds—from $18 billion in the early 1960's to $31 billion in the mid-1970's.[4]

These changes in consumer spending patterns continue the tendencies of the recent past. Spending for food, according to a recent Department of Labor study of the changes in consumer spending from 1950 to 1960, fell from 30 per cent of total expenditures for current consumption in 1950 to 24.5 per cent in 1960.[5] This was the most sizeable change brought to light in the study. Spending for automobile operation and purchases increased from 11.5 to 13 per cent of the

---

4. This total includes premiums paid for ordinary, group, industrial, and credit insurance.

5. Chase, A. E., *Changing Patterns of Consumer Expenditures 1950–1960,* Bureau of Labor Statistics, U.S. Department of Labor, 1964.

total. The largest percentage increase was in family expenditures for education. While still only slightly more than 1 per cent of all consumer spending, they doubled as a proportion of consumers' outlay during the decade.

III.

Since 1950, Americans have expressed their preference for higher living standards by spending 92 to 94 per cent of their personal income after income taxes. Net savings have fluctuated within the narrow limits of 6 to 8 per cent of disposable personal income. It is possible that the savings rate will increase somewhat with rising incomes. Nevertheless, in line with past experience, it is reasonable to expect that the social attitudes favoring this emphasis on more goods and services will continue through 1975. Our goal for consumer expenditures, accordingly, assumes that spending by consumers will absorb 92 per cent, and savings 8 per cent, of disposable personal income in the 1970's.[6]

As GNP rises to the expected near-trillion dollars by 1975, consumer expenditures per family are estimated to increase from the $5,850 they represented in 1962 to $7,800 a year in the mid-1970's. All told, consumer spending is listed at $594 billion in 1975 for the 8-per cent savings rate. This is one quarter of a trillion dollars more than in 1962.

The massive increases projected for consumer spending are attributable to three factors, namely, the expected increase in the number of families, the increases in spending likely to result from changes in the occupational structure

6. Since the research for this chapter was completed, the Department of Commerce has published revised estimates of the national income and product accounts which include several statistical and definitional changes reducing the earlier estimates of personal savings. The effect of these changes is to reduce personal savings as a share of disposable personal income by about a fifth in 1962. The revisions in the savings estimate do not substantively affect the projections or the discussion in this chapter. See *Survey of Current Business*, August, 1965, pp. 6–22.

which lead to higher incomes for many families, and the projected increases in spending per family because of our goal.

If consumption expenditures per family remained frozen at their 1962 levels, total consumer spending would still rise substantially in the next decade because of population growth. The 58 million families in 1962 are expected to increase to 71 million by 1975. To maintain the 1962 average family expenditures for the 1975 population would involve an increase in overall consumer spending of over $80 billion. Without any improvement in standards of living, consumer spending would rise from $357 billion in 1962 to $438 billion by 1975.

Another, and a much smaller, addition to consumer spending is likely to result from the larger incomes earned as more of the work force is employed in higher paying occupations. The occupational shifts expected in the next decade are extensions of the changes which have made up the "manpower revolution" of the past decade. Employment in the professional and technical groups, and in many service occupations, is likely to rise more rapidly than the increase in the total labor force. The proportion of operatives, laborers, and farmers in the work force is expected to decline.

The occupational shifts are estimated to increase personal income by over $20 billion a year in the mid-1970's. The growth in consumption expenditures from this larger income would reach $18 billion by 1975. These increases in consumer spending, together with the expenditures for maintaining the 1962 *status quo* in family consumption expenditures would occur even if overall standards of living were to remain stationary. Accordingly, they make up our hypothetical preempted estimate of consumer spending, i.e., the benchmark for assessing the additional expenditures required to achieve the higher living standards in our goals.

The consumer expenditures listed for the 8-per cent savings rate in the 1970's are summarized in Table 2–1. The projections presuppose an additional income tax cut, similar to the 1964–65 tax reduction, before 1970. The table also includes the estimates for the hypothetical preempted benchmark.

Table 2–1
Estimated Consumer Expenditures in 1970 and 1975, 8-Per Cent Savings Rate and Preempted Benchmark
(in 1962 dollars)

Item	Projections for 1970	1975
1. 8-Per Cent Savings Rate		
a. Average family consumption expenditures[a]	$6,950	$7,800
b. Total consumption expenditures (in billions)[b]	479	594
2. Preempted Benchmark Expenditures (in billions)		
a. To maintain 1962 per family expenditures	402	438
b. Greater consumption expenditures due to occupational shifts	12	18
c. Total[b]	414	456
3. Consumer Expenditures in 1962 (in billions) $356.7		

a. "Family" refers to "consumer units"—to families and to individuals living alone.
b. The totals for consumer spending include consumption expenditures by "consumer units" and spending for the institutional population—i.e., persons in state institutions, members of the armed forces, etc.

IV.

The estimates for the 8-per cent savings rate are stated in terms of aggregates. These aggregates serve to indicate the changes in average family consumption expenditures in the next decade which are consistent with consumer spending and saving preferences in the recent past. The averages do not show the extent to which standards of living for sizeable groups in the 1970's would be concentrated at levels far below the average. The problem obscured by the averages is the problem of poverty.

Like "need," poverty is difficult to define. It refers both to a type of status and also to actual deprivation. The poor are not simply the individuals who happen to be located at the lower end of the curve of income and property distribution. They constitute a subculture, cut off by their chronic lack of income from effective participation in the larger society as producers, consumers, or citizens.

Income, especially at the lower levels, is an inadequate measure of this status. The same low income may have one meaning for a retired couple free of debt and owning a home, a car, a savings deposit, and an insurance policy, and it may mean something very different for a recently established family with small children, just beginning to acquire a home, furniture, and a car. An income of $3,000 a year means one living standard for a rural family and another for a family living in an urban center such as New York or Chicago. Moreover, as family expenditures and standards of living rise, what is regarded as a poverty level of living also changes and becomes more costly.

Economists have attempted to shortcut the difficulties involved in defining poverty by assuming a particular level of income to be the dividing line between poverty and non-poverty. For operational purposes, the individuals or families below the cutoff income are regarded as the part of the population living in poverty.

The President's Council of Economic Advisers has suggested a cutoff level of a $3,000-money income for families, and $1,500 for individuals living alone as a "family" of one, as a currently relevant criterion for poverty for both the urban and the rural population. By this yardstick, one fifth of American families was living in poverty in 1962, and the poor included a total of 33 to 35 million persons.[7] By 1970 and 1975, the cutoff income for poverty is likely to rise, probably to the neighborhood of $4,000 for families and $2,000 for individuals living by themselves. What is regarded as a poverty income in the early or mid-1960's will probably be considered destitution by the mid-1970's.

No matter which precise cutoff serves as the criterion for inadequate incomes, the families in the poverty group share an over-representation of a common body of characteristics which help to explain their status. The frequency with which

7. *Annual Report of the Council of Economic Advisers,* January, 1964, p. 59.

these characteristics occur in the general population and in poor families is described in Table 2–2. The data in the table refers to the $3,000 money income cutoff employed by the Council of Economic Advisers.

Table 2–2
Selected Characteristics, All Families and Poor Families, 1962*

	PER CENT POSSESSING CHARACTERISTIC	
Characteristic	In all families	In poor families
1. Family Head 65 or Older	14%	34%
2. No Wage Earner in Family	8	30
3. Family Headed by Female	10	25
4. Family Head with 8th-Grade Education or Less	35	61
5. Nonwhite Family	10	22
6. Farm Families	7	16
7. Live in South	30	47

* Annual Report of the Council of Economic Advisers, January, 1964, p. 61. It is interesting to note that another study using a poverty cutoff income for families of $2,000 presents a similar list of distinguishing characteristics of poor families. See Lampman, Robert J., The Low Income Population and Economic Growth, Joint Economic Committee, U.S. Congress, 1959, pp. 9, 12.

Poverty is pervasive and the poor are to be found in many groups in the population. However, poor families are more likely to be headed by an aged person, a female, or an individual with less than an eighth-grade education. In addition, the poor are more likely to be engaged in farming and to live in the South. Wherever found, poverty in the United States is largely attributable to low productivity, old age, unemployment or lack of a family member able to work, broken families, and to the caste barriers created by segregation.

Poverty is over twice as prevalent among nonwhite families as among whites. The median income of all nonwhite families in 1962, $3,300, was only 10 per cent more than the $3,000 figure used by the President as the criterion for poverty.[8] The Council of Economic Advisers has estimated that our society loses as much as $20 billion annually in potential

8. Manpower Report of the President, 1964, p. 276.

production because of employment discrimination and the poorer educational opportunities available for Negroes, Puerto Ricans, Spanish-Americans, and Indians.[9] Since the end use of nearly two thirds of production is current consumption, it can reasonably be assumed that one of the costs of discrimination in the mid-1960's was to reduce consumption by approximately $13 billion a year.

V.

The changes associated with economic growth have also been the changes associated with a reduction in poverty. They include the rising productivity brought about by technological change and higher average levels of education. Outmigration from the South and inmigration to the West Coast, and the movement of Negroes from the rural South to the urban areas have had a similar effect. The sharecroppers of the South and the dustbowl farmers of the Middle West, the leading examples of rural poverty before World War II, have largely disappeared as many of the individuals in these groups have moved to other areas and occupations.

The effects of economic growth in reducing the proportion of the population in the poverty group since World War II are described in Table 2–3.

Table 2–3
Percentage of Families with Poverty Incomes
1947, 1955, 1962*

| | PER CENT OF FAMILIES WITH MONEY INCOMES[a] | |
Year	Less than $3,000[b]	Less than $2,000[b]
1947	32%	18%
1955	25	15
1962	20	12

a. Pertains to families, excluding unattached individuals.
b. In 1962 dollars.
* *Annual Report of the Council of Economic Advisers*, January, 1964, p. 59.

9. *Annual Report of the Council of Economic Advisers*, January, 1965, p. 167.

Since 1947, the percentage of families in the $3,000-or-less group has declined by two fifths and the proportion in the less-than-$2,000 group by one third.

There is some evidence that the composition of the poor population has been changing in ways which would tend to make it more difficult for economic growth to eliminate poverty in the future. Families headed by persons over 65, or by females, or by other persons not in the labor force, have become a larger part of the poor. The low incomes of others are linked with grossly inadequate education, or with obsolete job skills or lack of skills, or to residence in "pockets of poverty." Economic growth, by itself, would be unlikely to improve the earnings or employment prospects for many of these families.

The variety of reasons why people are poor, and the changes in the importance of each reason, make it apparent that there is no single or simple remedy for poverty. About half the poor families are still headed neither by an aged person nor a woman. Seventy per cent include at least one earner.[10] The greater earnings and employment opportunities associated with vigorous economic growth are essential if these families are to move to higher income levels. For many persons in the poverty group, retraining, adult literacy education, redevelopment programs, or better medical care could remove the disabilities which perpetuate low productivity and, consequently, low income. For families without earners or would-be-participants in the labor force, social security and public assistance—or, perhaps, the family allowances considered in the next section—are likely to provide basic support. And, whatever the specific causes of poverty, rapid growth in output would increase the public and private resources available for overcoming the handicaps responsible for low earnings, or for financing more adequate social welfare benefits for families without earnings.

---

10. *Annual Report of the Council of Economic Advisers,* January, 1964, p. 73.

VI.

Economic growth, even with the support of the policy measures for removing the handicaps creating poverty, could not be expected to generally eliminate poverty in the near future. Moreover, in a society in which average family incomes would be in the neighborhood of $10,000 a year, the social gap represented by a family income of less than $4,000 or $3,000 would be considerably greater than if these same low incomes were compared with the 1962 average income of about $7,300. With the same income in the 1970's as in the early 1960's, the poor will be relatively poorer in the next decade.

Direct public financial assistance to families with chronic low incomes in the past generation has been largely confined to relieving destitution. It is unlikely that the present pattern of welfare assistance will be extended far in the future. The public assistance grants, according to the U.S. Commissioner of Welfare, Ellen Winston, "are inadequate throughout the nation."[11] State welfare payments to families with dependent children have averaged $1.15 a day per child. Yet, if present tendencies in public assistance caseloads continue, one out of six children in the U.S. will be helped by public assistance before they reach 18. Unemployment compensation and the retirement and survivors benefits available through Social Security have also lagged behind the general rise in incomes and living standards. Commissioner Winston has proposed that state welfare agencies help define what a reasonable floor to income would be— "one that no family should fall below." To indicate the probable cost of providing a floor of this type to the incomes of destitute families, the goal for consumer expenditures includes a system of family allowances. These payments could be expected to vary with the size and age composition of the families receiving the allowances. However, in the light of the anticipated increases in average income and GNP, a

---

11. *The Washington Post,* December 9, 1964.

typical family income of less than $3,000 in 1970 and $3,300 by 1975 can reasonably be taken to represent destitution. This sum translates into a weekly income of approximately $60. It would purchase the equivalent of a minimum economy-plan family budget as described by the Social Security Administration in the early 1960's.[12]

The allowances considered would be sufficient to raise family incomes to the destitution cutoff levels. They would replace the present public assistance payments, and would supplement old age pensions, disability compensation, unemployment insurance, or substandard earnings from work. The cost the allowances would add to the consumer expenditures goal represents the additional consumption of goods and services brought about by the greater purchasing power of the poor. The allowances figure in both the consumer expenditures and the social welfare goals.

The cost estimates for the family allowances are indicated in the table which follows.

Table 2–4
Estimated Cost of Family Allowance Program, 1970 and 1975
(dollar totals in billions of 1962 dollars)

Item	Projections for: 1970	1975
1. Estimated Population in the Groups Eligible for Allowances (in millions)[a]		
a. Families	5.9	6.1
b. Individuals unattached to families[b]	3.6	3.8
2. Estimated Increase in Personal Income to raise Incomes to Destitution Cutoff	$8.7	$9.9
3. Estimated Increase in Consumer Expenditures from Greater Incomes[c]	$8.3	$9.4
4. Increase in Consumer Expenditure as % of GNP	1.1%	1.0%

a. The population estimates assume that 25 per cent more families will be eligible for the allowances than would be the case if economic growth were to continue removing families from the low income groups at the same rate as in the past two decades.
b. The cutoff income for unattached individuals is half that for families—i.e., $1,650 in 1975.
c. Assumes 95 per cent of the additional income is spent for consumer goods and services.

12. *Annual Report of the Council of Economic Advisers,* January, 1964, p. 58.

The cost of the family allowances for eliminating destitution is listed at about 1 per cent of GNP in the next decade.[13] Cost would be higher, perhaps closer to 2 per cent of gross national product, if persons earning less than the cutoff incomes, working as domestics, farm laborers, or hospital attendants were generally to quit working at substandard earnings and attempt to live on the allowances instead.[14] Costs could be reduced below the amounts in the table if the "war on poverty," expansion of educational opportunities, or a lessening of discrimination in employment succeeded in increasing earnings for large numbers of the poor.

The effects of the family allowances program on the overall economy could be roughly similar to those of the 1964–65 income tax reductions. The initial rise in consumer spending would add to incomes elsewhere in the economy, and these incomes would again be largely spent. Taking into account the feedback effects stemming from the successive rounds of spending, the national income would increase by several times the amount of the income supplements. If there were considerable excess capacity and unemployment in the economy, this additional spending would serve to increase production and employment. If the economy were already operating at full capacity, the program, like other large increases in total spending, would have an inflationary potential.

The family allowances would do little to eliminate the causes of poverty and destitution. They would merely compensate for their effects. The proposal underscores, to quote

13. To allow for the fact that not all families with any particular low income are living in poverty or destitution, the cost estimates assume that 90 per cent of the consumer units with substandard incomes would qualify for allowances.

14. It could be contended that virtually all persons at work earning less than the income allowance would cease work. The complex problems of administration in this type of program, or the social desirability of encouraging employment at substandard earnings are beyond the scope of this paper. Moreover, rising productivity and more extensive union organization in many of these occupations is likely to substantially reduce the number of persons at work earning substandard incomes in the 1970's.

the President's Council of Economic Advisers again, that "conquest of poverty is well within our power."[15] For destitute families headed by an aged person, or for families with young children headed by a female, the allowances would create a more liberal floor to standards of living than is otherwise available. For Americans who are destitute because of unemployment, lack of skill or education, or because of their race, programs for increasing employment opportunities or earning capacity would remove the causes of their poverty. For these individuals, the allowances are an alternative only insofar as the handicaps which keep them impoverished are not removed.

VII.

The standards for our goal take it for granted that consumers' freedom of choice in determining how they will spend their income will continue as an important national objective. Yet it is apparent that consumers often lack the information needed for making intelligent choices. Consumers are typically unaware of the full cost of a credit transaction because of the non-standard ways of reckoning interest charges. Similarly, the design of packages frequently makes it difficult to determine the volume of contents in the package. In determining the serviceability of the contents for their intended purpose, consumers are seldom able to obtain or to interpret the engineering specifications and laboratory tests widely used to guide industrial or government purchases.

Much has already been done by Government, by industry, and by consumer groups to improve the information at the disposal of consumers and to protect them against fraud and dangers to their health. The Federal meat inspection service's work, for example, is a leading instance. Accurate listing of interest charges is primarily a matter of legislation,

---

15. *Annual Report of the Council of Economic Advisers*, January, 1964, p. 77.

social attitudes, and trade association codes. However, it would also be encouraged if consumers had more information on how to reckon true interest charges. As personal income and R & D expenditures rise in the coming decade, the spectrum of consumer goods and services, and especially of the durable goods usually purchased on credit, will widen and become more complex. Expansion of consumer information services could make a significant contribution to raising living standards at a minimum cost. If the equivalent of one half of 1 per cent of consumer expenditures were spent for expanding these services, we would be spending approximately $300 million more for this purpose in 1975.

VIII.

The projections for the consumer expenditures goal include the expenditures listed for the 8-per cent savings rate and the cost of the consumer information services. This total must be increased because of the increases in consumer expenditures generated by the pursuit of other goals. The family allowances system and other proposals considered in the social welfare goal, and the greater expenditures by consumers for medical care in the health goal, are the largest items in these additions. Inclusion of the additional expenditures from the other goals raises the estimate of consumer spending to nearly $660 billion in 1975.[16]

The benchmark estimate of the cost of freezing 1962 living standards for another decade is also incomplete since it, too, includes consumer expenditures from the preempted estimates for other goals. The largest single item arises out of expenditures for automobile purchases and operation. Even

16. Part of the consumer expenditures which also represent expenditures for other goals are implicitly included in the totals for the 8-per cent savings rate. The amounts by which consumer expenditures included for the other goals exceed the amounts which are implicitly present in the projection for the 8-per cent savings rate have been added to the cost projections for the consumer expenditures goal. For further discussion of this problem, see Appendix A.

with constant living standards, these expenditures would rise by considerably more than population because young people are expected to make up a larger proportion of the population in the 1970's. These adjustments raise the hypothetical preempted benchmark estimate to $473 billion by 1975.

The items which enter into the cost of our standard for the consumer expenditures goal are summarized in Table 2–5.

Table 2–5
Estimated Spending for Consumer Expenditures Goal, 1970 and 1975
(in billions of 1962 dollars)

| | Projected Expenditures in | |
Item	1970	1975
1. Consumer Expenditures for 8% Savings Rate Estimate	$478.5	$594.0
2. Additional Consumption Expenditures from Other Goals	53.9	65.3
a. Social welfare	21.1	26.4
b. Health	14.9	15.2
c. Housing[a]	5.8	7.2
d. Transportation	5.6	7.5
e. Education	4.4	6.2
f. Other[b]	2.1	2.8
3. Consumer Information Services	0.2	0.3
4. Total Consumer Expenditures Goal	532.6	659.6
5. Consumer Expenditures as % of GNP[c]	67.5%	67%
6. Consumer Expenditures in 1962 . . . . $356.7		

a. Expenditures for housing repair and upkeep.
b. Includes consumer expenditures generated by subsistence allowances in manpower retraining goal, and expenditures included as consumption in the national income accounts, which result from the operations of nonprofit organizations.
c. Refers to GNP growing at 4.1 per cent a year from full-capacity base in 1962.

The estimates for the consumer expenditures goal represent expenditures for a "high consumption" economy. As a percentage of GNP, consumer expenditures would rise from 64 per cent in 1962 and 1963 to 67 per cent of the far larger gross national product anticipated in the 1970's. In terms of dollars, consumer spending in 1975 would be almost one fifth greater than the entire GNP in 1962. The higher living standards made possible by these rising expenditures would affect virtually all aspects of American society, and their effects would be most evident in the low income groups. However, the bulk of the greater spending by consumers would be generally distributed throughout the income ladder.

High levels of private consumption, in turn, can be expected to increase the demand for public services and facilities. As private living standards rise, the deficiencies in public health, educational, or recreational facilities will loom larger in people's expectations. With more cars and income, travel and vacations will become far more frequent. If public facilities continue to lag behind, to quote John K. Galbraith, "the family . . . [with] its air-conditioned, power-steered, and power-braked car out for a tour [will pass] through cities that are badly paved, made hideous by litter, blighted buildings, [and] billboards. . . . They [will] picnic on exquisitely packaged foods from a portable icebox by a polluted stream."[17] Further, if highway construction fails to keep pace with the growth in automobile ownership, urban families will lack the incentive to picnic in parks or in the countryside because highway congestion will cause traffic to come to a nerve-wracking standstill.

All sixteen goals included in this study add an anticipated $350-odd billion to the cost of maintaining present levels of performance in our society for the next decade—the basis for our hypothetical preempted estimate. Half of this increase, 53 per cent, is made up of the additional consumer expenditures for the higher living standards anticipated for the 1970's. Improving standards of living for all groups in the population is the most costly and comprehensive of all our national objectives.

---

17. Galbraith, J. K., *The Affluent Society*, Houghton Mifflin Co., Boston, Massachusetts, 1958, p. 253.

CHAPTER 3

Private

Plant

and

Equipment

I.

Our objective in private plant and equipment is to create the productive capacity for industry and agriculture and the facilities for non-profit organizations needed to pursue the nation's goals in the 1970's. Creating this productive capacity is not an independent goal but rather a means for supporting all the goals. We treat it as a separate goal because the construction of plant, equipment, and facilities, while adding to productive resources, is also one of the major claimants on the use of resources. In order to estimate the amount of resources required for all goals, the expenditures for the productive capacity needed to pursue them must be included. Our estimate of the private outlays for plant and equipment which is consistent with the pursuit and achievement of all goals amounts to $152 billion in 1975, compared with actual outlays of $49 billion in 1962.

Private capital outlays of this magnitude could provide the productive capacity to support a GNP of over $1.1 trillion a year in the mid-1970's. This is the amount of output that would be needed to fully achieve our goals by 1975. It would imply a steady rate of growth in GNP of about 5.5 per cent a year. Since it would probably require massive increases in productivity, or "forced-draft" economic growth to sustain an annual growth rate of 5.5 per cent for over a decade, full achievement of all our aspirations by 1975 does not figure as a feasible alternative.

If we assume a growth rate of 4 per cent a year or slightly higher as a reasonable representation of the economy's potential performance allowing for human error and incomplete fulfillment of plans, we would be pursuing all our goals, but at a slower pace, in the 1970's. We would require, correspondingly, less productive capacity. A 4-per cent rate of growth would imply an estimated $102 billion in private capital outlays in 1975. These outlays would provide the plant, equipment, and facilities consistent with the $981 billion GNP projected for 1975 with this rate of increase in output.

Our society's ability to produce is limited by the stock of plant and equipment, and by its composition in terms of age, type, and location. However, many goals and policies, in addition to outlays for plant and equipment, contribute to growth in our capacity to produce. More and better educational opportunities increase the effectiveness with which the labor force utilizes the existing plant. Better physical and mental health raises manhour productivity and the size of the work force, and it reduces the number of hours lost each year because of illness. Urban development programs make it possible to build new and more efficient plants in metropolitan areas by increasing the availability of transportation, land, and water, and by improving housing and parking facilities for employees. Policies for eliminating discriminatory barriers based on race are essentially grounded in our national ideal of equality of opportunity. They also serve to raise output by encouraging utilization of employees where their productivity can be greatest, and by increasing the productivity of nonwhites through enlarged opportunities for education and training.

Government fiscal and monetary policy can exert a powerful influence on growth in the economy, by affecting the rate at which industry adds to productive capacity, or by expanding the demand for goods and services. Corporate tax and depreciation policies can also serve to encourage private capital outlays. The respondents to the *McGraw-Hill Survey of Business Plans for New Plant and Equipment* attributed over a billion dollars of the investment planned by their firms in 1964 directly to changes in the tax laws in the early 1960's, allowing a 7 per cent tax credit on purchases of certain types of new plant and equipment, and liberalizing the rules governing depreciation allowances for tax purposes.[1] The direct and indirect effects of the recent income tax reduction in stimulating demand were probably the largest single factor in the reported plans of the firms participating in the McGraw-Hill survey to raise the share of plant and equipment expenditures devoted to expansion of capacity by 10 per cent beyond the 1963 level in 1964.

Research and development is also a strategic factor in economic growth. R & D encourages private expenditures for new types of plant and equipment or for additional productive facilities to manufacture new products. In 1963, according to the McGraw-Hill survey, 18 per cent of all business expenditures for plant and equipment—some $7 billion

---

1. *16th Annual McGraw-Hill Survey, Business Plans for New Plant and Equipment*, 1963, Table III.

—represented spending for automated machinery associated with self-regulating controls.[2] Twenty-five per cent of the 1962 sales of the manufacturers surveyed were in new products not made ten years earlier. Modernization of outmoded plant and equipment, and continued introduction of new products, is likely to create large-scale opportunities for private capital expenditures in the next decade.[3]

Slow growth in demand for goods and services creates unutilized capacity, which discourages private investment in expanding productive facilities. Capital expenditures by manufacturers in 1961 and 1962 were retarded by a level of operations, as described by the McGraw-Hill survey, approximating 83 per cent of capacity.[4] This was 9 points below the rate at which the firms reporting preferred to operate. "For the entire economy," the President's Council of Economic Advisers points out, "what appears as unavoidable excess capacity is in fact avoidable deficiency of demand."[5]

The relationship of private capital expenditures to the pace of growth in GNP is illustrated by experience since World War II. From 1947 to 1954, GNP, in constant dollars, grew at an annual rate of 3.8 per cent. Business fixed investment averaged 11 per cent of GNP a year. In the 1955–1960 period, output grew more slowly, at a rate of 2.4 per cent a year. Spending for business plant and equipment fell to 9.8 per cent of GNP. With continued slow growth, this proportion fell to under 9 per cent in 1962 and 1963.[6]

Rapid technological change, translated into additional plant and equipment, raises the productivity of the workers

---

2. *17th Annual McGraw-Hill Survey, Business Plans for New Plant and Equipment,* 1964, pp. 7–8.

3. The 1963 McGraw-Hill survey reported that over a fifth of the industrial plant and equipment in the United States was technologically outmoded. *16th Annual McGraw-Hill Survey,* 1963, Table X.

4. *Ibid.,* Table VII.

5. *Annual Report of the Council of Economic Advisers,* January, 1962, p. 130.

6. Derived from *Annual Report of the Council of Economic Advisers,* January, 1962, p. 129.

employed, and increases their earning power and standards of living. The same changes also create the problems of displaced workers, declining industries, and depressed areas. "A commitment to accelerated growth," as the Council of Economic Advisers observes, "is at the same time a commitment to solve . . . such problems."[7] National goals in area redevelopment, education, or manpower retraining constitute attempts to find remedies for these problems which facilitate rather than retard the economy's capacity to grow.

II.

The forces which have influenced private spending for plant and equipment in the early 1960's reflect essentially the same forces which have influenced expenditures for our other goals. They include urbanization and the growth of metropolitan areas, technological change, rising living standards, transportation bottlenecks, the emergence of new national objectives such as the space effort, and greater emphasis on needs in health, education, and recreation.

The distribution of the $49 billion spent for private capital expenditures in 1962 is summarized by economic sector in Table 3–1.

About 30 per cent of all plant and equipment expenditures in 1962 represented spending by firms in manufacturing. Manufacturing industries practically doubled their productive capacity between 1950 and 1962. Spending for construction of commercial buildings, warehouses, office buildings, and stores has also shown a large gain, increasing, in constant dollars, by 7 per cent a year since 1950.[8] This increase is partially due to the growth of suburban shopping centers and office buildings, and to the movement of wholesale distributors to outlying parts of metropolitan areas. The efforts

---

7. *Annual Report of the Council of Economic Advisers*, January, 1962, p. 109.

8. *The Construction Industry and Its Capital-Goods Requirements; A Ten-Year Projection*, National Planning Association, 1963, p. 16.

Table 3–1
Private Expenditures for Plant and Equipment, 1962*
(in millions of 1962 dollars)

Sector	Expenditures in 1962
1. Manufacturing	$14,700
2. Mining	1,100
3. Transportation including Mass Transit[a]	2,900
4. Public Utilities	5,500
5. Communications	3,600
6. Trade, Services, Finance, Construction	9,500
7. Agriculture	3,800
8. Private Non-Profit Organizations[b]	3,500
9. Other[c]	4,300
10. Total	48,900
11. Outlays as % of GNP	8.8%

a. Does not include spending for passenger cars, trucks, trailers, or airplanes by firms which are not primarily engaged in transportation services.
b. Refers to plant expenditures only.
c. Includes business purchases of passenger cars and capital outlays charged to current expenses.
* Derived from *Survey of Current Business*, July, 1964, Tables 35 and 37; *Statistical Abstract*, 1964, Table 899.

of private and public groups to check the decline of the downtown areas of central cities by rebuilding civic centers or constructing new ones has added to these expenditures.

The $3.5 billion listed for non-profit organizations understates the true total because it includes only the expenditures for construction of plant. Private expenditures for the construction of hospitals, educational, religious, and cultural facilities have risen from 11 per cent of private non-residential construction in 1948 to 17.5 per cent in 1962.[9] Much of this increase has contributed to changing suburban developments from clusters of homes into viable communities.

The long-term tendency to concentrate capital expenditures more heavily on equipment than on plant has continued in the recent past. In 1929, slightly over half of all spending for business facilities was spending for plant, and something less than half was spending for equipment. By the early 1960's, spending for plant had declined to about

---

9. *Ibid.*, p. 28.

40 per cent of the total and equipment expenditures had risen to almost 60 per cent.[10] Investment in new equipment, according to the Council of Economic Advisers, "serves as a vehicle for technological improvements, and is perhaps the most important way in which laboratory discoveries become incorporated in the productive process."[11]

Technological changes and considerations of employee welfare and efficiency have also encouraged expenditures for plant by influencing the design and location of plants. Drab, high-rise factory buildings within the central city have been replaced by one- or two-story plants spread out over large expanses of land in the outlying parts of the metropolitan area or beyond it. These plants economize the movement of men and materials within the building. To reduce shipping time and costs, they are usually located close to transportation facilities such as express highways. Metropolitan land utilization programs have encouraged construction of new plants by creating industrial parks readily accessible to sources of water and power and to transport. The new plants are typically attractive structures emphasizing function, and providing for employee needs with cafeterias, good lighting, parking space, adequate office space for white collar workers, and pleasant surroundings.

More than 50 per cent of the spending for business facilities from the mid-1950's to the early 1960's, according to the National Planning Association's *National Economic Projections Series,* has consisted of spending for replacement and modernization, and under 50 per cent has represented expenditures for expansion.[12] The distinction is often difficult to draw in specific instances since the technological changes which prompt modernization usually involve the installation of more advanced equipment with a capacity greater than

---

10. Derived from *National Economic Projections Series,* 1962, National Planning Association, p. II–16.

11. *Annual Report of the Council of Economic Advisers,* January, 1962, p. 129.

12. *National Economic Projections Series,* 1962, p. II–16.

that of the equipment which has been replaced. However, expenditures for expansion are more sensitive to increases in demand which create near-capacity levels of operation. Firms may engage in substantial replacement-modernization spending, as in the early 1960's, in spite of the presence of considerable unutilized productive capacity in their industry.

The 9 per cent of GNP represented by private spending for plant and equipment in 1962 and 1963 reflected the slow growth of demand in the economy. This rate of spending over the next decade could probably not sustain a growth rate of more than 3 per cent a year.

III.

A growth rate in GNP of 4 per cent a year or somewhat higher (measured in constant prices from the full capacity level of production in the base year) is generally identified with full employment. Past experience with changes in the relationship of capital stock to output make it possible to estimate the private capital outlays for creating the productive capacity needed to produce the trillion-dollar output projected for 1975 with this pace of growth over the next decade.[13] The estimates assume a continuation of the decline in stocks of plant per dollar of output and approximately the present value of stocks of equipment per dollar of output.

The expected private capital outlays are summarized in Table 3–2.

Keeping the economy growing at 4 per cent a year would require an estimated level of private capital expenditures in 1975 that is more than 100 per cent greater than in 1962. Attainment of this growth would involve increasing private capital outlays from under 9 per cent of GNP in the early

---

13. Taking into account the anticipated increases in the labor force, in productivity, and the expected decline in hours of work, the volume of employment required to produce this amount of output is consistent with an unemployment rate of slightly under 4 per cent of the civilian labor force.

Table 3–2
Estimated Plant and Equipment Expenditures
to Achieve Economic Growth, 1970 and 1975
(in millions of 1962 dollars)

Sector	Actual Expenditures in 1962	Projected Expenditures for the 4% Growth Rate		% Increase 1962-1975
		in 1970	in 1975	
1. Manufacturing	$14,700	$25,200	$32,500	121%
2. Mining	1,100	2,000	2,200	100
3. Transportation including Mass Transit[a]	2,900	5,900	7,400	155
4. Public Utilities	5,500	9,600	12,200	122
5. Communications	3,600	5,900	7,500	108
6. Trade, Services, Finance, and Construction	9,500	15,000	18,600	96
7. Agriculture	3,800	4,900	5,200	37
8. Private Non-Profit Organizations	3,500	6,700	9,000	157
9. Other	4,300	6,600	7,700	79
10. Total	48,900	81,800	102,300	109
11. Total as % of GNP	8.8%	10.4%	10.4%	

a. Expenditures by commercial carriers only.

1960's to almost 10.5 per cent of the larger gross national product anticipated in the 1970's.

The largest percentage increases in private capital outlays in this portrayal of a growing economy are listed for non-profit organizations, transportation, public utilities, and manufacturing. Within manufacturing, sizeable increases are projected for the electronics industry, chemicals, food processing and canning, and in the manufacture of scientific instruments.[14] These industries are likely to be characterized by substantial growth in output, productivity, and company-financed R & D expenditures. Not surprisingly, the smallest percentage increase for any of the major sectors is listed for agriculture.

A dynamic economy can be expected to increase spending for both the expansion and the modernization of plant and

14. See *American Industry in 1976 and 1985*, National Planning Association, 1964, pp. 3–4.

equipment, and this tendency influences the estimates for the 1970's. Expenditures for expansion of productive capacity are projected to rise to 55 per cent of the total private capital outlays in 1975. A continuing emphasis on expenditures for equipment, reflecting greater R & D spending by industry, is also anticipated for the next decade.

On an economy-wide basis, productivity, using GNP per manhour as an indicator, is expected to increase by about 3 per cent a year over the next decade. Growth in the capital stock per worker is the source of a large part of the productivity increase. How rapidly the capital stock per worker is likely to rise will depend mainly on the pace of GNP growth. The significance of economic growth for the increase in the stock of plant and equipment per worker in the private economy is summarized in Table 3–3 by projecting the impact of slow and vigorous growth in the coming decade.

Table 3–3
Average Annual Rate of Change, Private Capital Stock, Private Labor Force, and Capital Stock Per Worker
1961 to 1975*

Average Annual Rate of Change in	AVERAGE ANNUAL RATE OF INCREASE, 1961 TO 1975	
	3% Annual Growth in GNP	4% Annual Growth in GNP
1. Total Private Capital Stock	2.4%	3.5%
2. Private Labor Force	1.5	1.7
3. Capital Stock Per Member of Private Labor Force	0.9	1.8

* Derived from *National Economic Projection Series*, 1962, p. II-15; 1963, p. I-21.

The stock of plant and equipment can be expected to increase more rapidly than the labor force, so that capital stock per worker in the private economy is likely to grow by approximately 1 to 2 per cent a year to 1975. The percentage increase in capital stock per worker is twice as great with 4-per cent growth in GNP as it is in an economy growing at the slow 3-per cent rate. The larger increase for the 4-per cent rate partially reflects a greater degree of mechanization in producing goods and services. It also arises from a shift in the combination of products and services accompanying more rapid growth.

While these projections point to rising capacity and earning power per worker, if the experience since World War II continues, the gains from overall economic growth will be unevenly diffused through the private work force. Even in a rapidly growing economy, "pockets of poverty" and unemployment would be likely to persist in areas bypassed by economic advance and among the poorly trained and poorly educated members of the labor force. With slow growth in GNP, the "pockets of poverty" in isolated segments of the labor force would be diffused throughout the economy by a rising volume of unemployment.

Spending for plant and equipment represents the setting aside of resources which could otherwise be utilized to satisfy current private and public needs, and employing these resources in uses which will yield increased output for greater satisfaction of needs in the future. The $102 billion listed for private capital outlays symbolizes an equivalent quantity of resources set aside to assure growth. These resources will not be available in 1975 for raising standards of living or for the pursuit of other goals. But the resources set aside each year to expand and modernize productive capacity make it possible to more effectively pursue our objectives in health, education, or living standards after the additional capacity is in operation. Since the outlays for plant and equipment are part of the costs of growth, they are treated as preempted expenditures in the study. Achieving a dynamic economy with a sufficiently larger volume of output to permit substantial improvements over present performance standards is estimated to preempt a tenth of GNP for the construction of private plant and equipment in the 1970's. However, the improvements which are possible with these additions to productive capacity are lesser improvements than those representing the aspirations spelled out in the standards for the sixteen goals.

IV.

The aspiration standards for the sixteen goals imply considerably larger increases in spending for private plant and equipment in the next decade than the expenditures listed to assure growth. They imply greater capital expenditures for specific goals, i.e., urban development, transportation, or natural resources, as well as a sizeable overall increase in productive capacity to create the $1.1 trillion volume of output required for full achievement of our objectives.

Table 3–4 summarizes the private plant and equipment

Table 3–4
Estimated Private Expenditures for Plant and Equipment
for Goals, 1970 and 1975
(in millions of 1962 dollars)

Sector	Expenditures in 1962	Projected Expenditures 1970	1975	% Increase 1962 to 1975
1. Manufacturing	$14,700	$35,700	$47,900	226%
2. Mining	1,100	2,700	3,300	200
3. Transportation[a]	2,900	8,500	10,500	262
4. Public Utilities	5,500	13,800	18,100	229
5. Communications	3,600	8,300	11,000	206
6. Trade, Service, Finance, Construction	9,500	21,000	27,300	187
7. Agriculture	3,800	6,000	6,800	79
8. Private Non-Profit Organizations	3,500	10,700	15,000	329
9. Other	4,300	9,700	11,700	172
10. Total	48,900	116,400	151,600	210
11. Total as % of GNP	8.8%	14.8%	15.5%	

a. Expenditures by commercial carriers only.

expenditures implied by the standards for all the goals in 1970 and 1975. All told, these capital outlays are listed at $152 billion in 1975. This is $50 billion more than the estimate of the capital expenditures required to sustain a dynamic economy in the mid-1970's, and over $100 billion more than private capital outlays in 1962.

As in the estimates of capital outlays for growth, the largest increases are projected for non-profit organizations, transportation, public utilities, and manufacturing. Two goals contribute heavily to the increases listed for these sectors and for several others. They are urban development and transportation. The private non-residential construction called for in urban development is expected to cost over $30 billion a year by 1975. This would include spending to rebuild the commercial and cultural facilities of the downtown areas, and large sums to provide suburbs with additional shopping centers, office buildings, public utilities, and recreational centers. Outlays growing out of urban development are primarily responsible for the large percentage increase listed for construction by non-profit organizations. Part of these expenditures could be used to establish metropolitan research and development centers to improve the utilization of the resources which contribute to the economy of a metropolis, and to attract new science-oriented industries. The expenditures would also include private spending for museums, theaters, churches, and schools. Private outlays to construct medical centers and hospitals, very largely in urban areas, are projected to triple to $3 billion by 1975.

Business investment in transportation facilities is estimated to involve expenditures of $20 billion in 1975. This is about double the amount estimated for transportation in Table 3–4, since it includes spending for trucks, trailers, passenger cars, and airplanes owned by private firms in non-transportation industries as well as the expenditures by commercial carriers listed in the table. Outlays by the railroads to adapt their roadbed, routes, and equipment to the potential speed and tractive power of modern locomotives is anticipated to cost $2.4 billion a year in the 1970's. Spending for new types of transportation is listed as adding approximately $2 billion a year to private plant and equipment expenditures. The most likely candidates for greater spending in 1975, as seen in the mid-1960's, are gas turbine engines for motor vehicles, nuclear ships, hydrofoils, and supersonic airplanes.

In addition to the private plant and equipment outlays for urban development and transportation, private capital expenditures exceeding $2 billion a year are listed for the natural resources goal. Half of this spending would be undertaken to assure an adequate water supply for industrial use.

To attain the level of productive capacity and the additional facilities needed for the goals in the 1970's would mean increasing sharply the percentage of GNP used for private plant and equipment. The total outlay of 15.5 per cent of gross national product called for by our aspirations compares with an estimated 10.5 per cent to keep the economy growing by 4 per cent a year over the next decade, and the 9 per cent actually spent in 1962 and 1963.[15]

Taken by themselves, the costs of the business and non-profit facilities included in the projections for the private plant and equipment goal represent feasible objectives for the 1970's. We could afford to replace the old factory buildings with attractive modern structures located in industrial parks in the periphery of the metropolis, or we could replace the large ocean-going ships in our merchant marine with nuclear-powered vessels. The significant problem is how to accomplish these objectives, and to what degree, while simultaneously pursuing the goals concerned with private expenditures to raise standards of living, plus the many goals involving public spending to develop the nation's human resources and its security. Even with a trillion-dollar GNP, these competing claims would create a need for priorities—for choices—to balance our aspirations with our resources.

---

15. This estimate indicates that full achievement of the goals would require a considerable rise in the average and marginal capital-output ratios. However, it is difficult to compare the capital-output ratios for the goals with actual ratios or those estimated for growth, because achievement of the goals would presuppose a different composition of output and of capital outlays. There would be considerably heavier emphasis on transportation and construction by non-profit organizations, for example.

CHAPTER 4

Urban
Development

I.

Urban development is often referred to as "urban renewal." More fundamentally, it pertains to "human renewal" —to creating viable urban communities in a rapidly changing American society. Expenditures to enable people to live, work, move about, shop, and play in American cities in the 1970's are projected to rise to an annual total approximating $130 billion. Most of this total represents private expenditures.

Urban development is a "framework" concept rather than a specific activity or function. It provides a perspective for integrating the different activities which contribute to healthy urban growth into a meaningful whole. Development includes provision for the transportation networks which link the central city and suburb. It must also take into account needs for housing, schools, hospitals, industrial and commercial buildings, public utilities, recreational facilities, and a variety of government buildings. Since most of these facilities also figure as part of the requirements for other national objectives, many goals contribute to urban development.

The forces which have transformed America into a modern industrial society have also made our nation an increasingly urbanized society. In 1900, 40 per cent of the population lived in urban areas. By 1960, this proportion had grown to 70 per cent. Almost all of the population increase between 1960 and 1970, it is estimated, will be an increase in the population of urbanized areas.

The growth of the urban population is summarized in Table 4–1. The table also includes a projection of this growth to 1975.

Table 4–1
Growth of the U.S. Urban Population, 1900–1975*

Item	Actual			Projected	
	1900	1950	1960	1970	1975
1. U.S. Population (in millions)	76	151	179	209	226
2. Per Cent of Total Living in					
a. Urban areas	40%	64%	70%	74%	76%
b. Metropolitan areas[a]	31.5	56	63	68	71
3. Per Cent of Metropolitan Area					
Population in Central Cities	68	58.5	51	47	44.5

a. For years prior to 1950, areas whose principal city had a population of 50,000 or more are included as metropolitan areas.
* Sources: U.S. Department of Commerce, Bureau of the Census, and National Planning Association.

By 1975, over three fourths of all Americans will be living in urban areas. Most of the population increase in the coming decade is expected to take place in the suburbs. For every person added to the population of the central city, it is anticipated that 2 or 3 persons will be added in the suburbs.

As urbanization proceeds, expanding metropolitan centers will emerge to form a new social and economic unit—the megalopolis. The 500-mile stretch from Alexandria, Virginia, to Portsmouth, New Hampshire, including some 64 metropolitan communities, will constitute a northeastern megalopolis whose main outlines are already discernible. This area, covering 2 per cent of America's land area, contains 21 per cent of our population.[1] Other megalopolitan centers will form in the Chicago-Indiana-Wisconsin area, the Dallas-Forth Worth area, in San Francisco, and elsewhere. Problems of transportation, land and water use, recreation and housing will be common to all parts of these units for which at present there is no equivalent political or administrative entity.

Advances in transportation technology have served as the strategic variable in determining the scale of urbanization. Urban growth in the nineteenth century was at first heavily influenced by natural waterways and canals, and, later, also by railroads and steamships. Since World War I, the automobile, the truck, and the highway have greatly speeded up the pace of urbanization and changed its nature. They have created the metropolitan area with its division between central city and suburb. Automobiles, trucks, and highways facilitate the growth of the suburbs, and they contribute to the decline of the central city. Since urban transportation is the critical element in metropolitan growth, it is singled out for detailed consideration in this chapter.

I I.

We are already spending large sums for objectives which relate to community development. Total private and public spending for urban facilities in 1962 is estimated at $64 billion. The breakdown of the expenditures is listed in Table 4–2.

The $64 billion spent for these facilities in 1962 represents a massive investment in housing, schools, industrial buildings, shopping centers, and highways. All told, this spending was about one fourth greater than the expenditures for national defense in the same year. However, the

---

1. President Johnson's Message on the Cities, March 2, 1965.

Table 4–2
Public and Private Expenditures
for Urban Facilities, 1962
(in millions of 1962 dollars)

Item	Expenditures in 1962
1. Urban Construction and Maintenance Excluding Transportation	$59,700
a. Residential construction	20,900
b. Industrial and commercial buildings	7,600
c. Public utilities	4,800
d. Sewer and water systems	1,700
e. Health facilities	1,100
f. Educational facilities	3,500
g. Recreational facilities	1,600
h. Other government buildings	2,200
i. Churches, private institutional facilities, and miscellaneous	1,500
j. Maintenance and repair	14,800
2. Urban Transportation Facilities	4,500
a. Railroad and transit facilities	100
b. Urban streets and highways	2,900
c. Highway maintenance	1,500
3. Total Expenditures for Urban Facilities	64,200

total includes a mass of individual details which are frequently unrelated to an overall program for meeting the needs of metropolitan areas. Their net result, in some instances, has been to make the city less hospitable to human habitation by adding to snarled traffic, polluted air, sterile housing projects, and a "churning destruction and frantic rebuilding."[2]

Cities, suburbs, and metropolitan areas are likely to figure prominently in national policy in the coming decade. The recent Supreme Court decisions directing the states to reapportion their legislatures and congressional districts to give greater representation to the urban population are a significant indication of this tendency. The legislation to establish a cabinet-level Department of Housing and Urban

2. *The State of the City,* New York Chapter, American Institute of Architects, 1964.

Development enacted by Congress in 1965 is a symptom of a growing awareness that urban needs and problems call for an effort which as a nation we have not yet attempted to make.

III.

The elements which create the need for large scale community development can be summarized in terms of shifts in the location of economic activity within the metropolis, changes in the makeup of the population in the central city and the suburb, and the mushrooming growth in the number of private automobiles. These factors intensify the problems of the central city, and they increase the separation between the urban core and the suburbs.

The truck and the highway diminish the cost advantages that induce firms to locate close to railroad terminals or ship docks—facilities usually located in the heart of the city. Part of the wholesaling trade has moved out of the congested high rent center of the city to its periphery or to the suburbs. New manufacturing plants, and especially the larger ones, are now generally built in outlying parts of the metropolitan area near highways where parking space is available. As middle income families have moved to the suburbs, suburban shopping centers have taken over much of the retail trade which would otherwise have taken place in the shopping district in the heart of the city. Between 1948 and 1954, years of heavy movement to the suburbs, the volume of retail trade in the central business districts of 24 metropolitan areas increased by less than 1 per cent. The retail turnover in the suburbs of these same areas increased by 53 per cent.[3]

The suburbs have become important centers of employment and economic activity as well as being places where people live. Much of the investment in commercial and industrial buildings in the past decade has been located in

3. Wilbur Smith and Associates, *Highways and Urban Growth*, 1961, p. 22.

the outlying areas. Many of the buildings in the central business district have been razed and their sites converted into parking lots. With these changes, the economic functions of the central cities of earlier periods become dispersed throughout the surrounding areas.

Since World War II, middle income white families have moved to the suburbs in large numbers. Upper income families have tended to remain in the central city along with single people, childless couples, older persons, and a growing number of nonwhites. The overall result, as President Johnson observed in his 1965 Message on the Cities, is that "the old, the poor, the discriminated against are increasingly concentrated in central city ghettos; while others move to the suburbs leaving the central city to battle against immense odds."[4]

Nonwhites now make up a majority of the central city population in only one of the ten largest cities—Washington, D. C. However, most of the increase in the population of the central cities since 1950 has been made up of nonwhites, and almost all of the population growth of the suburbs is composed of white persons. This differential in the growth of the central city and the suburb is summarized in Table 4–3.

The suburban population grew by three times as much as the central city population during the 1950's. Only one in twenty-five of the new suburbanites was nonwhite. Five out of eight of the additions to the central city were nonwhite.

Racial segregation has become an urban problem throughout the nation rather than a specifically southern problem. In 1950, about 60 per cent of the Negro population was living in cities. This proportion had increased to 73 per cent by 1960. By 1975, almost 85 per cent of American Negroes are expected to be living in cities.[5] Like most migrations, the movement of Negroes to the city is largely

---

4. President Johnson's 1965 Message on the Cities.

5. National Planning Association, *National Economic Projections Series, Regional Projections to 1976, Technical Supplement No. 8,* 1962, p. 181.

Table 4–3
Increase in White and Nonwhite Population, Central Cities and Suburbs, 1950 to 1960*

Item	Increase between 1950 and 1960
1. Amount of Increase (in millions)	
a. In central cities	5.6
b. Outside of central cities	17.9
2. Per cent of Population Increase in Central Cities made up of	
a. Whites	38%
b. Nonwhites	62%
3. Per cent of Population Increase Outside of Central Cities made up of	
a. Whites	96%
b. Nonwhites	4%

* Derived from *Our Nonwhite Population and Its Housing*, Housing and Home Finance Agency, 1963, p. 24.

made up of young people in the age groups establishing families. In some northern cities, the birthrate among Negroes of 40 to 50 per 1,000 compares to a national figure for whites of 24 per 1,000.[6] These birth rates for Negroes are as high as the birthrates associated with the population explosion in the underdeveloped nations.

Residential segregation within the metropolis reinforces segregation in education, in employment, and in human relations generally. Unemployment, low incomes, slum housing, crime and delinquency, broken families, and illiteracy make the urban nonwhite ghettos concentrations of social dynamite. Their young people are seldom motivated by educational programs geared to the culture and the vocational prospects of the white middle class. Because of changes in job requirements emphasizing higher levels of skill and education, many of the nonwhite unemployed are becoming unemployable unless they receive special retraining and education. Public welfare assistance has become the primary means of support for successive generations of urban

6. Grier, Eunice and George, "The Negro Migration," in *The Housing Yearbook*, 1962.

families with inadequate income, education, and job skills. Coping with the problems the urban slums represent will require large scale expenditures for education, for social welfare, for housing, and for public health activities. Expenditures are likely to accelerate in the next decade because of the large backlog of needs, the civil rights movement, and rapid population growth.

The exodus of the middle class population and of many businesses to the suburbs erodes the tax base of the cities at the same time that the pressures for greater expenditures intensify. Per capita municipal tax revenues increased between 1954 and 1963 by 43 per cent. Local government indebtedness, however, rose by 119 per cent.[7] Inadequate transportation, high crime rates, poor land use, or public health problems in the central city affect the entire metropolis. But the division between central city and suburb along lines of income and race makes it difficult to translate common needs into metropolitan-wide loyalties and action.

IV.

The alternatives available in transportation heavily influence the concentration or dispersion of the urban population, the growth or decline of central business districts, land use, and public health. Consumer preference for the private automobile is the dominating fact in metropolitan transportation.

The automobile is the leading form of urban transportation for getting to work, for shopping, and for pleasure trips. Automobile ownership is as prevalent in American cities, other than special cases such as Manhattan, as in the nation at large. Families owning two or more cars in the United States are concentrated in the suburbs.

Some of the problems attributed to the automobile are the results of inadequate planning to take account of the per-

---

7. President Johnson's Message on the Cities.

vasive effects of mass utilization of the private automobile. Suburban sprawl is an instance. Much of the development of strips of land along highways has taken place in local jurisdictions without zoning regulations. The net result in many instances, as summarized in a recent study of New York metropolitan development by the American Institute of Architects has been the growth of "mile upon mile of nondescript, ill planned, ugly neighborhoods of declining value," or a chaotic suburban limbo of filling stations, shopping strips, and shoddy housing.[8]

The space requirements of the automobile frequently conflict with other efforts by cities to conserve space. Two thirds of the land in the central business district of Los Angeles in the late 1950's was used for streets, freeways, service ways, off-street parking, and loading.[9] The Institute of Public Administration estimates that the average journey to work by automobile at a speed of 20 miles an hour requires from 6 to 45 times as much road space per person as by a transit bus, and from 10 to 90 times the amount required by multiple-unit railroad cars.[10]

Investment in additional metropolitan highways often offers little more than temporary relief from congestion. After a short lapse of time the additional capacity is taken up by an increase in the number of automobiles using the highway. To cite the experience of Los Angeles again, the Hollywood Freeway was opened in 1954 and designed to carry an ultimate volume of 100,000 vehicles a day. It took one year for traffic to reach a daily level of 168,000 vehicles.[11]

Automobiles contribute most heavily to metropolitan congestion during the peak hours of travel to and from work.

8. *The State of the City.*
9. *National Transportation Policy,* Report prepared for the Committee on Interstate and Foreign Commerce, U.S. Senate, 1961, p. 592.
10. *Urban Transportation and Public Policy.* Institute of Public Administration, 1961. Ch. 1, p. 5.
11. *National Transportation Policy,* p. 597.

Sixty-four per cent of metropolitan area workers, according to a recent study, use the automobile to get to work.[12] In the heavily congested central business districts, in seven of nine metropolitan areas surveyed in the late 1950's, one third or more of the persons entering the district during the peak hours entered by private automobile or taxi.[13]

In the absence of adequate controls, automobiles, trucks, and buses have been a major source of air pollution. Rough estimates indicate that pollution from motor vehicle exhaust is responsible for 40 per cent of air pollution in New York City and from 65 to 70 per cent in Los Angeles.[14] There is a growing conviction among public health authorities that air pollution is a factor in respiratory diseases, lung cancer, eye ailments, heart disease, and other illness. It is also injurious to plant and animal life.[15] The Surgeon General of the United States has estimated that economic losses due to air pollution in the early 1960's cost the nation more than $7 billion a year.[16]

As automobile use has expanded in metropolitan areas since World War II, mass transit has undergone a spectacular decline. The history of subway and elevated transit, trolley and bus lines in the past fifteen years is a story of declining use, growing obsolescence of facilities, actual bankruptcies, and, more frequently, threatened bankruptcies averted by public assistance or abandonment of facilities or service. Commuter railroads have survived in many instances because of tax relief extended by state and local authorities.

The decline of mass transit patronage is summarized in

12. *Automobile Facts and Figures,* Automobile Manufacturers Association, 1963, p. 43.

13. *National Transportation Policy,* p. 599.

14. *Urban Transportation and Public Policy,* Ch. 1, p. 8.

15. *Motor Vehicles, Air Pollution, and Health,* A Report of the Surgeon General to the U.S. Congress, 1962, pp. 39–54.

16. "Air Pollution—A Nationwide Menace," in *New Medical Material Commentary,* February, 1963, p. 17.

Table 4–4. The figures in the table relate to all forms of mass transit other than commuting railroad service.

Table 4–4
Urban Mass Transit, Total Passengers
and Rides Per Capita, 1935 to 1960*

Year	Billions of Passengers	Annual Rides Per Capita Urban Population
1935	12.2	171
1950	17.2	195
1955	11.5	124
1960	9.4	95

* Source: American Transit Association, New York City.

Over half the cars in railroad commuter service in New York, Philadelphia, and Chicago in 1958 had been purchased before 1925. Most of the rolling stock of urban rail systems was acquired before World War II.[17] These increasingly obsolete facilities are heavily used only during the peak hours of travel. Peak hour subway patronage in New York and Chicago has made up more than half of the total patronage.[18]

Since mass transit offers great opportunities for economizing space and time in moving people within the metropolis, it is reasonable to anticipate that major steps will be taken to rehabilitate urban mass transit in the next decade. These steps can be expected to involve considerably more than simply adding to or replacing existing facilities. Many of the changes will represent extensions of present developments. Minibuses, used in Washington, D.C., have demonstrated their value in relieving congestion in downtown districts. The journey to and from work could be facilitated by express buses using specially reserved lanes, and by facilities for parking automobiles in large underground or multi-storied garages at the periphery of the downtown areas. By

17. *Urban Transportation and Public Policy*, Ch. 2, pp. 35–36.
18. *National Transportation Policy*, p. 599.

1975, many subway systems are likely to adopt the high-speed automated trains used recently on an experimental basis in New York City. These developments should be encouraged by the current interest in urban transit renewal as expressed in the mass transit legislation enacted by Congress in 1964.

The amount spent since World War II in developing new or improved mass transit technologies is unknown, but it is probably less than one million dollars annually. In spite of the absence of a large scale research effort, the technical knowledge exists to create new types of transit systems which offer good prospects for relieving congestion, especially in the central business districts. The long lead times in planning mass transit facilities, large investments in existing modes of transport, and the requirement that mass transit be fail-safe in its earliest public use are likely to rule out major overhauls in urban transportation technology in the next ten years. However, with an expanded research and development program, some of the innovations which are currently regarded as highly speculative possibilities would probably be candidates for use by 1975 or 1980.

Walk-on, walk-off conveyor belts, sometimes referred to as "moving sidewalks," and the "carveyor," illustrate these possibilities. Like minibuses, conveyor belts or the "carveyor" could do away with much of the need for large buses, taxis, and automobiles in the downtown business and shopping districts. They could also be used for short-distance movement of freight. At present, slow speeds of 1-1/2 or 2 miles an hour, and possible safety hazards, remain to be overcome before the conveyor belts are in widespread use.

The "carveyor" is made up of small car units, each seating six to ten people. The cars move on a separate automated track or on belts at speeds of about 15 miles an hour. Passengers board the cars at station points where the trains slow down to a speed of one mile an hour. Like the simpler conveyor belt, the "carveyor" requires more testing and development before it becomes a serious prospect for downtown passenger service.

Monorails have also been widely proposed as a solution for urban mass transit problems. Most monorail systems are, in effect, upside down railroads with cars and propulsion equipment similar to those used in standard operations. With the exception of a line built at Wuppertal, Germany over 50 years ago and special monorails at world fairs in Seattle and New York, they have not achieved widespread success. However, recent investments by U.S. firms in producing new types of monorail equipment could lead to improved facilities with good commercial prospects.

Other possible innovations in metropolitan transportation may include automated highways with electronic guidance and control systems. They could help relieve congestion on expressways by moving large numbers of people in individual vehicles in a highly channelized system. Hydrofoils are already in commercial service for suburban commuting and their use is likely to increase considerably before 1975.

Much of the metropolitan transportation development in the period since World War II has been concentrated on building additional highway facilities. Yet transportation is a system made up of different modes, each of which offers special advantages for particular communities, types of trips, and individuals.

Subway rapid rail transit is especially suited for large metropolitan centers and for commutation to the central business district. By 1970, there will probably be at least 29 metropolitan areas with populations exceeding one million. In the early 1960's, only five had rapid rail transit. Commuting railroads have an advantage in transporting passengers to the downtown district from outlying communities beyond the reach of subways. In turn, use of the existing railroad rights-of-way often supplies the most efficient and least expensive method for extending urban rapid rail systems to new areas. Bus travel is especially suitable for smaller metropolitan areas lacking the population density for subways, and as a feeder in the suburbs to rapid rail service. Automobiles offer inherent advantages for interurban trips, for social and

recreational travel, and for shopping and business trips outside the central downtown district. Automobiles also serve
as the sole means of local transportation in areas where low
population density could at best support infrequent bus
service.

By 1975, we will need urban transportation facilities for
the daily movement of 200 million people and over 80 million automobiles.[19] The solution to these accelerating transportation needs, according to one authority, S. S. Taylor,
"lies in discovering that complementary system of streets,
freeways, and transit lines which most effectively promote
. . . a truly functional pattern of land use."[20] Both the existing modes of mass transit, and the new transportation technologies, are likely to figure as essential components in this
complementary system in the 1970's.

V.

Mass transit, hospitals, water systems, schools, and houses
make up a composite whose ingredients are only indirectly
related to each other. Yet they all contribute to the overall
objective of community development—making the nation's
cities more hospitable places for human habitation. In part,
this objective is summed up in a recent report of the New
York Chapter of the American Institute of Architects discussing urban development in that city. The report points
out that

Neighborhoods . . . must be planned to create environments
which offer more than mere spartan utility, which have character and provide pleasure for those who live there . . . The
movement of (middle income) families to the suburbs must be
moderated . . . The city needs the good social influence of these
families, their buying power and their taxpaying ability. The

---

19. President Johnson's Message on the Cities.

20. Quoted in *National Transportation Policy*, p. 603.

city also needs to reduce the strain caused by commuters on highway and rail facilities.[21]

Urban development, of course, is concerned with all income groups and with the wholesome growth of both the central city and the suburb. It is also concerned with preserving the unique function of the city as a center offering business, professional, cultural, and educational facilities within ready reach of one another.

We are currently spending over 11 per cent of GNP for purposes which relate to urban development. Estimates of the expenditures required for meeting needs vary widely. They range from a figure of $4 billion to $7 billion a year in the 1958 Rockefeller Brothers Fund report for public expenditures, largely devoted to housing, to an estimate of $187.5 billion a year for private and public spending for slum clearance, highways, and other community facilities, presented in study published by the Committee for Economic Development. A report published by the National Planning Association in 1963 estimates the annual average investment required for urban renewal and development at $120 billion to $125 billion, largely made up of private expenditures.[22]

The estimates vary so markedly because of differences in what is included in the scope of development. The American Council to Improve our Neighborhoods defines development as including the "total of all the public and private actions which must be taken to provide for the continuous sound maintenance and development of the urban areas."[23] Our estimates of expenditures for development needs in the

21. *The State of the City.*

22. Rockefeller Brothers Fund, *The Challenge to America: Its Economic and Social Aspects,* 1958; Isaacs, R. R., "The Real Costs of Urban Renewal," in *Problems of United States Economic Development,* Committee for Economic Development, 1958; Wagner, P., *The Scope and Financing of Urban Renewal and Development,* National Planning Association, 1963.

23. *Urban Renewal Research Program,* American Council to Improve our Neighborhoods, New York, 1954, pp. 1–3.

1970's refer to the spending for facilities implied by this comprehensive definition.

Many of the objectives in development are not primarily questions of large scale expenditures. The elimination of the pattern of racial segregation that divides central city and suburb is a problem in legislation and in changing social attitudes rather than in spending. The cost of effective metropolitan planning organizations would amount to no more than a fraction of 1 per cent of the projected expenditures listed for urban development in the next decade. Moreover, while the expenditures pertain to physical facilities, it is apparent that greater operating expenditures would usually be necessary to efficiently utilize the facilities. Improved school buildings, for example, would be of little avail if they were staffed by badly paid, poorly prepared instructors, teaching an outmoded curriculum.

Since most of the expenditures for urban development are part of the cost of other goals, the estimates for these goals offer a basis for many of our projections in community development. The sums listed for urban housing, education, health, shopping centers and industrial buildings, or for pure water, are the share of the total expenditures anticipated for these objectives which are attributable to urban needs. This distribution takes into account the percentage of the total population expected to be living in cities in the next decade, and the increase in population projected for the urban areas. The allocation of the global totals also recognizes the special needs for more and better schools, housing, and health facilities for the rapidly growing urban nonwhite population. The estimates for the standards for these goals are discussed in detail in the individual chapters dealing with each goal.[24]

The most comprehensive analysis of capital requirements for urban development has been presented by Dyckman and

---

24. See Chapters 3, 6, 7, 10, and 12 for a discussion of the other goals which figure in the projections for urban development.

Isaacs in their study, *Capital Requirements for Urban Re-development and Renewal*, published in 1961.[25] Our projections for the items which are not included in mass transit or as parts of other goals are derived from the Dyckman and Isaacs estimates. However, they have been adapted to the framework of 1962 prices, GNP growth rates, and population increase assumed in this study.

Expenditure totals including as many components as those listed for urban development mean little unless they can be related to a reference point. The cost of extending the present level of development activities for the larger population living in urban areas in the 1970's is the basis for our benchmark, or preempted estimate. These expenditures would enable us to do no more than we are currently doing to relieve traffic congestion, blighted neighborhoods, or suburban sprawl in the next decade. All told, population growth would raise the cost of continuing this hypothetical *status quo* from $64 billion in 1962 to over $83 billion in 1975.

Perpetuation of the *status quo* bears little relationship to needs or to the growing concern with urban problems. The expenditures needed for our redevelopment objectives would raise total annual spending by an additional $47 billion by 1975.

Improvement of transportation facilities is probably the critical component in the plans and programs for rebuilding our cities, although it accounts for only a small share of the expenditure projections. It is reasonable to assume that consumers' preference for their automobiles will continue in the next decade. The problem for metropolitan communities will be to allow for this preference without choking the central cities with automobiles, and using up most of the available land for highways and parking facilities. Expenditure for urban streets and highways to accommodate the 80-odd million automobiles likely to be owned by the urban popu-

---

25. Dyckman, J. W., and Isaacs, R. R., *Capital Requirements for Urban Development and Renewal*, McGraw-Hill, 1961.

lation in 1975 is expected to increase to $10 billion. The figure includes both highway construction and maintenance.

The Institute of Public Administration has estimated that rehabilitating urban mass transit would cost $10 billion, spread out over the 10-year period, 1961 to 1970.[26] This sum includes the cost of replacing all obsolete rolling stock, the cost of proposals for expanding existing transit systems in six major cities, and expenditures for new mass transportation systems receiving consideration in four large metropolitan areas. The need for improved transit in many other cities, together with continued obsolescence of equipment and population growth in the next decade, are likely to lead to a comparable volume of expenditures in the 1970's.

Further development of new transportation technologies and restoration of the art of walking could make it possible to create areas free of automobiles, large buses, and trucks for most of the day in the central business districts. Initial costs for a carveyor system in Los Angeles have been estimated at $4 million a mile. Expenditures for facilities incorporating the new transport technologies are projected at $300 million to $400 million a year in the 1970's.

In order to reduce hazards from air pollution, the estimates include the cost of equipping motor vehicles with devices to control exhaust and crankcase fumes. Four new devices to reduce exhaust fumes have been approved by the California Motor Vehicle Pollution Control Board. Currently they range in price from $50 to $120.[27] Similar protection is available for eliminating crankcase fumes. If the cost of both devices fell by half through further research and mass production over the next ten years, we would be spending $700 million to $800 million a year in the 1970's to equip new motor vehicles in urban areas with the two controls. These figures are about one tenth of the estimated annual economic loss from air pollution in the early 1960's. By the

---

26. *Urban Transportation and Public Policy*, Ch. 2, p. 66.
27. *Wall Street Journal*, June 18, 1964, p. 28.

end of another decade, however, improvements in the combustion engine or its replacement, perhaps by fuel cells, may do away with most of the pollution currently attributable to motor vehicles.

The expenditures listed for the aspiration standards in urban transportation and for the other facilities in urban development are summarized in Table 4–5.

Table 4–5
Estimated Public and Private Expenditures for
the Urban Development Goal, 1970 and 1975
(in millions of 1962 dollars)

Item	Expenditures in 1962	Projected Expenditures for Aspiration Standards in 1970	in 1975
1. Urban Construction			
Excluding Transportation	$59,700	$97,900	$116,900
a. Residential construction	20,900	34,300	42,500
b. Industrial and commercial buildings	7,600	14,000	17,600
c. Public utilities	4,800	7,000	7,700
d. Sewer and water systems	1,700	2,700	3,100
e. Health facilities	1,100	4,300	5,700
f. Educational facilities	3,500	5,900	5,200
g. Recreational facilities	1,600	2,800	3,300
h. Other government buildings	2,200	3,600	3,800
i. Churches, private institutional facilities, and miscellaneous	1,500	2,500	3,200
j. Maintenance and repair	14,800	20,800	24,800
2. Urban Transportation	4,500	11,100	12,800
a. Railroad and transit construction	100	1,100	1,100
b. New urban transportation methods	—	400	400
c. Urban streets and highways	2,900	5,800	7,000
d. Highway maintenance	1,500	3,100	3,500
e. Air pollution control	—	700	800
3. Total Expenditures for Urban Facilities	64,200	109,000	129,700

The standards imply a level of spending for urban development that rises from 11 per cent of GNP in 1962 to between 13 and 14 per cent in 1975. Expenditures would approximately double in this period. As in 1962, housing makes up the largest item in the totals, and spending for industrial and commercial buildings is the next largest. These are also the areas which are very largely composed of private expenditures. Since spending for urban mass transit had almost come to a halt in the early 1960's, the modest increases projected for the standards constitute a sizeable percentage increase.

While the $130-billion total listed for the urban development goal in 1975 is an enormous sum, it pertains, after all, to the requirements for facilities of the preponderant segment of our society. The projected total probably underestimates overall urban needs in the next decade, because it includes only physical facilities. Estimates on this massive scale are reasonable anticipations of the costs of our goal, because the nation's problems in education, race relations, housing, social welfare, health, recreation, and water supply are primarily urban problems.

CHAPTER 5

Social
Welfare

I.

Programs and objectives in social welfare are currently
undergoing reexamination and change. Mass unemployment
and poverty in the 1930's led to the establishment of Social
Security and nationwide public welfare assistance. The general poverty and unemployment associated with the Great
Depression has been superseded by a new problem—the persistence of substantial islands of poverty and joblessness in
what is otherwise the world's most productive and prosperous
society. The improvement of existing welfare systems, and the
planning of programs to cope with new problems, is projected to increase public and private expenditures for social
welfare from $38 billion in 1962 to $92 billion by 1975.

In the past generation our nation has followed three routes
in remedying economic distress. One has been the route of

promoting economic growth and full employment. More rapid growth expands opportunities for individuals at all economic levels, including the poor. Another route, typified by the recent programs in manpower retraining, has concentrated on increasing the earning capacity of low-income individuals through programs intended to enhance their productivity and employability. A third route has been to provide benefits to individuals without income or with an inadequate income because of old age, unemployment, disability, and dependency. These benefits are available on an insurance basis, as in Social Security, or on the basis of need, as in public assistance. It is this third alternative which makes up the traditional social welfare system.

The reexamination of programs and objectives in the mid-1960's implies far-reaching changes in the nation's approach to poverty. The "war on poverty" largely represents an experiment to shift the emphasis from programs for relieving poverty to measures for removing its causes. These measures transcend the traditional content of social welfare and, accordingly, they are considered in the chapters dealing with goals in education, health, housing, area redevelopment, and manpower retraining.

Within the framework of the social welfare system, periodic extensions of benefits and coverage in the public insurance systems and in private group insurance reflect a progressive broadening of concepts of equity. These extensions also stem from the rise in overall income levels and in the cost of living. There has been widespread dissatisfaction with public welfare assistance. The present assistance programs tend to perpetuate poverty and public assistance from one generation to its successors. The public assistance grants, according to the U.S. Commissioner of Welfare, Ellen Winston, have generally failed to provide "the minimum decent levels of living that families and children need if they are going to break the cycle of poverty and dependency."[1]

---

1. *The Washington Post*, December 9, 1964.

I I.

Expenditures for social welfare have risen sharply in dollars and in relation to GNP. They increased, in current dollars, from $12 billion in 1950 to $38 billion in 1962. Measured by GNP, social welfare spending rose from 4 per cent of GNP in 1950 to 7 per cent in 1962. The benefits these expenditures supported are summarized in Table 5–1.

Table 5–1
Public and Private Social Welfare Expenditures, 1962
(in millions of 1962 dollars)

Program	Expenditures in 1962[a]
1. Old-Age, Survivors, and Disability Benefits	$28,200
a. OASDI	13,350
b. Railroad retirement system	1,050
c. Government employees benefits	3,350[b]
d. Veterans benefits	3,650
e. Workmen's compensation	950
f. Temporary non-occupational disability compensation	2,350[c]
g. Private group pensions	2,150
h. Private group life insurance	1,350
2. Unemployment Compensation	2,950[d]
3. Public Welfare Assistance	5,500[e]
4. Private Social Service	1,600[b]
5. Total, Social Welfare Expenditures	38,250

a. These figures exclude medical benefits.
b. Estimate.
c. Includes temporary non-occupational disability programs in four states, railroad system benefits, and group compensation programs and formal sick leave in public and private employment.
d. Excludes temporary extended Federal benefits paid by program terminated in 1962.
e. Includes transfer of money income in public assistance programs, and social service assistance, surplus food distribution, and emergency aid.

Of the $38-billion total in 1962, approximately five sixths was made up of public spending, and one sixth of private spending. OASDI payments, the old-age, survivors, and disability benefits financed through the Social Security system, were by far the largest element in social welfare expenditures.

While American social welfare expenditures are large and

rising, the benefits paid create a proportionately lesser claim on the nation's resources than in most other industrial nations. In the most recent period for which comparable information is available, the late 1950's, public expenditures for social security amounted to 6 per cent of the national income in the United States. For the West European nations, public social insurance spending ranged from 9 per cent of national income in Switzerland, to almost 19 per cent in France, and to 21 per cent in West Germany.[2] Part of this differential stems from the inclusion of family allowances and medical care in the social security systems of these European nations. In addition, the private group benefit plans in the United States take the place of some of the public benefits in these nations. More fundamentally, the differences reflect a history of unprecedented social and economic mobility in the United States. Until the 1930's, this mobility tended to minimize the emphasis on public or private group action to assure economic security.

III.

Progress in updating the public and private old-age, survivors, and disability insurance systems would affect more Americans than changes in any other welfare program. Over 90 per cent of all persons employed in 1962 were covered by OASDI, the basic public system. Two thirds of the population aged 65 and over were receiving benefits from the system in that year.

Advances in medical technology have increased the share of the population represented by older persons. There were 12 million people in the United States aged 65 and over in 1950 and 17 million in 1962. They are expected to increase to 21 million by 1975. Creating a place for an expanding population of older persons in the United States will re-

2. Gordon, M. S., *The Economics of Welfare Policies*, 1963, Table 5, pp. 19–20.

quire greater availability of medical care, research in geriatrics, changes in manpower policies, and specialized housing
and community facilities. The standard of living for most of
the aged in the next decade will be determined by their pension benefits from public and private sources, and especially
from OASDI.

The typical monthly OASDI pension for a retired couple
in 1962 was $128.[3] A study published in the *Social Security
Bulletin* in the early 1960's estimated that an elderly couple
required $233 to $280 a month, varying with place of residence, to maintain a "modest but adequate" standard of
living in American cities.[4] The average OASDI benefit was
about half that amount.

While successive amendments have increased OASDI pensions and expanded coverage, benefits have not kept pace
with rising income levels. When Social Security was first
established in 1935, the maximum earnings creditable for
contribution to the system in any year was $3,000. Compar-
able creditable earnings today would have to exceed $9,000.
The maximum in 1965 was $4,800. In 1965 Congress raised
the ceiling to $6,600 beginning in 1966.[5] Failure to increase
pension benefits and the ceiling on creditable earnings commensurately with the increases in average wages and salaries
has meant that the ratio of benefits-to-earnings has declined,
especially for employees with above average earnings.[6]

Lagging OASDI benefits have served to encourage the expansion of private, usually collectively bargained, group
pension plans. They now cover approximately two thirds of
the employees whose employment circumstances are suitable
for private group insurance. The reserves in the private pension and deferred profit-sharing plans amounted to $61

3. *Statistical Abstract,* 1964, p. 289.

4. *Social Security Bulletin,* December, 1960, pp. 26–36.

5. See provisions of H.R. 6675, *Social Security Amendments of 1965.*

6. The average retired worker's monthly OASDI benefit declined from
21 per cent of monthly earnings in manufacturing in 1940 to 19 per cent in
1960. *The Economics of Welfare Policies,* p. 57.

billion in 1962. They paid an average monthly pension of $86 to a retired worker in that year.[7]

If the benefits paid in the private systems continue to increase at the same rate they did in the past decade, the average pension would rise to $100 a month by 1970. It can reasonably be expected that the private systems will include virtually the entire eligible work force before the end of the decade. If the OASDI benefits in 1970 were 20 per cent larger than in the early 1960's, a typical retired couple with a combination of public and private pensions would be receiving a retirement income of about $250 a month in the early 1970's —an amount equaling the "modest but adequate" standard of living for an elderly couple in an American city in 1960. To provide a standard of living for retired persons that would rise with overall levels of earnings and national well-being in the next decade, it would also be necessary to substantially increase the maximum creditable earnings and the ceiling on pensions in OASDI.[8]

Aside from OASDI, the Railroad Retirement System offers similar, and typically more liberal, benefits for the employees in a declining industry with a higher-than-average concentration of older workers. Over 6 million Federal, state, and local government employees are in public service retirement systems. Many state and local employees are in both the public service programs and in OASDI. A large percentage, perhaps most, of the state and local plans are inadequately financed. Some, particularly teacher retirement plans, require

---

7. *Statistical Abstract*, 1964, p. 294.

8. The Social Security amendments of 1965 proposed to increase the minimum monthly retirement benefit for a retired couple, both aged 65, by 10 per cent, and the maximum, by 1971, by 32 per cent. Beneficiaries generally would receive an immediate 7 per cent increase. The estimates of OASDI expenditures for the social welfare goal assume a 20-per cent increase in benefits for all OASDI programs by 1970 and an increase in the ceiling on maximum creditable contributions to $9,000 a year.

heavy employee contributions while paying modest benefits. A comprehensive national system of old age and disability insurance would create important advantages to persons both while they are employed and when they retire. The system's capacity for raising revenues would rest on the entire economy rather than on a single industry, state, or local unit of government. Benefits could be adjusted more readily to changes in earnings or in the cost of living than in the more limited public systems. Credits earned in the system could be transferable throughout the economy. These advantages would be realized by absorbing the railroad system into OASDI and by extending OASDI coverage to all public employees. The employees in these systems would continue to receive the benefits they currently provide. Future additions to benefits would be part of the general increases channelled through the nationwide social security system.

The changes considered for the retirement programs would affect the largest component in old-age and survivors insurance. Other changes could include expansion of the private group life insurance plans financed by employers, trade unions, and fraternal associations. This inexpensive group life insurance has taken the place of the high-cost "industrial insurance," formerly the mainstay of the insurance purchased by individual wage earners. Expanding the coverage of group life insurance to include all the eligible labor force, and increasing benefits to an average that is twice the annual wage or salary of the deceased, as is considered for the social welfare goal, would enable group life insurance to protect families deprived of their main or only wage earner from sudden or drastic changes in their standard of living.

Probably the most neglected feature of disability insurance is protection against loss of income from short-term illness. The total income loss from these illnesses in 1962 was almost $10 billion. Four states, the railroad system, and many individual employers pay compensation for loss of income due to non-occupational illness. However, nationally only one fourth of this income loss has been compensated for by group insurance and formal sick leave programs.[9] Coverage is erratic and usually unavailable for low-income employees who have the least reserves. Nationwide protection against loss of income from illness could be obtained by adding short-term non-occupational disability insurance as a regular part of OASDI in the place of the present programs.

The measures discussed suggest possibilities for expanding old-age survivors and disability benefits in the coming decade. The changes considered are estimated to raise total public and private spending for this type of insurance to $70 billion a year by the mid-1970's. The programs supported by these expenditures and the anticipated cost of each are described in Table 5-2.

Table 5-2
Estimated Private and Public Expenditures for
Old-Age, Survivors, and Disability Insurance,
1970 and 1975
(in millions of 1962 dollars)

Program	Projected Expenditures in 1970	in 1975
1. Expansion of Existing OASDI Benefits	$34,000	$45,500
2. Addition of Short-term Illness Compensation to OASDI	3,600	3,900
3. Railroad Retirement System	(a)	(a)
4. Government Employees Benefits[b]	3,600	3,950
5. Veterans Benefits	4,050	4,250
6. Workmen's Compensation	2,100	2,300
7. Private Group Pensions	5,400	6,950
8. Private Group Life Insurance	3,600	3,950
9. Total, Old-age, Survivors, and Disability Benefits	56,350	70,800

a. Absorbed into OASDI.
b. The estimates for government employees refer to continuations of current benefit schedules.

The proposals for old-age benefits deal with the cost of improvements widely regarded as desirable. Yet there are other changes in our retirement systems, perhaps of equal

---

9. *Trends*, 1964, U.S. Department of Health, Education, and Welfare, p. 81.

importance to the aged, which are only secondarily matters of cost. It is far from self-evident that compulsory retirement at age 65 or at any specific age increases economic efficiency or broadens the social choices open to older persons. So long as unemployment is high, there is a tendency to create job openings for younger employees by instituting arrangements for compulsory retirement at a fixed age, usually 65. These arrangements are measures for redistributing the available employment rather than programs intended to serve the needs of older workers.

IV.

Our objective in unemployment compensation is to offset the human and economic losses that result from unemployment by providing sufficient benefits to enable the unemployed to continue their non-deferrable expenditures for food, shelter, utilities, time payments, and medical care. This means reversing the long-term tendency for unemployment compensation payments to decline as a percentage of earnings, a decline in weekly benefits from an average of 42 per cent of earnings in 1939 to 35 per cent in 1962.[10] Raising the percentage of wage loss compensated for in this way would help sustain the unemployed, and would aid in stabilizing the economy by checking the decline in purchasing power when production falls.

The present unemployment system lacks sufficient scope to sustain the unemployed or the nation's purchasing power. Many individuals who lose their employment are kept from receiving compensation by limitations on coverage or eligibility. Farm laborers are an outstanding example. Others exhaust their benefits before finding work again. A survey in 1962 indicated that almost three fifths of the unemployed were not receiving benefit payments in the week of the

---

10. *Handbook of Unemployment Insurance Financial Data*, U.S. Department of Labor, Bureau of Employment Security, No. U-73, May, 1964.

survey.[11] As a result of the restrictions on coverage or eligibility, or the limited duration of the benefits, only a small proportion of the wage loss resulting from unemployment is offset by unemployment insurance. According to one noted labor economist, R. A. Lester, writing in 1962, the compensation payments have offset about a fifth of the wage loss from unemployment.[12]

The limitations in the unemployment compensation program have their greatest impact on nonwhite workers, the poorly educated, older employees, and the inhabitants of depressed areas. They are the groups most heavily exposed to unemployment—and to long-term unemployment. They also frequently encounter severe handicaps in finding work once they lose their jobs.

The present unemployment system is designed to bridge short periods of time between losing one job and finding another. It is less effective in dealing with long-term unemployment or with sharp increases in unemployment resulting from cyclical downturns. In the 1958 and 1961 recessions some 2-1/2 million unemployed persons exhausted their benefits. Long-term unemployment has become an increasingly serious problem. The percentage of the unemployed without work for 27 weeks or more increased from 4 per cent in 1952 and 1953 to 13 per cent in 1963.[13]

Long-term unemployment and modest levels of benefits have prompted trade unions to bargain for employer-financed supplemental unemployment compensation programs. These plans typically supplement the public system's compensation until the total benefit reaches 60 or 65 per cent of the unemployed worker's previous take-home or gross pay. Some plans pay benefits for as long as 52 weeks. Currently, about two million persons are employed in firms offering the supple-

---

11. Bureau of Employment Security, U.S. Department of Labor, 1962.

12. Lester, R. A., *The Economics of Unemployment Compensation*, 1962.

13. *Manpower Report of the President*, 1965, p. 209. In 1964, the percentage of the unemployed without work for 27 weeks or more dropped slightly to 12 per cent. *Monthly Labor Review*, September, 1965, p. 1070.

mental compensation.[14] While the private plans have helped in many specific situations, they generally lack the reserves to cope with continuously contracting employment in one firm, or successive layoffs followed by full shutdowns, as at Studebaker in 1963. Under these conditions, the funds become insufficient, and benefits are either curtailed or discontinued.

Both Presidents Eisenhower and Kennedy proposed legislation to expand unemployment compensation benefits. The Johnson Administration has recommended legislation to broaden coverage, to raise the minimum compensation benefit to 50 per cent of weekly earnings, and to increase the ceiling on unemployment payments, by gradual steps, to two thirds of earnings, up to a maximum of $67 weekly. The current Administration's proposals would add up to 26 weeks of Federal unemployment benefits to the compensation available under the state systems. Changes similar to these recommendations provide the basis for the unemployment compensation objectives considered for the social welfare goal.[15] The costs these changes could be expected to add in the 1970's would depend on the volume of unemployment. If unemployment were to decrease to 4 per cent of the civilian labor force in 1975, the compensation payments are anticipated to reach $4.7 billion.

V.

OASDI and unemployment compensation offer insurance protection for specific risks. Their benefits are available to all persons who are covered as a matter of right. In addition

14. *Digest of Nine Supplemental Unemployment Benefit Plans, Early 1963*, Bulletin No. 1365, U.S. Department of Labor, Bureau of Labor Statistics, 1963.

15. For the Administration's proposals, see H.R. 8282, *Employment Security Amendments of 1965*. The estimates for the social welfare goal assume a shorter maximum length of benefits, but they include benefits to all who had demonstrated attachment to the labor force during the two years prior to their claim.

to these insurance programs, all levels of government contribute assistance based on need in money, in kind, and in professional services. Private philanthropic contributions also support social service assistance for the needy, the handicapped, and the physically or emotionally ill.

The Federal Government furnishes the bulk of the funds for state programs for financial aid to families with dependent children, and to the aged, the blind, and the disabled. General assistance to the needy is the sole responsibility of state and local governments. In 1962, seven million persons received $3.3 billion in aid from these programs, excluding the payments for medical care. Other public assistance programs emphasize benefits in kind and professional services rather than cash payments. They include the surplus food distributed to needy families, the school lunch program, emergency aid, veterans' welfare assistance, child welfare services, and vocational rehabilitation for the handicapped. Expenditures for this assistance amounted to $2.2 billion in 1962.

The necessity for a continuing public assistance program has been generally accepted since the 1930's. The present programs are primarily intended to relieve the poverty caused by chronic unemployment, poor education or health, physical or mental disability, old age not compensated for by OASDI, or lack of a family wage earner. The Special Advisory Committee on Public Assistance summed up the status of public welfare assistance in the early 1960's, noting that "we are . . . impressed with the great progress of the public assistance programs over the past quarter of a century and with the serious gaps and inequities that still remain in coverage, in adequacy of . . . assistance, and in availability of high quality services."[16]

The gaps and inequities can be suggested briefly. All but

16. *Report of the Advisory Council on Public Assistance,* Senate Document No. 93, January, 1960.

three states have residence requirements which exclude many destitute families from receiving assistance. Seven states meet emergency needs only, rather than providing assistance to meet a standard. The assistance supplied by half the states does not meet needs as the states themselves define them. Average assistance per family in December, 1962, was $126 in the aid to dependent children program, and $26 per recipient in the wholly state-supported general assistance programs.[17] Assistance of these dimensions reflects both a lack of funds, and a residue of a belief, more prevalent in an earlier period, that benefits should be set low enough to deter actual or potential welfare recipients from seeking or remaining on public assistance.

The public assistance programs supply relief, but they do little to mobilize the energies or the resources of the poor to increase their earning capacity or employability. Neither do they encourage low-income individuals to engage in the traditional American practice of self-help through organization. Not surprisingly, the search for new approaches in social welfare affects public assistance more than any other aspect of our welfare system. The "war on poverty" has marked the beginning of a concerted national effort to treat the causes of poverty rather than to remedy its effects. The measures in the anti-poverty program are concentrated on breaking up the transmission of poverty from one generation to its successors. The Youth Act, for example, aims to provide work and job skills, along with basic education, to teen-agers from low-income families. It also furnishes part-time employment to enable young people to complete high school or attend colleges and universities. And, unlike public assistance, the Economic Opportunity Act requires representation from the low-income population on the boards of the local agencies administering the programs financed through the Act. While these programs are small in com-

17. *Trends*, 1963, HEW, p. 149.

parison with the scope and deep roots of poverty in our
society, they are significant as indicators of new directions
in social welfare.

The possibilities for creating employment opportunities,
rather than providing relief, are demonstrated, in another
context, by the Vocational Rehabilitation Act. One third
of a million persons received vocational rehabilitation aid
in 1962. Assistance includes psychological counseling and
testing, tuition for training courses, medical treatment, and
help in job placement. One hundred thousand persons were
rehabilitated through the program in 1962 at a cost of about
$130 million. The earnings of the individuals who were re-
habilitated increased from $44 million a year at acceptance,
to $211 million when their cases were closed.[18]

In addition to the public programs, private social agencies add to our resources for rehabilitation and therapy.
They offer specialized care for children, family services,
and community facilities and trained personnel for recreation and group work. The private agencies are largely supported by philanthropic and religious bodies. Their expenditures in the past decade have averaged 3/10 of 1 per cent
of GNP.[19] Although this spending is a small share of the
social welfare total, the impact of the private agencies is
greater than the expenditures imply. They have pioneered
in developing social work techniques. Their standards and
techniques often influence the public programs.

With perspectives and plans for coping with poverty
changing rapidly, there is little relevance to projecting the
cost of the present public assistance programs for another
decade. The remedies available for coping with the poverty
remaining in the 1970's will be those defined as "reasonable" in an economy capable of producing an annual gross
product of a trillion dollars.

18. *Trends,* 1963, HEW, pp. 97–98.

19. Derived from Karter, T., "Voluntary Agency Expenditures for Health
and Welfare from Philanthropic Contributions," *Social Security Bulletin,*
February, 1958.

Objectives which currently appear to be far-reaching and speculative may appear in a different light in another decade. To illustrate the cost magnitudes involved in these possibilities, the different public assistance programs could be merged into an overall plan to establish a system of family allowances for relieving destitution in the 1970's. The allowances could take the form of a "negative tax" or subsidy for families receiving less than the critical income. The subsidy would supplement unemployment compensation, OASDI benefits, and substandard earnings from work.

The family allowances plan is considered in detail in connection with the consumer expenditures goal (see Chapter 2). The costs projected for the allowances are based on the assumption that by 1975 an income of less than $3,300 will represent destitution for most American families. Raising family incomes to approximately $60 weekly by providing the allowances is estimated to add almost $10 billion a year to the income of the low-income population in the mid-1970's, and about $9.5 billion to their expenditures for goods and services. Costs would probably be lower if economic growth, together with the "war on poverty," succeeded in reducing that part of the population whose incomes are low enough to require augmentation to something less than the 6 million families and almost 4 million individuals anticipated for 1975. The costs could be higher if persons receiving the allowances, who were employed in low earning positions, were generally to cease work.

The expenditures projected for private and public social welfare assistance including the family allowances, are summarized in Table 5–3.

VI.

The expenditures listed for the social welfare goal include the costs of rationalizing and expanding the social and group insurance programs, of expanding private social service assistance, and of attempting a new approach in public assistance.

These expenditures are projected to total $92 billion in 1975, or $54 billion more than the comparable total in 1962.

Even if there were no new decisions to enlarge programs, benefits, and coverage, large-scale increases in social welfare expenditures could be anticipated for the next decade because of growth in population and labor force. Maintaining the present programs and benefit levels for the larger population expected in 1975 would increase spending for social welfare to $55 billion, or $17 billion more than in 1962.[20] This projection of the cost of extending the *status quo* is our hypothetical preempted benchmark estimate for social welfare expenditures in the mid-70's.

The breakdown of the expenditures for the social welfare goal is described in Table 5–4.

As in the early 1960's, spending for old-age, survivors, and disability benefits is far and away the largest item in the projections for social welfare expenditures. The dimensions of these expenditures, both in the 1960's and in the estimates for the 1970's, make it apparent that public and private group action have to a large extent taken over the role of providing financial protection against the risks associated with old age and disability.

The expenditures for the social welfare goal in 1975 would be exceeded only by the sums listed for the goals in consumer expenditures, urban development, and for private plant and equipment. Government spending for social welfare would rank first in the public expenditures for all sixteen goals. The estimates for the social welfare goal refer to a gross national product growing at an annual rate of 4 per cent (measured in constant prices from the full-capacity level of production in 1962). If the economy were to grow more slowly, social welfare expenditures would probably be considerably larger. This is especially true for unemployment

---

20. This estimate assumes that the ratio of beneficiaries to population or labor force would remain constant for the next decade.

Table 5–3
Estimated Private and Public Expenditures for
Social Welfare Assistance, 1970 and 1975
(in millions of 1962 dollars)

		Projected Expenditures
Program	1970	1975
1. Public Programs	$9,700	$11,000
a. Vocational rehabilitation	200	250
b. Child welfare services	550	600
c. Veterans social service assistance[a]	250	250
d. Family allowance program[b]	8,700	9,900
2. Private Social Service	4,700	5,900
3. Total, Public and Private Expenditures	14,400	16,900

a. The estimates assume that approximately half the social service activities for veterans will be provided as part of other programs.

b. The estimates for the family allowance program are based on the assumption that 90 per cent of the families earning less than $3,000 in 1970 and $3,300 in 1975 will receive allowances raising their income to these levels. For individuals living alone—the unattached individuals—the destitution cut-off incomes are half the amounts listed for families.

Table 5–4
Estimated Expenditures for Social Welfare Goal,
1970 and 1975
(in millions of 1962 dollars)

	Expenditures in 1962	Projected Expenditures	
Program		1970	1975
1. Old-Age, Survivors, and Disability Benefits	$28,200	$56,350	$70,800
a. OASDI	—	37,600[a]	49,400[a]
b. Other public programs	—	9,750[b]	10,500[b]
c. Private group insurance benefits	—	9,000[c]	10,900[c]
2. Unemployment Compensation	2,950	4,100	4,700
3. Public Welfare Assistance	5,500	9,700	11,000
4. Private Social Service	1,600	4,700	5,900
5. Total Expenditures	38,250	74,850	92,400
6. Social Welfare Expenditures as % of GNP	6.9%	9.5%	9.4%

a. Includes, in addition to current OASDI benefits, temporary non-occupational disability benefits, Railroad Retirement System benefits, and increases in benefits beyond 1962 benefit rates for government employees.

b. Includes benefits for government employees at 1962 benefit rates, workmen's compensation, and pensions and compensation for servicemen and veterans.

c. Includes benefit payments from private group old-age and disability insurance and from private group life insurance.

compensation and the family allowances.[21] Retirement benefit payments would also increase as older workers who were
unemployed or earning low incomes decided to retire, frequently before 65, and live on their pensions.

The social welfare goal is basically concerned with "the
promise of American life," and with translating this promise
into a closer approximation to reality for Americans who are
unemployed or who, for other reasons, are living in poverty.
Social welfare is only one of the institutions for pursuing
this objective. For the aged, the dependent, and the disabled,
social welfare is likely to remain our primary institution for
assuring minimum adequacy in standards of living. The extent to which the social welfare system will be utilized to
serve the needs of other groups in the population will depend
on the scope and effectiveness of our planning for growth,
for full employment, and for programs to raise the earning
capacity of low-income individuals in the next decade.

---

21. If GNP were to grow at an annual average rate of 3 rather than 4
per cent, the expenditures projected for the family allowances would rise by
$2.7 billion in 1975, from $9.9 to $12.6 billion. If the unemployment rate
were double the 4 per cent of the civilian labor force assumed to be unemployed in projecting unemployment compensation payments in 1975, unemployment compensation expenditures would rise by almost $5 billion.

CHAPTER 6

Health

I.

The health needs of individuals and of society have altered radically over the past fifty years. Our nation has progressively narrowed the gap between the potentialities of the modern health technologies and the availability of health services. Our goal in health is to accelerate this process by facilitating access to adequate medical care for all Americans. Realization of this goal is estimated to raise expenditures for health and medical care from $32 billion in 1962 to $85 billion by 1975.

The scientific revolution which has transformed industry and defense has made especially striking advances in medical care. Since 1900, the life expectancy of a child born in the United States has been lengthened by a quarter of a century. However, relatively few years have been added to the life expectancy of a person reaching age 45. Conquest of infectious diseases has exposed older Americans to a range of chronic conditions limiting their activities. Three in particular—heart disease, cancer, and stroke—now constitute the major causes of death. They account for two thirds of the deaths in the United States.[1]

The incidence of disease strikes most heavily in the below-4 age group and in persons 45 and over. The population included in these groups has increased from 30 per cent of the total in 1900 to 40 per cent in 1960. Changing demographic composition and greater emphasis in medical care on chronic diseases—coupled with advances in antibiotics and chemotherapy—have made possible a taken-for-granted revolution in the organization of health services. In 1900, one doctor visited many patients in their homes. Today the preponderance of medical care is received in hospitals, offices, and clinics. The traditional doctor-patient relationship is being replaced by the "many specialists in many places at many phases of life" type of illness-patient relationship. Full-time specialists now comprise at least half of all physicians— compared with one sixth thirty years ago.

Specialization has been accompanied by new types of health services and by the development of large and complex organizations to increase efficiency in supplying health care. As society becomes more urban and industrialized, public health activities grow in importance. Health hazards from industrial chemicals and pesticides, or from traffic accidents, require control by the community along with control of pollution of air, water, and the upper atmosphere. New medical specializations such as geriatrics and psychiatry flourish in response to changing needs and new knowledge. Concepts of private practice change as solo practice shifts to organized group practice. Clinics, such as the Mayo Clinic in Rochester, Minnesota now bring together under one roof the full range of specialists, services, and supporting activities essential for the application of modern medical knowledge. Perhaps the most promising development is the growth of teaching hositals, which are affiliated with medical schools. These schools

---

1. "Advancing the Nation's Health," President Johnson's Message to Congress, January 7, 1965.

typically operate large modern medical centers providing a high quality of medical care, and integrating care for patients with research. They frequently set the standards for high quality medical care in their communities.

Expectations in health services have grown rapidly as rising educational levels make more people aware of medical advances, and as higher incomes develop a capability to pay for more and better health services. Expenditures for health and medical care have increased sharply in the past generation. Total expenditures, public and private, rose, in 1962 dollars, from under $7 billion in 1929 to $32 billion in 1962 and $33 billion in 1963.[2] On a per capita basis, they increased from $60 per person in 1929, to $128 in 1950, and to $173 in 1962.

Many factors other than those just described have contributed to the rise in health expenditures. The cost of health services to consumers has risen. In the past thirty years we have transformed the manner in which we use and pay for health services. A generation ago the financing of health care was left primarily to the individual, with some assistance from private philanthropy and limited public relief measures. This relatively simple structure has been replaced by an intricate combination of public, private, and non-profit resources for financing medical care.

Today, direct payment by consumers still predominates as a means of financing medical services, but it is a diminishing share of the total. A rising proportion of health expenditures is paid for by third parties through voluntary health insurance and government participation. In 1948, less than one tenth of private consumption expenditures for health were paid for by health insurance. By 1962 they were over one fourth of the private consumption total.[3] The Federal Government supplies medical care directly to a wide variety

2. *Trends,* 1963, U.S. Department of Health, Education, and Welfare, p. 26.

3. Reed and Rice, "Private Consumer Expenditures for Medical Care and Voluntary Health Insurance, 1948–1962," *Social Security Bulletin,* December, 1963.

of individuals—to members of the armed forces, veterans, Indians, and others. It also bears the predominant share of the costs for medical research and over two fifths of the costs of constructing health care facilities. State governments provide medical care to a different series of groups, such as the mentally ill, the retarded, TB patients, and the aged residing in state institutions. All levels of government pay for, but do not directly furnish, medical care for large numbers of people receiving various forms of public assistance. The public share in health expenditures has risen more rapidly in the past generation than the total. The ratio of private to public expenditures has shifted from 6 to 1 in 1929 to 3 to 1 in recent years. This 3-to-1 ratio has been relatively stable since 1950.

The complex of activities which make up the American mixed economy in health is summarized in Table 6–1. Table 6–1 presents the major components in health expenditures for 1962.

Greater life expectancy and better health serve the humanitarian values of our society. They also encourage economic growth by adding to the labor force and enhancing its effectiveness. It has been estimated that 13 million of the 67 million persons employed in 1960 were in the labor force in that year because of the substantial decline in death rates since 1900. The labor product of these people added more than 60 billion dollars to the national product in 1960.[4]

Our goals in health also involve the nation's objectives in research and development, urban development, civil rights, the "war on poverty," and international aid. Spending for health-related research by the Federal Government is exceeded only by the public R & D expenditures for atomic energy, defense, and the space program. Developing a network of health services is an essential ingredient in community planning for the suburbs and, even more so, for the

---

4. Mushkin, S., "Health as an Investment," *Journal of Political Economy*, Vol. LXX, No. 5, Part 2, 1962, pp. 145–147.

Table 6–1
Health and Medical Care Expenditures, 1962*
(in millions of 1962 dollars)

	Amount	Per cent of Total
1. Private Expenditures	$24,700	76.5%
a. Personal consumption expenditures for health and medical care	22,000	68.1
direct payment	14,400	44.6
insurance benefits	6,500	20.1
expenses for prepayment	1,100	3.4
b. Philanthropy	800	2.5
c. Non-profit medical research[a]	300	0.9
d. Industrial medical research[a]	500	1.6
e. Medical facilities construction	800	2.5
f. Other[b]	300	0.9
2. Public Expenditures	7,600	23.5
a. Health care and medical services	5,900	18.2
b. Medical research[a]	600	1.9
c. Medical facilities construction	600	1.9
d. Other[b]	500	1.5
3. Total Expenditures	32,300	100.0

a. These represent expenditures for *performance* of research rather than the *source* of funds for research. The industrial medical research is not reckoned as an end product in the national income accounts.

b. Public funds consist of medical benefits under workmen's compensation and temporary disability insurance. Private expenditures consist of industrial inplant health services.

* Derived from *Social Security Bulletin*, October, 1964.

slum dwellers in the central cities. The recent Supreme Court decision outlawing segregation in publicly supported hospitals symbolizes the implications of medical care for civil rights. Part of our foreign aid has consisted of modern medical technology and research to encourage its adaptation to the needs of the developing countries. Along with the longer life expectancy and the improved productivity resulting from better medical care, the export of medical technology has been a major element in the rapid rates of population increase which have frustrated economic progress in many of these nations.

II.

The far-reaching advances in medical care exist side by side with abundant evidence of unmet needs and new needs

created by social change or medical progress. As a nation we
have recognized the problems these needs create by such
measures as support for the construction of hospital facilities
through the Hill-Burton Act, or in the rapid growth of private health insurance. Yet much remains to be done to
translate the advances in medical knowledge into medical
services which are available to all. Wider use of the available
knowledge in cancer, for example, could save the lives of
approximately 150,000 cancer patients each year.[5]

Older persons have probably suffered most from insufficient medical care. They tend to have low incomes, large
medical costs, and a high incidence of major and catastrophic
illnesses. Persons 65 and over comprise less than 10 per cent
of the population. They account for 20 per cent of the nation's expenditures for personal health services.[6] In 1962,
only half of the elderly had any health insurance coverage,
and much of the coverage was inadequate.[7] The potentialities of the newly developing field of geriatrics are unlikely
to be available to most older persons from private insurance
or from their income and savings. Recognition of the special health problem of the aged was responsible for the
enactment of Medicare in 1965. This legislation expands
the Social Security insurance program to provide hospitalization, nursing care, home nursing services, and out-patient
diagnostic services for all Americans 65 and over.

Patients in mental hospitals were responsible for nearly
half of the days spent in hospitals by all patients in the
early 1960's.[8] Pilot studies have shown that the great majority of the mentally ill need not be institutionalized. The
resources of psychotherapy and drug therapy can be brought

---

5. *Annual Report of the Council of Economic Advisers,* January, 1965, p.
160.

6. *Financing Health Care for the Aged,* National Committee on Health
Care of the Aged, November, 1963.

7. *Annual Report of the Council of Economic Advisers,* January, 1965, p.
160.

8. *Trends,* 1963, HEW, p. 29.

to bear more effectively if the mentally ill can be treated in their own communities. Here, for most, therapy can be combined with productive employment and family life.

The late President Kennedy described the problem of mental illness in his message to Congress dealing with this subject in 1963. To quote the President,

Mental illness and mental retardation . . . occur more frequently . . . require more prolonged treatment . . . waste more of our human resources, and constitute more financial drain . . . than any other single [health] condition. . . . We as a nation have long neglected the mentally ill and the mentally retarded.[9]

In response to President Kennedy's urging, Congress in 1963 enacted the Community Mental Health Centers Act. It provides assistance in constructing community mental health centers supplying a full range of services for treating and rehabilitating the mentally ill in their own communities.

Neglect is by no means confined to the mentally ill. The President's Task Force on Manpower Conservation reports that "75 per cent of all persons rejected [by the Selective Service System] for failure to meet the medical and physical standards would probably benefit from treatment."[10]

The most effective way to identify the health problems of young persons, before they reach draft age, is by physical examination in connection with school health programs. At the present time only 6 per cent of all students in American elementary and secondary schools receive such examinations by physicians.[11] If the health needs of the 15 million children of low-income families are to be adequately served, enlargement and upgrading of school health programs could provide the strategic leverage.

Adequate dental care constitutes a widely prevalent and

9. President Kennedy's Health Message to Congress, 1963.
10. *One Third of A Nation*, The President's Task Force on Manpower Conservation, January, 1964.
11. *Statistical Abstract*, 1963, p. 309, Table 413.

oft-deferred health need. A recent study has reported that the average 16-year-old had approximately ten untreated decayed teeth.[12] Inadequate dental care is closely related to low income. Another study indicates that some three fourths of all families earning less than $2,000 spent no money on dental care in the survey year. Less than one fourth of the families earning $7,500 or over reported no spending for dental care.[13]

Hospital facilities present another important health need. Plans drawn up by states for aid under the Hill-Burton Act indicate a deficit of 155,000 general hospital beds in the early 1960's. The shortage is especially acute for adequate nursing home facilities for the aged.

Expenditures for medical research have mushroomed in the past decade, increasing from $148 million in 1950 to $1.3 billion in 1962. They are estimated to reach $1.7 billion in 1965.[14] In the past decade medical research has virtually eliminated polio, and it has greatly lengthened the life expectancy of children with acute leukemia. Medical research in the next decade will probably concentrate more heavily on mental illness and retardation, and on the chronic diseases which are the leading causes of death. Research is very likely to be more concerned with the public health problems associated with urban living. Air pollution is a leading instance. The hazards of nuclear energy and the adaptation of man to life in outer space can also be expected to create new areas for medical research.

Unmet health needs are especially concentrated among nonwhites. In the early 1960's, the life expectancy of the white population at birth was 71 years; for nonwhites, it was 64 years, or 10 per cent less. At age 45, the average white

12. "The Level of Dental Health," *Progress in Health Services*, Health Information Foundation, September, 1961.

13. Anderson, Collette, and Feldman, *Family Expenditure Patterns for Personal Health Services*, 1953 and 1958.

14. *Annual Report of the Council of Economic Advisers*, January, 1965, p. 160.

person could contemplate 30 remaining years, the nonwhite slightly under 27.[15] In the surveys of dental care discussed earlier, white persons averaged 1.6 visits to dentists a year. For nonwhites, the corresponding figure was 0.5.

Along with rising demands for health services, the cost of medical care has risen rapidly. Since 1955 medical care costs have increased about twice as rapidly as the overall Consumer Price Index. Table 6–2 presents these relationships.

Table 6–2
Percentage Change in Consumer Prices for
All Commodities and for Medical Care,
1955 to 1962*

Item	Per Cent Change in Consumer Price Index 1955-62
All Commodities	+ 13.0%
All Medical Care	+ 28.9
Physicians' Fees	+ 24.3
Hospital Daily Service Charges	+ 56.4
Hospitalization Insurance	+ 69.8

* *Trends,* 1963, HEW, pp. 23, 68. These tendencies continued in 1963. The overall Consumer Price Index rose by 1.2 per cent. Medical care costs rose by 2.2 per cent. *Trends,* 1964, HEW, p. 68.

The most striking increases in the cost of medical care have been in hospitalization charges and in the cost of hospitalization insurance. Rising hospitalization costs are largely responsible for the rise in charges for hospitalization insurance. Three fourths of private consumer expenditures for hospitalization in 1962 were paid for by health insurance. For the hospitals, however, health insurance was a less significant contributor. Only two fifths of total hospital costs were met by receipts from insurance payments.

The American performance in medical research and in the overall level of medical practice is outstanding. We have been less successful in diffusing the benefits of research or advances in practice to the general population. One sig-

15. *Trends,* 1963, HEW, p. 13.

nificant index of the diffusion of medical knowledge into
everyday use is the infant mortality rate. In the early 1960's,
almost a dozen nations reported lower infant mortality rates
than the United States.[16]

III.

With rising costs, expanding expectations, and unmet
needs, establishing more effective means for making medical
care generally available has become a matter of paramount
importance. For the United States, this issue has centered on
the financing of more comprehensive medical care for the
general population. A related issue is the problem of coping
with the financial burdens of illness in one age group—65
and over.

For the past fifty years, a controversy has raged between
organized medicine and groups advocating compulsory
health insurance or comprehensive group medical practice.
While the differences in principle have not been resolved,
a pragmatic evolution has transformed the financing of health
services in the United States over the past thirty years.

In 1933, the Federal Government, in a precedent-setting
regulation, established policies and procedures under which
medical care would be given to those receiving relief. Providing medical care for the indigent was recognized by the Government as a basic public responsibility, similar to the public
responsibility for assuring sufficient food, clothing, and shelter. The organized medical profession participated in formu-
lating these rules and gave them its sanction. In line with
this philosophy, the Federal Government has gradually assumed responsibility for subsidizing medical care for various
groups entitled to public assistance—the "indigent and neces-
sitous." Proposals that the Federal Government move beyond
subsidy of the medically indigent and extend social insurance
to the statistically predictable risks of illness for the population generally have not won legislative acceptance.

---

16. *Statistical Abstract,* 1963, p. 910, Table 1240.

Since World War II, the major progress in extending health protection to the population at large under 65 has come about through extensions of private insurance. As the war ended, unions found wage increases at first frozen and then frowned upon as inflationary. Benefits such as health insurance were acceptable as non-inflationary. Collective bargaining began to focus on fringe benefits including health and welfare plans. As a result, an immense private venture in the social financing of health care, unique among nations, has come into being.

By 1950, one half, and by 1962 more than three fourths, of the population were covered by hospital insurance.[17] Growth of health insurance reflects a steady broadening of types of coverage. However, relatively few of the current plans include coverage for comprehensive medical care. Hospital insurance is the component with the largest single percentage of consumer costs financed by insurance. Coverage for dental care and for mental illness is generally very limited.

Coverage in the present insurance plans correlates closely with family income. A study of short-stay hospital discharges several years back demonstrates this relationship. The higher the family income, the larger the proportion of discharges for which some part of the hospital bill was paid by insurance. The percentage of hospital discharges covered by insurance ranged from 40 per cent in the under-$2,000 group to 81 per cent of the families with annual incomes of $7,000 or more.[18]

Voluntary health insurance has introduced significant changes in the financing of medical care for all but the low income groups and the aged. Further developments in voluntary insurance are likely to involve increases in benefits, a broader population coverage, and more comprehensive programs to include coverage for dental care, mental illness, and other major illnesses.

---

17. *Source Book of Health Insurance Data,* 1963, Health Institute.
18. *Public Health Services Publication No. 584–B–30,* November, 1961.

I V.

Establishing access to adequate medical care for the entire population sets up a framework of response to the unmet needs and rising expenditures for health. These responses are likely to be influenced by the "mixed economy" sources of finance which are so well adapted to American experience. Since the standard in health is concerned with "adequacy," it pertains to a scale of "more or less," rather than to a utopian goal divorced from practice.

A minimum measure of adequacy in health care would assume that present standards will be continued through 1975. This is our preempted yardstick. It measures the cost of extending the *status quo* into the next decade. In 1962, expenditures for health and medical care amounted to $32 billion, or $173 per person. If health expenditures per person, public and private, remained at their 1962 levels in the 1970's, total spending for health and medical care would increase to $39 billion by 1975 because of population growth. We would be spending $7 billion more a year without increasing per capita expenditures for health services.[19]

The preempted measure is a crude minimum yardstick for health expenditures. It does not take into account changing health needs, or the dynamic changes in health services, or changes in the break between public, consumer, and insurance modes of payment.

Our standard in health refers to three underlying tendencies relating health expenditures to health needs and potentials. One is the *de facto* consensus making voluntary health insurance the primary means for financing medical care for persons under 65. A second is recognition of the

---

19. Conceptually, the preempted estimate should allow for increases in expenditures for health and medical care which are likely to come about because of changes in the age composition of the population or from rural-urban population shifts. They have been omitted because the historical data on which to base such a projection have not been available.

leading role of the Government in assuring adequate health facilities and health research. A third is the Government's added responsibility to continue expanding its support of medical care for the groups least able to afford it—the poverty groups and the aged. Extension of these three tendencies would provide access to adequate medical care for all Americans.

The Federal Government has statutory commitments to construct health facilities. The Hill-Burton Act provides public support for hospital construction, the Health Research Facilities Act in research, and the Health Professions Assistance Act does the same for medical schools. The Community Mental Health Centers Act establishes public responsibility for the construction of mental health centers. Public construction .outlays to realize national objectives in health are estimated at $4.8 billion in 1975, or some $4 billion more than in 1962.

The expenditures for hospital facilities constitute the largest element in the public construction estimates. The projections for the 1970's reflect the standard in the Hill-Burton Act of 14 hospital beds per 1,000 population. This would represent an increase from 11 beds per 1,000 in the early 1960's. Other public construction outlays would include the regional medical complexes proposed by President Johnson to speed up the translation of research in heart disease, cancer, and stroke into improved patient care. They would provide highly specialized services such as open heart surgery to patients, and their services would be made available to assist physicians in keeping abreast of the mass of new developments in medical knowledge and techniques.

Private construction for medical facilities is also expected to increase substantially, to $2.8 billion in 1975. A large volume of private construction would encourage expansion in two areas with critical backlogs in plant and equipment—nursing homes and group medical practice centers. The probabilities of attaining the projected levels of private con-

struction would be considerably enhanced if the Federal
Government were to provide mortgage insurance for long-
term low interest loans.

The National Institutes of Health have estimated that
77,000 professional health research workers will be needed
in 1970. Many of these researchers would be physicians and
many others would be psychologists, biologists, and specialists in new fields like biophysics or bio-engineering. Support
of the 77,000 health research professionals in 1970 is expected
to involve public and private expenditures amounting to $3
billion.[20]

In 1962, almost 13 million persons were entitled to receive medical care from the government. Most of these persons were veterans, members of the armed forces or their
families, or those receiving some form of public assistance.
Taking into account anticipated trends in population growth,
broken families, families with poverty incomes, and the size
of the armed forces, it is estimated that all levels of government—Federal, state, and local—will be spending over $16
billion in 1975 to provide adequate medical care to the members of the entitlement groups.[21] This sum includes an anticipated increase in expenditures for school health services
to enable school systems to require periodic physical examinations by physicians for all students in elementary and
secondary schools.

Health care for the aged could be made available through
Social Security, through direct payments for medical care
by the Government, or perhaps, for health care beyond the
provisions in Medicare, by public payments for private
health insurance. While the particular system employed

---

20. The cost of supporting these research workers and providing them with
facilities and nonprofessional assistance has been projected by NIH at
$39,000 per professional worker. *Resources for Medical Research,* National
Institutes of Health, January, 1963, p. 14.

21. For public assistance recipients under age 65, the largest single group
in the entitlement category, public expenditures for health care and medical
services per capita are projected to rise to $225 by 1975.

would determine where these costs showed up in the national income accounts, they need make little difference in the total cost of adequate health care for older citizens. In order to simplify the calculations, we assume that health care for older persons is financed directly by the Federal Government.

Medical assistance for the aged in the next decade can be expected to concentrate initially on protection against the heaviest costs of a serious illness—the costs of hospital and nursing home care, home health services, and out-patient hospital diagnostic services. This is essentially President Johnson's proposal in his recommendations to Congress preceding the legislation which established Medicare as part of Social Security.[22] The estimates for the health goal assume that the medical assistance would gradually be extended to include the range of illness and medical care services. A recent report by the Department of Health, Education, and Welfare indicates that a charge of $350 per person would cover 90 per cent of the hospital and medical care costs of the aged.[23] Allowing for an increase of about 50 per cent in per capita costs, to take account of progressive increases in the scope of medical care created by research in gerontology, the cost of the public medical assistance for persons 65 and over would total $7 billion a year in the mid-1970's. By that time only one third of the medical costs of the aged would still be financed by direct consumer payment, supplemented by private insurance.

For persons under 65, voluntary health insurance is likely to be the major resource for easing the burden of financing medical care. About 70 per cent of the population who do not receive medical care from the Government are covered by a combination of hospital and other medical insurance.[24] It is reasonable to anticipate that this coverage will grow to

22. President Johnson's Message to Congress, January 7, 1965.

23. *Blue Cross Blue Shield Non-Group Coverage for Older People*, HEW, Report No. 4, 1964.

24. *Source Book of Health Insurance Data*, 1962.

90 per cent by 1975. As comprehensive coverage gains in momentum, a greater proportion of the insurance will encompass benefits for mental illness and dental care. In 1962, private medical care expenditures for persons with a combination of hospital and regular medical insurance averaged something under $200. Again including a 50-per cent increase to allow for more comprehensive coverage, the total insurance benefits paid would grow from $6 billion in 1962 to $32 billion by 1975. The insurance benefits in 1975 are estimated to almost double the direct payments for medical care by private individuals.

V.

The changes discussed in the role of Government or in private health insurance indicate possibilities for implementing social choices in medical care in the coming decade. The directions of change the proposals imply are underscored by comparing actual health expenditures in 1962 with the projected totals for the health goal in the 1970's. These changes are described in Table 6–3.

The $85 billion listed as the cost of the health goal in 1975 represents an increase of $53 billion over the actual expenditures in 1962. This is equivalent to more than doubling per capita expenditures. Attaining the improvements in health and medical care included in the standard would also involve large increases in health personnel, and especially so in the number of doctors, dentists, and research workers. And, the near-tripling of expenditures for health could not lead to corresponding increases in medical care unless programs for expanding facilities in medical education were adopted well in advance to allow for the long lead times needed to educate professional manpower in the health professions.

President Johnson has proposed that our nation seek, as "a very ambitious, but attainable and realistic" goal, to add five years to the life expectancy of Americans in the forseeable

Table 6–3
Estimated Expenditures for Health Goal, 1970 and 1975
(in millions of 1962 dollars)

Item	Expenditures in 1962	Projected Expenditures for Aspiration Standards 1970	1975
1. Private Expenditures	$24,700	$50,200	$60,600
a. Personal consumption expenditures for health and medical care	22,000	45,200	53,800
direct payment	14,400	22,600	17,900
insurance benefits	6,500	20,300	32,300
expenses for prepayment	1,100	2,300	3,600
b. Philanthropy	800	1,200	1,500
c. Non-profit medical research[a]	300	800	1,000
d. Industrial medical research[a]	500	900	1,200
e. Medical facilities construction	800	1,800	2,800
f. Other[b]	300	300	300
2. Public Expenditures	7,600	17,900	24,800
a. Health care and medical services	5,900	11,700	16,600
b. Medical research[a]	600	1,300	2,100
c. Medical facilities construction	600	4,000	4,800
d. Other[b]	500	900	1,300
3. Total Expenditures	32,300	68,100	85,400
4. Health Expenditures as % of GNP	5.8%	8.6%	8.7%
5. Per Capita Health Expenditures	$ 173	$ 326	$ 378

a. These represent expenditures for *performance* of research rather than the *source* of funds for research.

b. Public funds consist of medical benefits under workmen's compensation and temporary disability insurance. Private expenditures consist of industrial inplant health services.

future. This would represent an extension from an average life expectancy of 70 to one of 75 years.[25] The measures considered for the health goal would help to achieve this objective by enlarging access to medical care for all, irrespective of race, age, or ability to pay. The equalization of opportunities for health care along the lines discussed would increase the percentage of GNP claimed for health by almost half.

25. *The New York Times,* August 5, 1965.

CHAPTER 7

Education

I.

Our goals in education are to foster individual fulfill-ment, to strengthen our free institutions, and to develop educated and trained manpower for changing labor force requirements. Spending by all educational institutions, pub-lic and private, amounted to almost $30 billion in 1962. Expansion of educational opportunities to achieve our ob-jectives is projected to raise this total to $82 billion by 1975.

Expenditures for education represent both a means for enrichment of personal life and an investment in human re-sources. These expenditures are likely to increase substanti-ally in the next decade as the pressures of technological change, rising educational aspirations, and the "war on pov-erty" are translated into greater demands on our educational system. The research revolution which tripled R & D spend-ing between 1953 and 1962 has left its imprint on curricula and enrollment at all levels of education. In recent years, to quote the National Education Association, "knowledge has multiplied in practically every area. Schools must teach, and man must know, many subjects and fields unexplored or of scant importance in past generations."[1] In higher education, the mushrooming growth of R & D has created a massive expansion in university-sponsored research. Many universities now operate elaborate research establishments, and they serve as major scientific and technical resources for Government and industry.

Technological and social changes since World War II have changed the relationship between work, education, and employment by increasing employment opportunities for the highly educated and the well-trained and curtailing them for persons with limited schooling. Growing public and private expenditures for health, R & D, space, and education have been intensifying these occupational shifts by adding to the demand for scientists, for many categories of engineers, for physicians and nurses, for medical and electronic technicians, and for teachers at all levels of education. Our educational objectives for the coming decade are being reformulated in an economic environment in which, to quote the National Education Association again, "the whole labor force must be prepared for a change to higher and more complex levels of skill."[2]

Educational aspirations for the nation's young people have been rising rapidly as personal incomes and the educational level of the older generation have increased. These aspirations have received renewed emphasis as part of the drive for greater equality of opportunity symbolized by the Supreme Court decisions on integration and the Civil Rights Act of 1964. But the quantity and quality of the available educational opportunity still varies widely from state to state, between city and country, and from metropolitan suburb to central city slum. For the year 1962, current educational expenditures per student in public elementary and secondary schools ranged from $229 in Mississippi to $629 in New

1. *Financing the Public Schools, 1960–1970,* National Education Association, 1962, p. 11.
2. *Ibid.*

York.[3] In some urban slums in the states with high per student expenditures, according to Dr. James B. Conant, former president of Harvard University, "over half of the boys between 16 and 21 are out of school and out of work."[4] These marked differentials in educational opportunity and their association with poverty and unemployment prompted Congress to enact Federal aid-to-education legislation in 1965. This legislation provides for expenditures of over a billion dollars a year to assist public elementary and secondary schools serving children of low income families.

The changes which are transforming job requirements and education are also increasing leisure. Average weekly hours of work for the total civilian economy fell from 44 in 1946 to slightly over 40 by the early 1960's. They are expected to decline further—to 37 by 1975.[5] Annual vacations, formerly confined largely to white collar workers, are now enjoyed by most members of the labor force. Greater leisure, higher personal incomes, and a rising level of educational attainment are creating a popular basis for a revival of the arts, for greatly increased international travel, and for more and more effective participation in community organizations.

The emergence of the developing nations after World War II adds to the tasks of education within the United States. To improve prospects for peace and international cooperation, our schools, at all levels, must broaden their students' horizons to include an understanding of the problems and the cultures of the majority of the world's population living in these nations. Schools and colleges are also likely to be increasingly called upon to supply technical assistance and to introduce new curricula, or establish new educational institutions in the developing nations. In addition, the impact of competitive coexistence with the communist nations in-

3. *Digest of Educational Statistics*, U.S. Office of Education, 1964 ed., p. 69.

4. Conant, James B., *Slums and Suburbs*, McGraw-Hill Book Co., New York City, 1961, p. 2.

5. *National Economic Projections to 1974*, National Planning Association, 1964, pp. 33, 57.

tensifies the need for more general education to promote our own cultural performance, and for more technical education to add to the skills required to increase our economic strength.

The skills and knowledge gained through education are the prerequisites for successful vocational training, and for intelligent social and political participation in a complex technological society. It is for these reasons that President Eisenhower's Commission on National Goals recommended in the early 1960's that "education at every level and in every discipline be strengthened and its effectiveness enhanced. . . . This is at once an investment in the individual, in the democratic process, in the growth of the economy, and in the stature of the United States."[6]

II.

Expenditures for education, like expenditures for R & D, have risen at a more rapid rate than GNP in the past decade. Expenditures for all levels of education more than tripled between 1950 and 1962, rising from $9 billion to $30 billion. As a claim on resources, these expenditures represent an increase from 3.5 per cent of GNP in 1950 to 5.5 per cent of the larger GNP in 1962.

Spending for education in 1962, public and private, is listed in Table 7–1 (see page 144). In addition to elementary and secondary schools, and colleges and universities, the table includes public libraries, since they are also an integral element in our educational system.

The $30 billion spent for education in 1962 increased to an estimated $34 billion by 1964.[7] Spending for education has been increasing rapidly because enrollments have grown, costs per student have risen, and because new demands have been placed on our educational system. As one index of

6. *Goals for Americans,* The Report of the President's Commission on National Goals, The American Assembly, 1960, p. 6.

7. *Digest of Educational Statistics,* 1964, p. 129.

Table 7–1
Expenditures for Education, 1962*
(in billions of 1962 dollars)

	Expenditures in 1962[a]
1. Elementary and Secondary Schools	$21.1
a. Current expenditures	17.8
b. Capital outlays	3.3
2. Colleges and Universities	8.3
a. Current expenditures	7.1
b. Capital outlays	1.2
3. Public Libraries	0.3
4. Total Expenditures for Education	29.7

a. 1962 refers to school year 1961-62.
* Sources: For public elementary and secondary schools, *Preliminary Statistics of State School Systems, 1961-62*, U.S. Office of Education, 1963, pp. 24-26; for private schools, *Digest of Educational Statistics*, 1963, p. 102; for higher education, *Preliminary Report of Financial Statistics of Institutions of Higher Education, 1961-62*, 1963, p. 4.

rising costs in elementary and secondary schools, current expenditures per student, in 1962 dollars, rose from $260 in 1952 to $401 in 1962.[8] Rising per student costs reflect higher teachers' salaries, changes in teaching techniques, as in the use of language laboratories, and changes in the curriculum, e.g., the "new math." More widespread use of supporting personnel, such as guidance counselors and librarians, has also contributed to the growth in costs. Population shifts from rural to urban areas or from the central cities to suburbs have increased school enrollments and expenditures by raising the share of the student population completing high school or enrolled in the more ambitious and more costly school systems.

The dimensions of spending for education as an investment can be measured by the nation's direct outlay on education, plus the earnings foregone by high school and college students who would have been working and earning income if they had not been attending school. Using this criterion, the gross investment in education in the United

8. Derived from *Digest of Educational Statistics*, 1963, p. 48 and *Statistics of State School Systems 1957–58*, U.S. Office of Education, 1961, p. 6.

States in 1957–58, the most recent year for which information is available, was one third of total investment in the entire economy.[9] Like other investments, the outlays for education contribute to economic growth. Recent studies by Denison, and others, suggest that a large share of the nation's economic growth in the past generation can be attributed to education.[10]

Along with greater expenditures, educational opportunities in the past generation have increased on an unprecedented scale. However, progress has been uneven for different groups, and needs have been expanding at least commensurately with opportunities. The percentage of the civilian labor force graduating from high school rose from 32 per cent in 1940 to 55 per cent in the early 1960's.[11] However, 60 per cent of the tenth grade students from low income neighborhoods in our fifteen largest cities in the mid-1960's were still dropping out before finishing high school. Attending college has become increasingly expensive. Currently, it typically amounts to nearly $2,400 a year in private colleges and universities, and about $1,600 in public colleges.[12] Consequently, family income remains a major factor in the decision to attend or not to attend college. A survey discussed by the Senate Subcommittee on Employment and Manpower —the Clark Committee—in 1963 showed that 13 per cent of the young people from families with annual incomes under $4,000 went on to college, compared with 47 per cent of those who came from families with incomes above $7,500. The net result, as summed up by the Committee, is that "the

---

9. Blitz, R. C., "The Nation's Educational Outlay," in *Economics of Higher Education*, U.S. Office of Education, 1962, p. 169.

10. See Denison, E. F., *The Sources of Economic Growth in the United States*, Committee for Economic Development, 1962, p. 73.

11. *Toward Full Employment*, Report of the Subcommittee on Employment and Manpower, U.S. Senate, 1964, p. 79.

12. "Toward Full Economic Opportunity," President Johnson's Message to Congress on Education, January 12, 1965.

Nation . . . is losing, through leakages in the educational system, a substantial portion of its brains and leadership potential."[13]

The demands on our educational system have been radically increased by the changes in requirements for employment in the past decade. A high degree of education or formal training, traditionally a requirement for only a minority of the work force employed in the professions, skilled white collar jobs, or highly technical crafts, is now becoming a condition for employment in many fields in which job oppportunities indicate a long-term tendency to expand. Between 1949 and 1962, for example, the American economy generated over 8 million additional jobs in occupations for which the median educational level was 12 years of schooling or more.[14] However, some two million jobs were lost in occupations for which the median was less than 9 years of school. While job opportunities increased for individuals at many different levels of education and skill in 1964, economic and social developments in our society are likely to continue concentrating job openings for the well-trained and the educated. As the supply of well-educated persons increases, the greater availability of educated manpower itself often becomes an important factor in raising the educational requirements for many types of work.

The changes in employment anticipated from 1962 to 1975, according to the 1964 *Manpower Report,* are described in Table 7–2.

The largest percentage increases in employment are anticipated in the professional and technical fields. The share of the labor force employed as laborers, farmers, or operatives, all low-education occupations, has been declining for the past two decades, and this decline is expected to continue.

---

13. Report of the Subcommittee on Employment and Manpower, U.S. Senate, 1964, p. 79.

14. Testimony of Sar Levitan, *Nation's Manpower Revolution,* Hearings, Subcommittee on Employment and Manpower, U.S. Senate, 1963, p. 688.

Table 7–2
Distribution of Employment by Occupational Group, 1962 and 1975*

Occupational Group	Median Years of Schooling Completed in 1962[a]	Per Cent of Total Employment	
		1962	1975
1. Total	12.1	100.0%	100.0%
2. White Collar Workers		44.1	47.8
a. Professional and technical workers	16.2	11.9	14.2
b. Managers, officials, and proprietors	12.5	10.9	10.7
c. Clerical workers	12.5	14.9	16.2
d. Sales workers	12.5	6.4	6.7
3. Manual and Service Workers		48.7	47.7
a. Craftsmen and foremen	11.2	12.8	12.8
b. Operatives	10.1	17.7	16.3
c. Laborers	8.9	5.2	4.3
d. Service workers	10.2	13.0	14.3
4. Farmers and Farm Laborers	8.7	7.2	4.5

a. In March, 1962.
* *Manpower Report of the President*, 1964, pp. 199, 244.

In the low-education occupations, employment is projected to increase for only one group—for service workers.

These changes in the labor force have redistributed the burden of unemployment by concentrating joblessness among the poorly educated. In 1962, persons with less than 5 years of schooling were five times as likely, and persons with 8 years of education more than three times as likely, to be unemployed as college graduates. Lack of education helps explain an unemployment rate among nonwhites double the rate for the general population. In 1962, for example, almost one third of nonwhite workers had not completed elementary school compared with one ninth among whites.[15] Achievement of formal legal equality unaccompanied by significant educational progress for nonwhites would be unlikely to affect their status as the group most heavily exposed to unemployment in the United States. Similarly, low educational attainment is a leading factor in poverty. Three fifths of

---

15. *Hearings*, Subcommittee on Employment and Manpower, 1963, pp. 1091, 1098.

the families earning less than $3,000 in 1962 were headed by persons with eight years of education or less.[16]

The relationship of education to unemployment and poverty has far-reaching implications for education, vocational training, and manpower policy. The training needed to prepare people for employment in the next decade, and for employment providing more than minimum earnings, will include both an increased emphasis on technical skills and more general education. In the early 1960's, by contrast, most employees outside the professions, according to the U.S. Department of Labor, had "just picked up" the necessary skills for their jobs or they had developed them through some combination of informal instruction and experience. For workers who did receive formal job training, high school vocational and commercial courses were the most important single source of training.[17]

"The quality of vocational education" in the high schools, according to the Clark Committee, "has been as disturbing as the quantity."[18] Few of the students taking vocational courses have been enrolled in occupations where employment opportunities indicate a long-term tendency to expand. The scope of the problem is underscored by the testimony of the Employment Security Administrator of the State of Illinois before the Committee. He states, "the equipment used in most . . . courses is outmoded and inadequate . . . There is, in most cases, no relationship between the skills the trade schools teach and the actual demands of the job."[19] John F. Henning, Undersecretary of Labor, points out that these problems are compounded by a tendency to make the vocational schools "the depository for students with disciplinary or intellectual problems."[20]

---

16. *Annual Report of the Council of Economic Advisers*, January, 1964, p. 61.

17. *Manpower Report of the President*, 1964, p. 70.

18. *Report*, Subcommittee on Employment and Manpower, 1964, p. 83.

19. Testimony of Samuel Bernstein, *Hearings*, Subcommittee on Employment and Manpower, 1963, p. 501.

20. Testimony of John F. Henning, *Ibid.*, p. 326.

After intensive hearings on the relationships between education, technological change, and employment, the Clark Committee concluded that "it would be a serious mistake to concentrate educational resources upon specialized occupational preparation at the high school level." Full employment in an increasingly complex industrial society, the Committee observed, requires "a sound basic high school education for everyone capable of assimilating it." Training for specific occupations, the Committee pointed out, "should to the extent feasible be postsecondary," and offered in junior colleges, technical schools, or through apprenticeship and on-the-job training.[21]

The shift in vocational training from non-theoretical skill training to programs combining basic education with scientific and technical studies is illustrated by the growth in two-year post-high school technical institutions and community colleges. The post-high school technical institutions provide instruction in physics and mathematics, and they prepare students for careers such as engineering aides, or electronic technicians and repairmen. The community colleges offer two years of traditional college education for students planning to transfer to four-year institutions. They also supply training in semi-professional fields, e.g., the graphic arts or medical and dental technology, and, increasingly, in skilled crafts, including printing or tool and die making. The community colleges often face problems in recruiting a collegiate level staff and in developing a curriculum of collegiate caliber. However, the pressing need for a two-year post-high school institution offering low-cost general education, and technical training closely related to the areas of expanding employment, can be expected to offer a favorable environment for growth in the character and the number of these institutions.

---

21. *Report,* Subcommittee on Employment and Manpower, 1964, pp. 78ff.

III.

Strengthening education at all levels, as proposed by President Eisenhower's Commission on National Goals, or the expansion of general and technical education, as recommended by the Clark Committee, indicate needs for large-scale increases in expenditures for staff and facilities. The sheer fact of enrollment increase caused by population growth would involve a sizeable growth in spending for education, even if the present educational system and the present standards remained unchanged.

The basic requirement for improving the quality and availability of education, as the late President Kennedy emphasized, is "more and better teachers—teachers who can be attracted to and retained in schools and colleges."[22] In 1962, there was a shortage of 134,000 teachers reported for elementary and secondary schools.[23] While enrollment in elementary and secondary schools increased by over half between 1950 and 1962, the number of college graduates qualified to teach in these schools rose by less than one fourth.[24] Changes in the requirements for teacher certification to give greater weight to liberal arts and science education would increase the supply of teachers and, frequently, of highly qualified teachers. In addition to improvements in compensation, changes in social status and in opportunities for professional fulfillment for teachers are also necessary for realizing our national objectives in education.

Programs already under way or under consideration for reducing the number of school dropouts, or for coping with the unemployment and social disorganization characterizing the white and nonwhite young population in the urban

22. *The Keystone in the Arch, Compilation of Major Remarks on the Subject of Education by the late John F. Kennedy*, U.S. House of Representatives, Committee on Education and Labor, 1964, pp. 50–51.

23. *Teacher Supply and Demand in Public Schools, 1962*, National Education Association, 1962, p. 21.

24. *Ibid.*, p. 12.

slums, will add to needs for a highly qualified instructional staff and for educational facilities. Again, the Clark Committee succinctly summarizes the problem. Students in the slums "enter the middle-class oriented school system at the age of 5 or 6 with almost insuperable handicaps. The school systems into which they come . . . are those with the lowest budgets, poorest buildings, greatest overcrowding, and the most inexperienced teachers." Remaining in school until minimum school-leaving age because of legal compulsion, these students drop out before high school graduation "illiterate, untrained, and unmotivated."[25] Meaningful education for students in the slum schools, as President Johnson pointed out in his 1965 *Message on Education,* "must begin with the very young."[26] Tests indicate that the child from the slum is usually a year behind in academic performance by the time he reaches third grade, and up to three years behind by the eighth grade. Pre-school programs have had considerable success in overcoming the initial language and cultural handicaps which characterize these children. However, in the mid-1960's, almost half the public school districts conducted no kindergartens. Public nursery schools were operated in only 100 of the 26,000 school districts in the United States.[27]

Colleges and universities also face serious shortages of qualified staff. It appears very likely that the demand for college teachers in the coming decade will outstrip the capacity of graduate schools to turn out Ph.D.'s. In addition, the National Education Association reported in 1961 that slightly less than half the persons receiving Ph.D. degrees in school years 1958–60 had remained in college teaching at the time of the report.[28] Rising enrollments coupled with the shortage

---

25. *Report,* Senate Subcommittee on Employment and Manpower, 1964, p. 80.

26. President Johnson's Message to Congress on Education, 1965.

27. *Ibid.*

28. *Teacher Supply and Demand in Universities, Colleges, and Junior Colleges,* National Education Association, 1961, p. 45.

of Ph.D.'s can be expected to lead to widespread recruitment of faculty with lesser preparation. This development will probably accentuate the division in higher education between a minority of institutions engaged in both teaching and research, and a majority concentrating on transmitting rather than adding to knowledge.

Shortages of facilities at all levels of education parallel the shortages of faculty. While some 348,000 public elementary and secondary classrooms were built between 1958 and 1962, there was still an accumulated backlog of almost 125,000 classrooms in the fall of 1963.[29] Recent school construction has been barely sufficient to accommodate the annual increment in enrollment. This lagging rate of construction is responsible for the perpetuation of double sessions and abbreviated school sessions. Moreover, the changes which have been influencing the public school curriculum and teaching techniques, like the pressure for improving education in the slums, serve to increase the need for school facilities and to raise construction costs.

The additional facility requirements for colleges and universities in the next decade will grow out of the need to replace obsolete and substandard buildings, and to provide for the expected growth in enrollments, especially in graduate and professional schools and in community colleges. Maintenance of the current population-physician ratio of approximately 750–1, according to the U.S. Office of Education, will involve construction of between 14 and 20 new medical schools in the 1960's.[30] The rapid expansion in university-sponsored research, particularly in the sciences and engineering, will also necessitate large investments in build-

---

29. *Fall 1963 Enrollment, Teachers, and School Housing in Full-time Elementary and Secondary Day Schools*, U.S. Office of Education, 1964, p. 28.

30. Mushkin, S., and Bokelman, W. R., "Student Higher Education and Facilities of Colleges and Universities," in *Economics of Higher Education*, 1962, p. 185.

ings and equipment. To purchase and install a nuclear re-
actor, again quoting the U.S. Office of Education, "represents
an investment of funds greater than would have been spent
for a whole scientific establishment half a century ago."[31]
   Like classrooms and laboratories, libraries are also an important intellectual and educational resource. The American
Library Association reported in the early 1960's that some
10 per cent of the population had no "legal access" to public
library service, and 62 per cent had "only inadequate service" available. Per capita library expenditures in 1962, including capital outlays, were $1.68.[32] Similarly, almost 70 per
cent of the public elementary schools had no libraries in the
mid-1960's. The libraries of half the four-year colleges fell
below accepted professional standards in the number of vol-
umes possessed.[33] Meeting the recognized standards for library materials in the elementary and secondary schools
would require a fourfold increase in current expenditures
in our major cities, and a doubling of per capita expenditures to attain standards of minimum adequacy in public
library service.

IV.

   The standards for our goal in education reflect the consensus of our national leaders, and of educational and
manpower experts, that our investment in people through
education must be increased. This consensus has gained
momentum as the educational implications of the new
technology have become apparent, as the civil rights movement has lent new urgency to our concern with poverty and
with equality of opportunity, and as the scientific and technical accomplishments of the Soviet society have challenged
complacency with past achievements.

31. *Ibid.*
32. *New Directions in Health, Education, and Welfare,* U.S. Department
of Health, Education, and Welfare, 1963, p. 185.
33. President Johnson's Message to Congress on Education, 1965.

President Eisenhower's Committee on Education Beyond
the High School summed up the essential ingredients in this
consensus for all levels of education as they appeared in the
context of the later 1950's. The committee observed that
"our institutions of higher learning, despite the remarkable
achievements in the past, are in no shape today to meet the
challenge. Their resources are already strained, their quality
standards are even now in jeopardy, and their projected
plans fall far short of the indicated need." Stressing the
central role of faculty, the committee proposed that "the
absolute highest priority . . . be given to raising faculty
salaries with the goal of doubling the average level within
five or ten years."[34]

Discussing education from the perspective of national manpower policy in the mid-1960's, President Johnson observed
that the gap between our educational resources and performance and the nation's needs was still a cause for concern.
The education of many of our people, the President commented, "[has] not prepared them adequately to qualify for
today's jobs . . . or to capitalize on new opportunities."[35]
Stressing the importance of removing the economic and
social barriers keeping many young persons from realizing
their educational potential, President Johnson proposed in
1965 that "we declare a national goal of full educational
opportunity."[36]

These restatements of national educational needs point
to substantial increases in expenditure if their objectives are
to be realized. The National Education Association, for
example, has stated that achieving the quality of elementary
and secondary education commensurate with our society's
demands on the educational system would involve an in-

34. President's Committee on Education Beyond the High School, *Second Report to the President,* 1957, pp. 3, 4.
35. *Manpower Report of the President,* 1964, p. XIV.
36. President Johnson's Message to Congress on Education, 1965.

crease in annual current expenditures per pupil from $341 in 1960 to $720 in 1970.[37]

V.

The nation's goals in education indicate broad objectives for the coming decade. Opportunities at all levels of education should be made available to all who can profit from them. The economic status of teachers must be significantly improved and more of the able college graduates attracted to teaching. Physical facilities must be expanded and modernized. College and university enrollment, for example, increased by 80 per cent from 1950 to 1962. Achieving our goals in higher education would mean an increase of 130 per cent from 1962 to 1975. In order to increase capacity to meet anticipated enrollment needs in the 1970's without a serious deterioration in the quality of higher education, the expansion must be planned and the facilities constructed in the meantime.

Universal education for American children virtually has been achieved for children in the 6 to 13 age group. Almost 100 per cent of the individuals in this age group were attending school in 1962. We are further from our goal in kindergarten and college enrollments and, to a lesser extent, in high school enrollment. Only two thirds of the 5 year olds were in school, overwhelmingly in nursery schools and in kindergartens in 1962. Students enrolled in colleges and universities amounted to one fourth of the population in the 18 to 24 age group.

We interpret our educational objectives to include 100- per cent attendance for the 5 to 17 age group at some level of education ranging from kindergarten to university. This means that all young persons would attend kindergarten, and would continue their education to include high school

---

37. *Financing the Public Schools, 1960–1970,* National Education Association, 1962, p. 16.

attendance and, for the overwhelming majority, high school graduation. In higher education, it is reasonable to anticipate an increase of about 50 per cent in the proportion of young people going to college. This increase represents a target reflecting present aspirations which is consistent with past experience.[38]

More young people would be attending school in the coming decade even if it were not our nation's objective to expand educational opportunity. Population growth alone would raise enrollments and educational expenditures. To indicate the increases in enrollments and in spending for education because of our educational goals, two estimates are presented for the 1970's. One shows the growth in school attendance if the 1962 enrollment-to-population ratios were to remain frozen to 1975. The other indicates the larger enrollments anticipated because of our objectives. These estimates, together with actual school attendance in 1962, are listed in Table 7–3.

Realization of our enrollment objectives would increase attendance in elementary and secondary schools by 1975 only moderately over the 1962 attendance. Enrollment in higher education would more than double. Most of the anticipated growth in enrollment represents an increase in the public schools. However, private elementary and secondary schools, largely parochial schools, are likely to continue enrolling about one seventh of all pre-college students. Rapid growth in the relatively inexpensive community colleges and in state and urban universities is expected to concentrate three fourths of the increase in college enrollment in publicly controlled institutions.

If actual enrollment approximated the constant ratio projection, and if teachers' salaries, curriculum, and capital outlays per student remained at their 1962 levels, educational

---

38. Figured as a percentage of the 18 to 24 age group, this is taken to mean that enrollment in colleges and universities would increase from 26 per cent of this group in 1962 to 35 per cent in 1970 and to 38 per cent by 1975.

Table 7–3
Enrollments in Education, 1962, 1970, and 1975*
(in millions)

	Enrollment in 1962	PROJECTED ENROLLMENT			
		Constant Ratio Estimates		Estimates for Education Goal	
		1970	1975	1970'	1975
1. Elementary	30.5	35.4	36.9	35.5	37.1
2. High School	14.7	17.0	17.8	18.5	19.4
3. Colleges and Universities	4.2	5.9	6.6	8.0	9.6
a. Undergraduate non-professional	3.1	4.3	4.8	5.6	6.7
b. Graduate and professional	1.1	1.6	1.8	2.4	2.9
4. Total, All Levels of Education	49.4	58.3	61.3	62.0	66.1

* 1962 data derived from the following U.S. Office of Education studies: *Fall 1963 Enrollment, Teachers, and School Housing in Full-time Elementary and Secondary Day Schools,* 1964, p. 14; *Digest of Educational Statistics,* 1963, p. 12; and *Opening (Fall) Enrollment in Higher Education,* 1963, p. 7.

expenditures would rise from the $30 billion spent in 1962 to $40 billion in 1975. Without any improvement in our educational standards, we would be spending $10 billion more a year for education because population growth would lead to larger enrollments.

The $40 billion estimate of the cost of extending the educational *status quo* through 1975 is our hypothetical pre-empted benchmark for education.[39] It serves as a base for projecting the additional costs involved in increasing the ratio of enrollment-to-population, adding more and better paid teachers, and building an adequate, modern plant for the 66 million students anticipated at all levels of education in the mid-1970's. The cost of achieving these objectives is projected at $82 billion in 1975, or over double the expenditures for the benchmark estimate.

Three fourths of the $42-billion increase in spending listed

39. Conceptually, the hypothetical preempted benchmark for education should also include the increase in educational expenditures expected to occur because of rural-urban population shifts. It has been omitted because the historical data on which to base such a projection has not been available.

as the cost of realizing the improvements included in our
aspirations for education represents additions to instructional
costs. The National Education Association has estimated that
a staff of 50 professionals—teachers, supervisors, counselors,
and librarians—is required per 1,000 students for effective
teaching in elementary and secondary schools.[40] This implies
an increase of about 20 per cent in the current average of
staff-to-students ratio. Accepting the Association's standard
as the basis for our estimate of faculty requirements in the
next decade, we would need an instructional staff of 2.84
million for the elementary and secondary schools in 1975,
an increase of one million over 1962.

In higher education, rapidly growing enrollments will
probably encourage changes in educational technology, i.e.,
widespread utilization of educational TV. The new technology will make it possible to teach more students than would
otherwise be the case. In courses where lecturing is the basic
teaching method, many students can be reached by an outstanding teacher through educational TV. These courses
will be combined with small advanced classes and seminars
emphasizing individual student participation. Allowing for
an increase of about 20 per cent in average class size because
of these changes, a staff of 528,000 teachers and administrators is estimated as the faculty required for the near-ten million college and university students anticipated in the goal
for education by 1975.[41]

Attracting an additional 1.2 million well-qualified faculty
members at all levels of education in 1975 will involve large
increases in compensation to make the earnings of teachers
more nearly equivalent to earnings in other professions. We

40. *Financing the Public Schools, 1960–1970,* National Education Association, 1962, p. 18.

41. These projections of faculty requirements imply an increase in average
class size in higher education from 19 in 1962 to 22.5 by 1975. The projections
for elementary and secondary education imply a decline in the number of
pupils per teacher in public elementary schools to 25 by 1975 and in public
high schools to 18.

interpret this increase as amounting to a doubling of teachers' salaries in the coming decade, as proposed earlier for college faculty by President Eisenhower's Committee on Education Beyond High School. If teachers' salaries doubled in the ten years following 1962, with a continued increase of 3 per cent a year thereafter, the average salary of the elementary and secondary instructional staff would increase from $5,750 in 1962 to $12,900 in 1975. For the instructional staff in higher education, the corresponding increase is from $7,600 in 1962 to $17,000 in 1975.

Rising enrollments, larger faculties, and existing backlogs and replacement requirements imply sizeable increases in expenditures for facilities. For elementary and secondary schools, an estimated 1.1 million classrooms will be needed between 1962 and 1975, representing an investment projected at $51 billion. In higher education, the comparable investment for instructional and research facilities, and for dormitories to house oncampus students, is expected to reach $33 billion. On an annual basis, these capital outlays are expected to approximate $6 to $7 billion in the 1970's.[42]

Expanding educational opportunity will mean increases in spending in many areas. Greater recognition of the need for vocational retraining, literacy education, and continuation education to enable doctors, lawyers, and engineers to keep up with advances in their fields is expected to quadruple spending for adult education and related community services. To keep pace with rising enrollments, college library expenditures are projected to grow to almost a billion dollars a year in the next decade. With greater urbanization and higher educational levels, it is reasonable to anticipate that a larger share of the population will use public libraries, and, on an average, read more books each year. Per capita public library expenditures, accordingly, are listed as tripling to $4.50 by 1975.

To reduce the influence of family income as a factor in

---

42. For sources used as bases for estimates of capital outlays, see Table 7–1.

determining who should attend college, expenditures by colleges for loans and scholarships are expected to double in the next ten years. This aid is in addition to National Defense Education Act Loans, or the expenditures by business firms to subsidize the education of their employees, or the work-study program begun by the Federal Government in the mid-1960's to enable students to earn up to $1,000 a year from part-time and summer work. Similar assistance would be extended to encourage students from low income families to complete high school or undertake vocational training.

About one half of the nation's basic research is carried on in college and university laboratories. Colleges and universities have been spending about 10 per cent of total R & D expenditures in the United States in the early 1960's with most of this research financed by the Federal Government.[43] Assuming these proportions continue, they will be spending something under $4 billion for research by 1975, roughly a tripling of their 1962 expenditures.

The expenditures for achieving the objectives included in the aspiration standard for the education goal in the 1970's are summarized in Table 7–4.

VI.

As a claim on resources, the $82 billion listed for the education goal would raise spending for education from 5.5 per cent of GNP in 1962 to over 8 per cent of the near-trillion dollar GNP anticipated for 1975. These increases in spending for education would reflect a change in national priorities. For all sixteen goals, education ranked eighth in order of expenditure in 1962. The estimates for the aspiration standard would raise spending for education to sixth place in the mid-1970's.

While the discussion of education for the purposes of this study has been in terms of its dollar costs, enlarging expendi-

43. *National Trends in R & D Funds, 1953–1962*, National Science Foundation, 1963, p. 2.

Table 7–4
Estimated Expenditures for Education Goal,
1970 and 1975
(in billions of 1962 dollars)

	Expenditures in 1962	Projected Expenditures for Aspiration Standard in 1970	in 1975
1. Elementary and Secondary, Total	$21.1	$43.4	$54.0
a. Instructional costs	11.3	28.5	38.1
b. Adult education and community services	0.1	0.6	0.7
c. Capital outlays	3.4	4.4	4.0
d. Other[a]	6.3	9.9	11.2
2. Colleges and Universities, Total[b]	8.3	21.8	27.2
a. Instructional costs	2.2	7.1	9.6
b. Libraries	0.2	0.6	0.9
c. Adult education and community services	0.6	1.6	2.2
d. Research	1.3	3.0	3.5
e. Student aid	0.2	0.9	1.3
f. Capital outlays	1.2	2.6	2.1
g. Other[a]	2.6	6.0	7.6
3. Public Libraries	0.3	0.8	1.0
4. Total, All Education	29.7	65.9	82.1

a. For elementary and secondary schools, this includes costs of administration and maintenance, fixed charges, health services, lunch programs, transportation, etc. For higher education, this also includes the costs of operating dormitories, student unions, and similar auxiliary enterprises.

b. Includes expenditures for community colleges and for post-high school technical institutes.

tures merely increases the means available for achieving our aspirations in education. It does not assure that the means will be effectively used. The $50-billion increase in spending listed for the education goal would be unlikely to achieve its purposes if the training of teachers is narrowly conceived, if the curriculum is insulated from advances in science and the arts, or if the freedom to teach and to learn is hedged in by bigotry or stifled by bureaucracy. Mass higher education, even with larger expenditures, is likely to deteriorate in quality if the university becomes transformed into the "multiversity"—a depersonalized department store of information and expertise.

Education in America has had many of the characteristics

of a secular religion. Widespread diffusion of educational opportunity has been our main channel for diffusing social and economic opportunity, and it has also served as the foundation of our technological dynamism. Education, from this perspective, is a dimension of all our goals. Expanding educational opportunity is the strategic ingredient in our programs for coping with poverty and racial discrimination. Assuring our future manpower needs for scientists and engineers, for doctors, for social workers, and for teachers depends on progress in education. And, the prospects for world peace in a nuclear age demand more widespread understanding of other societies than has ever been the case before.

CHAPTER 8

Transportation

I.

Our goal in transportation is to create an efficient and progressive transport system. Pursuit of this goal in the next decade is likely to be heavily affected by a family of technological changes expected to arrive in the 1970's. Expenditures for facilities and for R & D to create the kinds of transport capacity and the amount of capacity needed for an expanding and changing economy are estimated to rise to $75 billion in 1975.

Transportation is a strategic factor in economic growth and social change. Expenditures associated with transportation absorb one fifth of GNP.[1] The manufacture of transportation equipment uses one fourth of all steel produced and two thirds of all rubber.[2] New systems and extensions of existing modes of transportation expand the size of the market, and they make it possible to take advantage of the

---

1. President Johnson's Transportation Message, March 4, 1965.
2. Landsberg, Fischman and Fisher, *Resources in America's Future,* Johns Hopkins Press, 1963, pp. 142, 145.

economies of large-scale production and distribution. Inexpensive and rapid transportation has created the modern metropolis and megalopolis. It intensifies the forces that cause the rapid movement from place to place and from job to job which characterizes our society. Transportation, in this sense, is one of the great dynamic forces in American history.

The present transportation system in the United States is essentially a dual economy. One segment is made up of private automobiles and the other of commercial carriers. The impact of the private automobile on the manner in which people live, work, and spend their leisure is so great that one student of economic development, W. W. Rostow, uses the presence or absence of widespread automobile ownership as his criterion for the "takeoff point" to a mass consumption society.[3] Purchases of new cars in 1962 amounted to $20 billion of the $35-billion total spent for transportation facilities. Automobiles were also largely responsible for the $9 billion spent for highway construction and maintenance.

For the commercial carriers, the effects of the technological changes after World War II were apparent in the rapid growth of the trucking industry and the passenger airlines, along with a decline in the role of the railroads and the merchant marine. These changes created excess capacity and diminished earnings for railroads and shipping lines, and they caused loss of jobs for their employees. The consequences for the railroads and merchant marine transformed them into "sick" industries with ramifications extending throughout the economy. The railroads, especially in the East, pressed plans for mergers and abandonments of passenger service to shrink their facilities and personnel to the downward shifts in traffic. The shipping industry survived largely because of Federal subsidies. The advent of the jet airplane in the mid-1950's created similar problems of excess capacity

---

3. Rostow, W. W., *Stages of Economic Growth*, Cambridge University Press, 1960.

for the airlines which were eased in the 1960's by the overall growth in air travel.

High speed railroad passenger trains, nuclear ships, supersonic planes, hydrofoils, and, possibly electronic highways could open up new opportunities, and could also engender problems similar to those related to the growth of air travel in the past decade. Creating a viable transportation system in the 1970's will mean reconstructing the established modes, such as railroads, while also promoting the development of new transport modes. In addition, it will involve planning to accommodate an estimated 50 million more automobiles without intensifying already serious problems of land use, air pollution, suburban sprawl, accident hazards, and congestion.

II.

The changes in transportation show up strikingly in the distribution of traffic between the different carriers. The largest single element in commercial transport is the intercity movement of goods. What has happened to intercity freight is summarized in the table below.

The major shifts in these percentages are the decline in the railroads' share, and the rise in the percentage of traffic moved

Table 8–1

Distribution of Domestic Intercity Freight by Type of Carrier, 1950 and 1962*

	1950	1962
Total Intercity Freight in billion ton-miles	1,094	1,410
Percentage moved by		
rail[a]	57.4%	43.7%
truck	15.8	23.5
inland waterways	14.9	15.8
oil pipelines	11.8	16.9
air cargo	less than 1/10th of 1%	

a. Most of the decline in the railroads' share of intercity freight took place in the 1950's. From 1960 to 1963, the percentage of intercity freight carried by the railroads fell only from 44.3 to 43.6 per cent of the total. *Statistical Abstract, 1965, p. 559.*
* *Statistical Abstract, 1964, p. 570.*

by trucks and oil pipelines. Passenger traffic in this same period was dominated by the private automobile, and by the shift in long distance travel from railroads to airlines. The weight of these changes shows up in the data for intercity passenger traffic presented in Table 8–2.

Table 8–2
Intercity Passenger Traffic by Type of Carrier,
1950 and 1962*

	1950	1962
Billion Passenger Miles by		
private automobile	403	720
public carriers	70	81
Per cent of Public Carrier Traffic Moved by		
rail	46.3%	24.7%
buses	37.6	26.1
inland waterways	1.7	3.3
airways	14.4	45.9

* Statistical Abstract, 1964, p. 570.

Nine tenths of all intercity passenger traffic in 1962 was made up of people travelling in their own automobiles. Railroad passenger service survived in many areas, and especially in the eastern United States, because of subsidies or abatement of taxation, or because the railroads' earnings from other sources were sufficient to cover the deficit from moving people. Equally striking is the fact that air travel crossed the threshold in the 1950's and became a major mass transportation industry. Commercial air travel within the United States quadrupled from 1950 to 1962, growing from 10 to 38 billion passenger miles.

A greater tendency for Americans to visit other countries paralleled these changes. In 1963, three times as many Americans travelled to other countries as in 1950. By the early 1960's, 80 per cent of this travel was by air. The decline in travel by ship was exceeded by the downward spiral in the volume of freight handled by ships of U.S. registry. By the early 1960's, only about an eighth of the cargo tonnage in U.S. foreign trade was carried by these carriers.[4]

---

4. Part of this decline reflected a growing tendency to reduce costs by trans-

III.

National goals in transportation are made up of a range of public and private proposals for adapting to the changes which have affected the movement of freight and of people. At one end of the spectrum are the public programs for major changes in our transportation system, such as the late President Kennedy's Transportation Message of 1962, or President Johnson's recommendation to Congress in 1965 that the Government finance the development of a railroad passenger train to travel between Boston and Washington at speeds of more than 100 miles an hour. At another level are the goals of public bodies concerned with the prospects and problems of the industries they regulate. The Federal Aviation Agency's objectives for air transport in *Project Horizon* is an outstanding instance.[5] Programs formulated by industry spokesmen, like the plan of John W. Barriger, President of the Pittsburgh and Lake Erie Railroad, for reconstructing the railroads, are not to be overlooked. At yet another end of the spectrum are the millions of consumers voting with their dollars to perpetuate the automobile's sovereignty in passenger transportation.

President Kennedy's Transportation Message proposes two principles which define our objectives in transportation. The principles, to quote the Message, are

that users of transport facilities should be provided with incentives to use whatever form of transportation which provides them with the service at the lowest total cost, public and private . . . [and] to translate scientific knowledge into transportation engineering practice.[6]

---

ferring American-owned ships, and especially oil tankers, from U.S. registry to registry of other nations, such as Panama or Liberia.

5. *Report of the Task Force on National Aviation Goals, Project Horizon,* Federal Aviation Agency, 1961.

6. "Presidential Message to Congress on April 5, 1962," *The New York Times,* April 6, 1962, p. 18.

Following the President's Message, one element in our standard for the transportation goal is concerned with more effective use of the presently available technology. The other stresses the development of new transportation technology. Both take it for granted that consumers' preference for their automobiles will remain essentially unchanged for another decade, with the probable exception of greater use of mass transit in the central cities. Together, the two elements make up the goal of creating a more efficient and a more progressive transportation economy.

Aside from the expenditures for upgrading facilities, achievement of the objective of greater efficiency involves changing outdated regulatory policies based on the assumption that the railroads still enjoy a near-monopoly in inter-city freight, and eliminating subsidies and taxes which create uneconomic advantages for some carriers and equally irrational burdens for others. It also involves planning for transportation as a system made up of different modes, each of which has an advantage in particular uses. If efficiency were the criterion, railroads, for example, would concentrate on the long-haul movement of bulk freight, truckers would concentrate on short haul and local movements, and the two modes would be used cooperatively for less-than-carload long distance shipments.

Support for the innovations which will outmode much of the existing transportation system also figures as an important objective. Nuclear ships and supersonic planes are probably the leading innovations for the next decade. Others include hydrofoils, air cushion vehicles, gas turbine engines for automobiles and trucks, and, possibly by 1975, electronic highways. These innovations are now largely in the development or testing stage. They figure in our standard for the transportation goal because the prospects for introducing technological change in transportation are great, and they are more a matter of economy and desirability than of discovery of new basic principles or techniques.

I V .

The efficiency yardstick supplies a perspective for considering a cluster of changes which can be anticipated for the next decade. Improvement of transportation facilities, using the presently available technology, would introduce changes in the traffic distribution. It would also involve substantial capital expenditures. Reorganizing the present patchwork of piecemeal regulation, perhaps by creating a Federal Department of Transportation to regulate all interstate carriers, would also influence the distribution of traffic. Our estimate of the distribution of freight and passenger traffic which is consistent with the efficiency criterion is described in Table 8–3.

Table 8–3
Estimated Distribution of Intercity Traffic, 1962 and 1975

	1962	Projections for 1975a
1. Total Freight Ton-miles (in billions)	1,410	2,530
2. Per Cent of Freight Moved by		
rail	43.7%	40.9%
truck	23.5	24.3
inland waterways	15.8	16.5
pipeline	16.9	18.0
air	less than 1/10 of 1%	0.3
3. Billion Passenger Miles Moved by		
private automobile	720	1,400
public carrier	81	160
4. Per cent of Public Carrier Passenger Traffic Moved by		
rail	24.7%	18.5%
bus	26.1	17.5
inland waterways	3.3	2.1
air	45.9	61.9

a. The freight distribution projected for 1970 is nearly identical with 1975. For intercity passenger traffic, the distribution by mode is roughly similar to 1975.

The projections anticipate that the decline in the railroads' role as a mover of freight will probably continue in the next ten years, but at a considerably diminished rate. The railroads' share is expected to fall partially because they are likely to lose much of their coal traffic. While the railroads are competing vigorously to retain this freight, much of it will probably be lost as coal is increasingly used to generate electricity close to the mine source, while electricity is shipped long distances via high voltage power lines. Coal now shipped by rail can also be transported by pipeline in the form of a slurry, a mixture of finely ground coal and water. In addition, if efficiency were the guiding consideration, trucks would carry part of the less-than-carload shipments now transported by rail.

Greater use of containers is expected to strengthen the resistance of the railroad and water carriers to inroads by their rivals. The same container and cargo may be imported by ship, unloaded on a truck, shipped from its domestic point of origin by rail, and delivered to its destination by truck. Since the use of containers joins several transport modes in moving the same freight, it offers each an opportunity to concentrate in the area of its greatest advantage.

Along with greater use of containers, a thorough overhaul of railroad plant and equipment is essential for the railroads' survival. The basic roadbed and physical contours of most of the nation's carriers were designed in the nineteenth century, and they have not been significantly changed since. The speed of freight trains is typically limited by use of outmoded cars designed for the 50-mile an hour maximum of steam locomotives rather than the 70 or 80 miles possible with diesels. Many of the passenger cars were engineered for the capabilities of steam locomotives with a 70-mile an hour limit. Diesels can haul lightweight passenger cars at more than 100 miles an hour. Similarly, tunnels and bridges frequently reflect the engineering usages of an earlier generation.

Our estimates of the cost of reconstructing the railroads largely follow the outlines proposed by John W. Barriger in his book, *Super Railroads for a Dynamic America.*[7] Bar-

---

7. Barriger, John W., *Super Railroads for a Dynamic America*, Simmons Boardman Inc., 1950.

riger's objective was to create a railway system approximating the gradient of the least expensive type of transportation—water level routes. This would require massive expenditures to lower gradients, strengthen tracks, and reduce curvature. Present mountain routes would be renovated or circumvented by building a dozen tunnels 10 to 30 miles long. Newly designed freight cars would be hauled at speeds of 70 miles an hour by large diesels of 10,000 to 12,000 horsepower. Automated freight yards would replace the present units.

In 1962 prices, these and related proposals for passenger service would cost some $24 billion. Spread over a ten-year period, potentially 1968–1978, they would cost $2.4 billion a year. While the changes recommended by Barriger would utilize presently available technology, they could readily be accommodated to innovations such as the automatic crewless train or high speed passenger cars similar to those used in Japan. However, progress in reviving railroad passenger service is likely to require more thoroughgoing technological change than Barriger's program envisages.

The largest percentage increases in traffic are listed for air cargo, although air cargo is credited with less than 1 per cent of total freight ton-miles moved in the 1970's. However, air cargo offers an important advantage to firms interested in minimizing inventory costs or in developing one- or two-day factory-to-outlet deliveries on a national basis. The development of all-cargo jet planes, such as the Canadair or the Boeing cargo jets, should improve traffic prospects substantially by making it possible to reduce rates and improve service. By 1975, air cargo is likely to figure prominently in particular fields—for highly seasonal goods such as women's fashion items, or for moving machine tools, scientific instruments, or cut flowers.

In another ten years, passenger travel by air is expected to exceed the combined intercity passenger travel by rail, bus, and inland waterways by over half. This estimate of air traffic follows closely the projections of air traffic developed by public agencies as in the Federal Aviation Agency's study, *Project Horizon*. Expenditures for airports, ground facilities, navigation aids, and air traffic control are insufficient for air transport's status as a mass transportation industry. The need for computerized air traffic control systems to reduce accidents by minimizing the possibilities for human error has been pointed out in such studies as FAA's *Project Beacon*.[8] The wave of jets introduced in the late 1950's and early 1960's is likely to be largely replaced by similar and more powerful planes in the early 1970's, or, beginning in the mid-1970's, by supersonic airplanes. Rapid growth is also anticipated in the use of the smaller general aviation planes, and especially so by business firms owning their own planes.

As in the case of railroad passenger transportation, a reversal in the prospects for the merchant marine will probably await major changes such as automated or nuclear ships. Revival of passenger travel by ship could be encouraged by the development of high speed transoceanic ships carrying 5,000 to 10,000 passengers at low cost to Europe or Asia. These ships offer the possibility of mass transoceanic transportation with costs per person estimated as low as $100 for travel between the United States and Europe.[9]

The other carriers of freight—pipelines and inland waterways—are expected to roughly maintain their present share of the larger volume of traffic in the 1970's. Growth in the volume of pipeline traffic will probably reflect both the movement of coal in the form of slurry and new possibilities, such as shipping wood in chip form by pipeline. The advantage of inland waterways as inexpensive carriers of heavy bulk freight, such as cement, is likely to continue. Rising land costs are also likely to encourage construction of pipelines and improvements to internal waterways.

Updating our transportation system would involve spend-

---

8. *Report of the Task Force on Air Traffic Control, Project Beacon,* Federal Aviation Agency, 1961.

9. See "Transportation—Year 2000," by Morris Forgash, *Congressional Record,* January 12, 1965, p. 614.

ing $75 billion for facilities in 1975. As in the mid-1960's, the bulk of the expenditures, over half, represents spending to purchase new automobiles. Currently, more than two fifths of American families with annual incomes of $10,000 or greater own two or more cars.[10] Since average family income in the mid-1970's is expected to exceed $10,000, it is anticipated that over two fifths of all American families will become multiple car owners. All told, the number of automobiles registered is expected to increase by 50 million, from 66 million[11] in 1962 to over 115 million by 1975. Rising private expenditures for automobile purchases will lead to substantial increases in public spending for highways. Construction of additional highway mileage will accelerate the increase in car ownership and this, in turn, will lead to demands for new highway construction as roads become crowded again. The 50-million increase in automobile ownership indicates a probable need for the expansion of controlled-access highway construction in the 1970's on a scale similar to the Interstate System after that system is completed.

V.

Considerations of efficiency and the anticipated rapid growth in automobile use and air travel serve to illustrate problems and possibilities likely to be with us in the 1970's. By themselves, these considerations suffer from a static bias. If one assumes that the currently available technology is the framework for the future, the changes which are likely to transform our concepts of efficiency or desirability in transportation a decade from now are excluded from consideration. Planning a transportation system for a highly urbanized and mobile society, according to Robert A. Nelson, Director of the Northeast Corridor research project, makes it necessary "to learn not only what can be done to improve the

---

10. *Automobile Facts and Figures,* Automobile Manufacturers Association, 1963 ed., p. 38.

11. *Statistical Abstract,* 1964, p. 564.

present technology, but to try to speculate usefully on wholly new modes and systems of transportation."[12]

Many of the nation's programs in transportation are based on the expectation that a large-scale R & D effort, largely financed by public funds, makes it possible to plan technological change in advance for commercial production at a future target date. The project to develop the supersonic plane is an instance. Other innovations now in the development phase represent instances of the traditional evolutionary continuum in which modest efforts carried out by different sources, public and private, translate technical possibilities into commercial successes. Hydrofoils or gas turbine engines are examples. To reflect the impact of these changes on the transportation economy in the next decade, the cost estimates for our goal must take into account the innovations which can reasonably be expected to be in use by 1975.

Since the transportation innovations are not yet in everyday use, or, like hydrofoils, they are only beginning to gain commercial acceptance in the United States, the cost estimates, of necessity, are rough orders of magnitude. They represent the expected expenditures for R & D, plus the "breakthrough" costs, or the capital costs of the initial establishment of an innovation as a large-scale routine commercial operation. In two instances, the supersonic air transport and the nuclear ship, the projections are estimates of the costs of replacing the existing stock of equipment with the innovation which will outmode the existing facilities.

The prospects for technological change vary widely in the different transportation industries, mainly because of the great differences in their expenditures for research and development. At one extreme is the aircraft industry, with total R & D expenditures of almost $4 billion a year in the early 1960's, or about one fourth of net sales. At the other is the railroad industry with R & D spending totaling a fraction of 1 per cent of operating revenues.[13] This wide

12. *The New York Times,* March 5, 1965.
13. *Research and Development in Industry, 1960,* National Science Founda-

range of expenditures reflects both differences in company funds spent for research and the great differences in the Federal research funds available to the aircraft industry and the railroads.

The problems created by unequal expenditures for research are illustrated by the railroads. Since World War II, railway passenger traffic has declined sharply, although the carriers have spent large sums for new and improved passenger equipment. However, according to the authors of a recent authoritative study, the Doyle Report, in making these changes "the basic frames, trunk, and heavyweight design of earlier cars were continued for another 30 years—the average life of the cars."[14]

This lack of experimentation suggests that sizeable returns would result from greater research expenditures by the railroads. Currently, much of the research affecting railroads is carried on by the industries which supply them, and many improvements such as mechanization of maintenance have been adopted by the carriers. Manufacturing companies in the early 1960's spent slightly under 2 per cent of their sales for company-financed R & D.[15] If the railroads spent the same share of their operating revenues for R & D in the next decade, company expenditures could be expected to reach a level of over $300 million in 1975. This effort would very probably be supplemented by Federal funds.

Likely prospects for the railroad research effort include programs for standardizing and improving containers. The gas turbine locomotive and a revival of the work on atomic locomotives underway in the 1950's are other possibilities. A major research effort is essential if railway passenger service is to survive in many parts of the United States. Noting that intercity travel in the "Northeastern Corridor" between

tion, 1963, pp. 40, 64, 98; *Research and Development in Industry, 1961,* 1964, pp. 12, 40.

14. *Report of the Special Study Group in Transportation,* U.S. Senate, 1961, p. 293.

15. *Research and Development in Industry, 1961,* pp. 12, 40.

Washington and Boston is expected to increase by 150 to 200 per cent between 1960 and 1980, President Johnson recommended in 1965 that Congress authorize an R & D program to develop high speed passenger train service in the Corridor.[16] The objective of the research would be to introduce a system of noiseless electric trains travelling at speeds of 125 to 150 miles an hour, connecting the major cities in the Northeast on a near-commuter basis. With this system, travel by train would frequently take little more time than travel by plane in the East, including the trip to and from airports and railroad stations as part of the total travel time. Since these trains would move at double or more the speed of automobiles, they could ease highway congestion by diverting part of their traffic to the railroads. Once developed for the eastern United States, the high speed train could be utilized in other regions.

Smaller R & D expenditures for hydrofoils or air cushion vehicles are expected to create new transportation modes more or less competitive with ships, airlines, and railroads. The hydrofoil is intended to increase the speed of surface ships. By placing hydrofoils beneath the hull of a conventional looking boat, a speed can be reached in which the lift of the foils raises the hull completely above water and support is then supplied by the more efficient submerged foil. Speeds are intermediate between ships and planes.

A study prepared by the Stanford Research Institute suggests that the economic advantage of the present generation of hydrofoils for the United States lies in their potential as high speed ferries in intercity service for a range of up to 200 miles.[17] The next generation of hydrofoils will probably include large automated oceangoing vessels accommodating containerized cargo and moving at speeds of up to 100 knots. Abroad, hydrofoils offer the underdeveloped countries an

---

16. President Johnson's Transportation Message, March 4, 1965.
17. "The Economic Feasibility of Passenger Hydrofoil Craft in U.S. Domestic and Foreign Commerce," prepared by the Stanford Research Institute for the U.S. Department of Commerce, 1961.

opportunity to create an inexpensive transportation system. For countries lacking an extensive rail and road network and critically short of the large capital sums needed to create these facilities, the far less costly hydrofoils should offer attractive possibilities.

Hydrofoils are already in everyday use in Italy, Japan, Egypt, and the Soviet Union. The Soviet Union in the early 1960's was operating a hydrofoil fleet of some 300 units. United States participation has been limited. Total expenditures in 1962 were reported at less than $30 million. With the experience gained since the launching of a 90-ton ship, the *Denison,* in 1961, by the Maritime Commission, the smaller- and medium-sized craft are likely to be in everyday commercial use by 1970. Expenditures to build a hydrofoil fleet growing at 36,000 tons a year in the 1970's are estimated at approximately $400 million annually.[18]

Air cushion vehicles at present offer a more speculative prospect than hydrofoils. They are lifted above the surface, whether water, land, ice, or swamp, by air pressure. Once above the surface, the propulsion for movement is supplied by a second set of engine-driven propellers or turbines. In 1960, the British operated their version of the ACV, the Hovercraft, in commercial service at 60 knots on a 15-mile run carrying 15 passengers. In the United States, the major experimentation centers on the 20-ton Hydroskimmer. It is capable of flying at a height of 1-1/2 feet for a range of some 150 miles at a speed of 70 knots.

Many technical problems remain to be solved before the ACV's are in common use. Their potential for increasing the mobility of tactical units by reducing dependence on highways, railroads, airfields, or port structures is likely to encourage military development. For civilian use, the Maritime Administration is planning to build an experimental craft with a capacity roughly equal to the new all-cargo jets.

---

18. With this level of construction, we would be adding to our hydrofoil fleet at a rate equal to 3 per cent of the 1960 tonnage of oceangoing vessels under construction.

And, like hydrofoils, the ACV's offer the prospect of inexpensive transport to the underdeveloped countries. Experience with the Hovercraft indicates that air cushion vehicles will probably be in operation in the United States by 1970. The annual R & D costs and capital outlays for a fleet growing by 3,000 tons a year is estimated at $100 million by 1975.

Prospects for the older and better known helicopters appear more clouded than for hydrofoils and the ACV's. So far, high costs have confined the civilian uses of helicopters to general aviation and to limited local airport-to-airport service. The V-STOL craft are likely to be military developments in the period covered by this study.

Gas turbine engine and electronic highways are the two innovations directly affecting motor vehicles which are likely to be in use by the mid-1970's. Other innovations, such as engines powered by fuel cells, will probably be in the research and development stage in the next decade. Gas turbine engines offer lighter weight, simplicity, and smoother operation, plus the ability to operate on low priced fuels, such as kerosene and diesel fuel. Automobile and aircraft manufacturers have been experimenting with these engines for virtually every type of motor vehicle from passenger cars to fire engines. Heavy duty trucks are among the likely users of the gas turbine engines. They can effectively exploit the potential of the new engines in steady operations over long distances at high speeds. Completion of the Interstate Highway System in the early 1970's will provide a nationwide network of roads suitable for these vehicles. If 2 per cent of the trucks and buses, and 1 per cent of all passenger cars were equipped with gas turbine engines each year in the 1970's, we would be spending about $750 million in 1975 to acquire them.

Electronic highways are a more remote possibility than gas turbine engines. They offer opportunities for reducing accidents, increasing the capacity of highways, and enhancing the pleasure of driving, by enabling the driver to read, nap, or watch television en route. The automated highways operate by means of wire loops carrying a small current buried at close intervals in road lanes. When a car passes over each loop, it generates a signal which is passed on to the control system and, in turn, impulses are fed back to the special guidance equipment installed in the car. The potentialities of electronic highways are best realized on long stretches of turnpike, such as the Interstate System, or on especially hazardous parts of standard highways where safety would benefit most from guidance by automatic controls.

To adapt the electronic system to existing highways is expected to cost about $100,000 per mile. The guidance devices for the automobiles could probably be turned out in mass production for some $200. Automating 1,500 miles of highway a year, and installing the guidance devices in 750,000 automobiles annually in the mid-1970's, is projected to amount to about $300 million.

VI.

Innovations such as the hydrofoils or air cushion vehicles fit in with existing transportation modes and serve as rivals or feeders into their systems. In these respects they differ from nuclear ships and supersonic planes. Their purpose is to render obsolete the existing types of transportation equipment which they would replace *en masse*.

Some 75 per cent of the privately owned U.S. merchant fleet consists of vessels built during World War II.[19] These vessels will become obsolete about the turn of the decade. New equipment which has not been developed and proven before that time is unlikely to be introduced in the next generation of American ships. Faced with the prospect of block obsolescence, nuclear ships offer an alternative to the high construction and operating costs which have largely priced American shipping out of world markets. They also offer prospects for eventually ending the U.S. subsidies to

19. *U.S. Transportation Resources, Performance and Problems,* National Academy of Sciences, 1961, p. 287.

shipowners which totalled about $300 million annually in the early 1960's.

A report prepared for the Maritime Administration in 1963 considered the possibility of constructing a 14,000-ton nuclear "warehouse" ship.[20] It would travel at speeds of 30 knots, compared with the 18 to 21 knot speed for a comparable conventional cargo ship. The nuclear vessel would be flexible enough to handle bulk cargo, palletized or containerized cargo, and roll-on-roll-off trucks. Aside from a speed advantage, the nuclear ships would free space for cargo by eliminating space and weight requirements for fuel oil. Since these ships are virtually independent of fuel supplies outside of home ports, their cruising range would be far greater than conventional vessels. It is estimated that the annual cost, including capital and operating costs, for the ship considered would be about one third higher than for a conventional 21-knot ship, and about the same as for a non-nuclear ship travelling at 30 knots.

The first American nuclear ship, the *N.S. Savannah,* was launched in 1962. The Russians preceded the United States with a nuclear icebreaker, the *Lenin,* introduced in 1957. In 1962, the Federal Government opened a nuclear ship servicing facility which can service some 20 ships a year.

A vessel with a propulsion system as different as the nuclear ship would very probably do more than extend the range, speed, and cargo potential of conventional ships. It has been suggested that nuclear ships use their power plants for low cost in-transit processing of fish or food and chemicals. Submersible cargo ships, or sea trains, could revolutionize our concepts of international shipping. The vessel's power plant would be a separate above-water unit coupled to underwater trailers made up of highly collapsible containers. Trailers consigned to a particular port could be

---

20. For a summary of this report, see "Iron Men and Atomic Ships," *Business Week,* June 8, 1963.

uncoupled and transported to the dock area by tug, thereby minimizing the often lengthy stays required for port stop-overs. By standardizing containers, a world-wide transportation system could be established, providing a continuous flow of goods from a point of origin in one continent to their destination in another.

Cost estimates for nuclear ships have been reduced to such an extent that extrapolations of present costs to the 1970's are likely to lack relevance. Allowing for continued cost reductions, replacement of the present oceangoing merchant marine of the United States over a fifteen-year period, beginning in 1968, is estimated to require expenditures of approximately $1 billion annually in the 1970's. Converting the naval fleet to nuclear power would involve additional expenditures. The possibilities for a nuclear navy are discussed in Chapter 9.

Development of supersonic transport planes (SST) has been adopted as a national program largely to be underwritten by public funds. Implementation is expected to involve expenditures of $1 billion to develop an SST, preferably a Mach 3, ready for regular passenger service in the early 1970's. Emphasis on an American supersonic plane has been prompted by the steps taken by the British and French governments to develop the *Concorde,* a Mach 2.2 plane scheduled for service in 1970. Knowledge that the Russians have been experimenting with at least a prototype SST has also influenced American planning.

United States participation in transatlantic air traffic fell from 63 per cent of the number of passengers in 1950 to 40 per cent in 1960. An American SST is presented as the alternative to similar traffic losses in the 1970's.[21] Experience gained with the supersonics would be useful in developing the next generation of air transports, the Mach 6 hypersonics. If the *Concorde* is developed, but an American SST is not,

---

21. *Project Horizon,* Table 1, p. 108.

the nation's air carriers would probably purchase about 100 *Concordes* in France and Britain.[22] Assuming the supersonic planes become available in the early 1970's, and replace subsonic jets on long flights in the course of the decade, we would be spending over $700 million for SST's in 1975.

Not surprisingly, opinions differ as to the feasibility of the SST as a commercial venture a decade from now. An independent study of the Mach 3 planes estimates they would cost the U.S. airlines some $300 million more in direct operating cost annually than the subsonic jet planes they would replace. The Federal Aviation Agency suggests "if at the end of Phase II [detailed design phase] it is clear that the required economies cannot be attained, the development program should be re-evaluated and probably terminated."[23] Aside from the costs to the air carriers, the SST would create new problems for the population arising from the noise level of the plane, the sonic boom. Full realization of the savings in time on flights within the United States would require both speedier planes and more adequate provision for rapid city-to-airport transportation.

The costs for the transportation innovations are summarized in Table 8–4. The estimates include both the R & D expenditures and outlays for facilities.

The cost estimates for the innovations include some $500 million in each year for R & D; the rest represents outlays for plant and equipment. These projections are an incomplete representation of the expenditures required to continue the technological revolution in transportation. The cost of the new modes would be partially offset by reductions in expenditures for the existing modes for which they are substitutes. To replace the conventional merchant marine by nuclear ships in the 1970's, we would be spending about $1 billion more a year to purchase nuclear ships, and about

---

22. This estimate is derived from data in *An Economic Analysis of the Supersonic Transport*, Stanford Research Institute, 1963.

23. *Supersonic Transport Development Program*, Federal Aviation Agency, 1963, p. 24.

$500 million less for conventional craft. The capital costs could be minimized if investment decisions in the next decade would weigh in their calculations the probabilities inherent in the new technology. Capital outlays for conventional oil tankers, for example, could represent an investment in equipment likely to be outmoded by nuclear tankers before it has depreciated through normal use.

Our cost figures are also incomplete because they do not allow for the social costs the changes considered would impose on employees. Since two SST's are estimated to carry as many passengers in a year as five subsonic jets, fewer air crews would be required for the supersonics. Hydrofoils are potential competitors for ships and railroads, and nuclear ships are intended as replacements for conventional vessels. The new transportation modes typically require fewer employees per million passenger or ton-miles than the established modes because they are faster, or more automated, or they have a greater carrying capacity in proportion to their bulk. The loss of employment and earnings of the displaced employees is also part of the cost of technological change.

Table 8–4
Estimated Expenditures for Transportation Innovations, 1970 and 1975
(in millions of 1962 dollars)

Mode	Type of Change	Projected Expenditures in 1970	in 1975
Railroads	R & D Program	$ 260[a]	$ 330[a]
Hydrofoils	breakthrough	375	380
Air Cushion Vehicles	breakthrough	65	65
Gas Turbine Engines	breakthrough	750	750
Electronic Highways	breakthrough	15[a]	325
Nuclear Merchant Ships	replacement of oceangoing fleet	1,020	1,020
Supersonic Planes	replacement of long-haul jet planes	150[a]	750
Total		2,635	3,620

a. R & D only.

VII.

Total expenditures for our transportation goal, including both the new and the established technology, are estimated at $75 billion in 1975, or more than double the 1962 outlays. Spending for transportation plant and equipment in the mid-1970's is expected to be $8 billion larger than spending for national defense, assuming no disarmament, and $13 billion more than private and public expenditures for housing.

We would be spending large sums for transportation in the next decade if the industry's technology and traffic patterns were frozen in the pattern of the mid-1960's. If facilities for moving freight grew at the same pace as output, and automobile ownership and air travel increased proportionately with population, especially in the young adult age group, we would be spending an estimated $56 billion for transportation equipment and plant in 1975. The improvements and the new technology included in the standard for the transportation goal would add almost $20 billion to the cost of continuing the *status quo* for another decade.

The cost projections for our standard in transportation are described in Table 8–5, which follows.

As in the early 1960's, over five sixths of all the expenditures listed for transportation in the 1970's are for motor vehicles and highways. The magnitudes involved in introducing the new technologies are only a small part of the costs estimated for the transportation goal. However, these expenditures would rise substantially as the degree of breakthrough increased. Costs for the gas turbine engine alone would probably equal the expenditures estimated for all our innovations if, and when, they generally supplanted the standard engine.

Our projections relate to a nation in which economic and social distances are rapidly shrinking. The barriers to moving goods and people are likely to diminish further as transportation resources are used more efficiently and innovations

Table 8–5
Estimated Expenditures for Transportation Goal,
1970 and 1975
(in millions of 1962 dollars)

Mode	Expenditures 1962	Projected Expenditures 1970	1975
1. Railroads	$ 1,050	$ 2,650	$ 2,750
2. Motor Vehicles	32,200	49,850	65,000
automobiles	19,850	30,050	38,800
trucks, buses, trailers	3,600	5,950	7,400
highways[a]	8,750	13,850	18,800
3. Waterways	1,000	2,400	2,800
ships	700	2,000[b]	2,300[b]
inland waterways	300	400	500
4. Oil Pipelines	150	250	400
5. Airways	750	2,300	3,450
air carriers	200[c]	1,100[b]	1,800[b]
general aviation	150	300	400
airports	300	550	750
air navigation	100	350	500
6. Hydrofoils	—	350	400
7. Air Cushion Vehicles	—	50	100
8. Total	35,150	57,850	74,900

a. Excludes local city streets.
b. Includes expenditures for transportation innovations and for the currently available facilities.
c. Figure cited for year 1962 is atypical; corresponding expenditures in 1960 were $500 million.

are introduced. Reduction of these barriers would facilitate pursuit of many goals. Building a modern highway network in Appalachia would help to end the isolation which has depressed the region's economy. For this reason, expenditures for highway construction are the largest item in President Johnson's recommendation in 1964 for Federal aid to that region.[24] Inexpensive air transportation would make the national parks and forests of the western states accessible to the population of New York or Chicago. A reconstructed railroad passenger service could encourage urban development by providing rapid transit to and from work for the

24. Expenditures for highway construction in President Johnson's recommendations to Congress amount to $840 million. Letter from President Johnson to Speaker of the House and President of the Senate, April 28, 1964.

commuters in the suburbs of our large metropolitan areas. Air travel, and an automated, and probably nuclear, merchant marine would strengthen the bonds of trade and travel linking the world's wealthiest nation with the newly industrialized societies of other continents. Better transportation would tend to raise standards of living in the southeastern United States by assisting that region to shed its status as an underdeveloped enclave within the larger economy.

Our nation's goals in transportation are largely concerned with commercial carriers and public facilities. Yet the largest element in the transportation economy is made up of individual consumers with their preference for private automobiles. Accomodation of the role of the automobile with the nation's objectives for other transport modes, or in land use, public health, or urban development, is likely to figure as the major challenge in transportation planning in the next decade.

CHAPTER 9

National

Defense

I.

The criteria for adequacy in expenditures for the defense goal differ in an essential respect from the criteria for the other goals. Expenditures to build more health centers or schools are regarded as desirable because of the improvements in health or education resulting from such spending. Expenditures for military installations, equipment, or personnel are a means to other goals which are the desired objective—peace and national security.

The level of defense expenditures in the 1970's is likely to reflect the extent to which developments in the next decade encourage a greater emphasis on relaxation or on tension in international relations. Since the costs of defense are a major claimant on the nation's resources, estimates of spending for defense must be included for both possibilities in order to indicate the disposable resources for pursuing the other goals.

The standards for the defense goal refer to these two possibilities. One alternative extrapolates to the 1970's the signs
of diminishing international tensions in the early 1960's—
e.g., the test ban treaty. These developments are taken to
indicate a basis for arms reduction following the lines of
Stage I of the United States disarmament proposals at Geneva in 1962.[1] Expenditures for a level of defense equivalent
to partial disarmament are projected to decline from the
$51 billion spent in 1962 to $39 billion in 1975.

The other possibility proceeds from the assumption that
the present tensions between the United States and communist China will continue, and that new trouble spots will
arise in various parts of the globe. Under these circumstances,
it can be expected that the armaments buildup would be
resumed before 1970. The estimates for the high defense alternative project a steady expansion in defense capabilities,
primarily through technological advances in weapons systems, but also by increasing mobility and firepower for conventional forces. The expenditures for this possibility would
rise to $68 billion by 1975.

I I.

Events in the early 1960's have offered a reasonable basis
for anticipating improved prospects for partial disarmament.
The ban on atmospheric nuclear testing is the most tangible
realization of these tendencies. Another significant symptom
is the almost simultaneous, although independent, cut in
defense expenditures by the United States and the Soviet
Union, i.e., the announcement by both countries in April,
1964, of an intention to reduce the production of enriched
nuclear materials. The prospects for disarmament are enhanced by the depolarization of international relations. Divisions in the communist world, and the beginning of "poly-
centrism" in what had been the monolithic Soviet bloc in

---

1. *Outlines of Basic Provisions of a Treaty on Disarmament*, U.S. Arms
Control and Disarmament Agency, 1962.

Europe, add to the likelihood of depolarization. Similarly, a tendency toward independent political action within the Atlantic Alliance, and the growing voice of the underdeveloped nations in world affairs, make it less likely that the nations will be divided into two antagonistic power blocs a decade from now. Currently these developments have been partially reversed by the war in Vietnam.

Several years ago the Arms Control and Disarmament Agency of the Federal Government drew up a draft disarmament treaty which was submitted by the United States to the Geneva Disarmament Conference in 1962. Stage I of this draft treaty is the basis for our disarmament standard. Stage I provides for a reduction in the number of military personnel on active duty to 2.1 million in 1970. This total would be expected to fall to 1.8 million by 1975. Stocks of major armaments, including missiles and missile sites, bombers, antimissile systems, tanks, artillery, and combatant ships, would be reduced by 30 per cent. Production of new armaments in these categories would be limited to replacements. Production of fissionable material for use in nuclear weapons would be halted along with underground nuclear weapons tests. Similarly, the use of weapons of mass destruction in outer space would be prohibited.

The proposals in Stage I could be realized by several routes. They could be adopted as the result of a bilateral agreement between the United States and the Soviet Union, perhaps joined by other nations. The impetus to disarmament could come from an international accord sponsored by the United Nations. Perhaps the simplest and most likely method is unilateral but interdependent action. The United States would reduce its armaments independently of formal agreements as it became apparent that the Soviet Union was similarly engaged.

The Stage I disarmament alternative is conceived as a "separable first step" for relieving world tensions. Recent advances in military technology add relevance to the separability of the Stage I program. Equipment for our divisions could be stockpiled in Europe or elsewhere and manned quickly by airlift. The Administration's program for developing the C-5A transport plane capable of carrying 750 passengers could represent a dramatic step forward in increasing the worldwide mobility of our military forces.[2] Satellite and aerial photographic surveillance opens up new possibilities for inspection.

If it were successfully implemented, Stage I could lead to more far-reaching changes patterned after Stages II and III, which could include destruction of remaining inventories of nuclear weapons, elimination of overseas military bases, and large-scale reductions in military equipment and personnel. The national armed forces remaining at the end of Stage III would be restricted to the levels required to maintain internal order and protect personal security. International security in this disarmed world would be assured by a progressively strengthened United Nations Peace Force. The changes in Stage II and III would require elaborate international cooperation for their realization, and they go beyond the scope of the alternatives considered for defense in this study.

The reduction in forces for the Stage I alternative are conceived as being carried out over a three-year period. If a decision were taken in 1966, for example, implementation would proceed in 1967–1969 and the process would be completed by 1970. The probable impact of this type of partial disarmament for defense expenditures is summarized in Table 9–1 (page 191).

With partial disarmament, defense spending in 1975 is estimated at $12 billion less than in 1962. The bulk of the savings occurs in procurement as inventories of weapons are reduced. However, the full repercussions of disarmament for procurement spending would not be felt immediately. Initially, the obsolete items in the reduced inventory would be replaced by technologically more advanced equipment—

---

2. President Johnson's Message to Congress on National Defense, January 18, 1965.

e.g., the F-111 (TFX) would be produced until it entirely replaced the more limited F-110. Expenditures for operation and maintenance fall only slightly because the more complex weapons remaining in 1970 will require more elaborate maintenance than their 1962 counterparts. Expenditures for military construction decline since few new bases or missile sites would be added. Expenditures for military aspects of atomic energy fall by more than half. This decline reflects the cessation of nuclear tests and of the procurement and processing of fissionable materials.

Total expenditures for the smaller number of military personnel are listed to remain at approximately their 1962 levels. The estimates for military compensation include an allowance for an annual pay increase of 3 per cent. They also take into account the larger retirement and reserve expenditures likely to follow arms reduction as personnel released from active duty transfer to these components. Expenditures for military R & D are expected to continue at a high level, as a kind of insurance during the early years of the reduced levels of forces and weapons. Research efforts

Table 9–1
Estimated Expenditures for the National Defense Goal, Partial Disarmament Alternative, 1970 and 1975*
(in millions of 1962 dollars)

Component	Actual Expenditures 1962	Projected Expenditures 1970	1975
1. Military Personnel	$13,100	$13,500	$12,500
2. Operation and Maintenance	11,500	10,600	10,050
3. Procurement	15,000	9,950	5,850
4. Research and Development	6,450	8,250	7,400
5. Military Construction	1,250	550	550
6. Civil Defense	150	150	150
7. Military Aid to Other Countries	1,550	1,000	1,000
8. Atomic Energy (military)	2,300	1,300	1,000
9. Other	150	600	550
10. Total Defense Expenditures	51,450	45,900	39,050

* From *The Budget of the United States for the Fiscal Year 1964*, Table 18. Military functions of the Atomic Energy Commission have been estimated independently.

to improve surveillance techniques would probably intensify. R & D would also be utilized to develop a backlog of weapons possibilities which could be introduced into the defensive system if a changing international situation restored the arms buildup. With time and continued improvements in international relations, the R & D programs would taper off.

The projections of defense expenditure for partial disarmament constitute estimates of the minimum levels of defense spending which are expected to be consistent with national security in the 1970's. The magnitudes in these projections, therefore, also make up our hypothetical preempted benchmark estimate for defense spending in 1970 and 1975.

III.

The disarmament alternative represents an opportunity to translate widespread aspirations for social and economic progress into a closer approximation to reality in the next decade.

However, aspirations for world peace could be frustrated if, as nuclear technology becomes more generally diffused and less costly, many nations (including communist China) come to possess substantial military nuclear capabilities. The potentialities for adding to international tensions inherent in the proliferation of nuclear weapons would be accelerated if the United Nations were to lose the effective support from many countries which has enabled it to serve as a force for peace in Suez or on the borders of Israel. In the underdeveloped areas of the world, disappointments in popular expectations that living standards will rise significantly in the near future could make these nations inviting targets for civil strife or invasion. Guerrilla warfare in the new nations, especially in southeast Asia, might expand and grow into regular military operations involving other countries. The possibilities for strife and guerrilla warfare would become intensified if communism were to succeed in identifying itself with nationalism and social change in the less developed countries. While the split in the communist bloc has probably tended, to date, to reduce international tensions, it could serve to promote them if China and Russia were to compete in encouraging "wars of liberation" in Africa, Asia, or Latin America. If these circumstances were to materialize, considerations of national security would very probably lead the United States to increase its defense expenditures.

The expenditures listed for the high defense alternative assume a moderate upward tendency in military expenditures, with an increase averaging slightly more than a billion dollars a year. This is about the same average annual increase as in the 1955–60 period. Defense spending rose more rapidly in the early 1960's, increasing by $8.5 billion between 1960 and 1964. The policy of the Kennedy Administration contributed to the upward impetus by reequipping conventional forces for greater firepower and mobility, and by expanding the nuclear submarine fleet. This increase was also partially due to the introduction of the intercontinental ballistic missile. For fiscal 1965, President Johnson has indicated a decline in defense expenditures of $2 billion, made possible by the military cost reduction program adopted several years earlier, and by the fact that we had already achieved a high level of defense preparedness. The greater expenditures listed for the next decade are expected to occur because of the need for defense against possible dangers posed by the ICBM, or by space and underseas activities. In part, they also grow out of the continuing role of conventional forces in the undeclared twilight wars represented by guerrilla warfare.

Spending for the high defense alternative is expected to increase to $68 billion in 1975. This represents an increase of $16 billion over 1962. The major components of this expenditure are described in Table 9–2.

The largest increases in defense expenditures are listed for research and development, operation and maintenance, and higher pay and allowances for military personnel. The armed forces on active duty are projected to decline gradually from 2.85 million in 1962 to 2.4 million by 1975. As

Goals, Priorities, and Dollars

Table 9–2
**Estimated Expenditures for National Defense Goal,
High Defense Alternative, 1970 and 1975
(in millions of 1962 dollars)**

Component	Actual Expenditures 1962	Projected Expenditures 1970	Projected Expenditures 1975
1. Military Personnel	$13,100	$16,250	$17,800
2. Operation and Maintenance	11,500	12,850	16,850
3. Procurement	15,000	14,750	15,100
4. Research and Development	6,450	9,550	11,050
5. Military Construction	1,250	1,050	1,950
6. Civil Defense	150	600	600
7. Military Aid to Other Countries	1,550	1,550	1,550
8. Atomic Energy (military)	2,300	2,150	1,950
9. Other	150	800	700
10. Total Defense Expenditures	51,450	59,550	67,550

in the civilian economy, military technology tends to increase capabilities by the use of more and more complex equipment per member of the military force. The increases of 3 per cent annually in pay schedules and allowances for military personnel represent the equivalent of the productivity increases in the civilian economy.

Operation and maintenance expenditures are projected to increase by about $5 billion. These costs will rise because of the technical complexity of the new weapons systems. Much of the growth in operation and maintenance costs is attributable to one of the new systems, the Nike-X anti-missile system.

Military procurement spending is expected to remain at about the 1962 level in the 1970's. After inventories of existing weapons and of weapons likely to be adopted which are now in the development stage are built up, procurement of these weapons is assumed to taper off to replacement levels through 1975.[3] If procurement costs were confined to the present weapons technology, procurement spending would

---

3. Present (1964) programs to add Minutemen missiles or Polaris submarines to our defense capabilities should be completed before 1970. By that date we should have 1,200 to 1,300 Minutemen and a fleet of about 40 Polaris submarines.

be listed as declining to $9 billion in 1975. The additional $6 billion projected for procurement spending is for new weapons to add to defense capabilities in the 1970's.

As our stockpile of nuclear weapons increases to a level where further additions add little to overall military effectiveness, the procurement and production of nuclear materials will fall off. Large expenditures will still be required to keep establishments such as Oak Ridge and Hanford in running order and to make nuclear weapons more reliable and resistant to countermeasures.

With unconventional weapons rapidly becoming conventional, confinement of weapons systems in the 1970's to those which now appear likely to be adopted minimizes the forces making for change in defense technology. We do not know which prospective new weapons will prove to be feasible choices in another decade. To illustrate the possibilities involved and their probable impact on defense spending, the projections include cost estimates for the following, as examples: active missile defenses, nuclear surface ships and improved nuclear submarines, and enlarged defensive space activities. Updating present weapons systems and adding the advances in military technology is expected to increase spending for military R & D to $11 billion in 1975, an increase of two thirds over 1962.[4]

By 1970, it is possible that we will have perfected the Hard-Point Defense System. This anti-missile system is designed to intercept and destroy missiles approaching "hardened" military objectives, e.g., missile launching sites or underground command posts. As of now, technical difficulties associated with a general anti-missile system have not been resolved. However, the more limited purposes of the Hard-Point Defense System, as compared with the gen-

---

4. The R & D estimate takes into account the testing and further development of systems which are already under development. These include, among others, the F-111 (TFX) plane, V-STOL transports, the Typhon shipboard missile system, and the Poseidon missile to increase the striking power of of missile-carrying nuclear submarines.

eral system, may put it within reach before 1970. Establishment of the Hard-Point Defense System is estimated to cost approximately $600 million a year.[5]

Three fourths of the Navy's fleet was built during World War II. If we wish to avoid a situation in which these vessels all become obsolete at once, substantial shipbuilding expenditures must be programmed well in advance. Atomic power offers great advantages to the surface fleet and it will undoubtedly play an increasing role in the future. Nuclear aircraft carriers are currently quoted as costing about 20 per cent more than conventional carriers, and estimates for smaller vessels run to 30 or 40 per cent more. To offset higher construction costs, nuclear carriers could carry more aircraft than their conventional counterparts and as much as 50 per cent more fuel and ordnance for their planes. A greater percentage of nuclear ships could be on duty at any given time, and they could travel faster than the non-nuclear carriers. The cost of converting the fleet to nuclear power over a twelve-year period for the larger combatant ships, their auxiliary vessels, and for the special port facilities required is estimated at $2.5 billion a year.[6]

For the period after 1970, we have listed systems responsive to the three major defense needs growing out of modern technology: an anti-missile system for protection against ICBM attack, the Satellite Inspector as a defensive weapon in space, and a new deep-diving submarine to provide capabilities in an increasingly important area—the ocean depths.

---

5. The total cost of establishing the Hard-Point Defense System is estimated to be in the neighborhood of $2.5 billion. It is assumed that the system is introduced over a four-year period.

6. The House Armed Services Committee has estimated the cost of a shipbuilding program to modernize the conventional fleet at $24 billion. See *Composition of the Fleet and Block Obsolescence,* Armed Services Committee, U.S. House of Representatives, 1962. Converting the fleet to nuclear power is estimated to raise overall ship costs by 25 per cent, or $6 billion. Total costs for the new fleet, including the nuclear vessels, over the twelve-year period are projected to amount to $30 billion.

All of these systems are probably beyond our present capabilities.

The anti-missile system now being studied is called Nike-X and it is intended for the general defense of industry and population centers. Project Defender is the R & D effort investigating methods to overcome the technical difficulties associated with radar recognition of targets and resistance to countermeasures. If this research is successful and the Nike-X is adopted, the total construction and procurement costs for a nationwide system are estimated at $20 billion.[7] Assuming the system were installed in the 1972–1975 period, annual outlays would average $5 billion.

In the recent past, our nation has been reluctant to spend the large sums required for overall shelter protection. This reluctance is mainly attributable to the widespread belief that the protection afforded by the fallout shelters would be of limited value in a nuclear conflict. Active missile defenses of the Nike-X variety could be expected to stimulate interest in fallout shelters, since the defenses against nuclear attack the Nike-X provided would be integrated with the additional protection the shelters might offer. Secretary of Defense McNamara has proposed a system of shelters to supply fallout protection for the population by 1968,[8] a system exected to require some 240 million shelter spaces. Allowing for the larger population and the additional spaces needed by 1975, the cost of providing shelter spaces for the population is projected at $14 billion, one fourth to be borne by the Federal Government. If the shelters were built in the eight years after 1967, their construction costs, together with the expenditures for operating the civil defense system, are estimated to add $600 million a year to defense

---

7. More recent estimates based on developments in military technology and a reevaluation of defensive needs have reduced this estimate to as low as $10 billion. *Wall Street Journal,* July 26, 1965.

8. Statement of Secretary of Defense Robert S. McNamara before House Armed Services Committee, January 30, 1962.

spending.[9] These costs do not include the expenditures required to develop more effective and probably more expensive shelters to protect against blast and fire as well as radiation.

The Satellite Inspector illustrates the defensive possibilities of the new space technology. It is a space craft which could be used to place two men in orbit to inspect, repair, disarm, or destroy objects in space. The craft could serve non-military uses such as repairing communications satellites. Negative buoyancy submarines are possible successors to the Polaris submarines. For lift, they would rely on "wings," such as hydrofoils have, and on their forward motion. This type of submarine could operate at great depths where detection and destruction by surface ships would be difficult if not impossible. It would be equipped with a low-flying missile powered by a nuclear ram-jet engine, traveling at several times the speed of sound. Adding the Satellite Inspectors and negative buoyancy submarines to military capabilities in 1975 is estimated to cost $1.5 billion.[10]

The full impact of the changes in weapons systems resulting from new military technology is not expected to make itself felt before 1975. They add approximately $3 billion to the cost of defense in 1970 and $14 billion by 1975. The new weapons are intended to increase capabilities, and especially defensive capabilities, in the event of a nuclear war. Yet it is difficult to conceive of a nuclear conflict as a rational instrument of policy for any nation. The U.S.–U.S.S.R con-

9. It is assumed that 265 million shelter spaces would be needed in 1975. Cost per space for the shelters built in private homes are estimated at $100, and $40 per space for the shelters in public facilities. In addition, about $150 million a year is included for operating the civil defense system. Total expenditures for the private shelters, after allowing for government incentive payments to encourage their construction, would amount to $11 billion.

10. Costs for introducing the Satellite Inspectors over a four-year period are projected to average about $300 million a year. This figure includes the cost of 10 GEMINI capsules and 50 boosters. The cost of building six of the negative buoyancy submarines is estimated at $1.2 billion in 1975, or approximately 50 per cent more per submarine than for the Polaris submarines.

frontation through the Cuban missile crisis in the early 1960's
tested the recognition on both sides of the irrationality of
nuclear warfare. However, there has been little recognition
of the irrationality of more limited wars on the part of the
nations which have initiated them. The wars which have
been fought since World War II, as in Korea, have been
primarily land wars fought by conventional or guerrilla
forces. The bulk of the projected expenditures in the high
defense alternative, accordingly, is made up of spending for
conventional forces and updated versions of present weapons
systems or weapons currently undergoing development.

IV.

Both the partial disarmament and the high defense alternatives list defense spending as a smaller share of GNP in
the 1970's than it is currently. The extent to which defense
expenditures would be expected to fall below the 9.3 per
cent of gross national product they represented in 1962 is
summarized in Table 9-3.

With partial disarmament, the proportion of GNP accounted for by defense falls to 4 per cent by 1975. For the
continued arms buildup in the high defense alternative, de-

Table 9-3
Spending for Defense Goal as a Share
of GNP, 1970 and 1975

	In 1962	In 1970 Partial Disarmament Alternative	In 1970 High Defense Alternative	In 1975 Partial Disarmament Alternative	In 1975 High Defense Alternative
Expenditures for Defense (in millions of 1962 dollars)	$51,450	$45,900	$59,550	$39,050	$67,550
Defense spending as per cent of GNP[a]	9.3%	5.8%	7.6%	4.0%	6.9%

a. The percentages for the 1970's refer to a projected GNP in 1962 dollars of $787 billion in
1970 and $981 billion in 1975.

fense spending declines to 7 per cent. By the mid-1970's, the difference in defense expenditures projected for the two alternatives amounts to $28 billion.

If expenditures for defense can be expected to constitute a declining portion of an expanding GNP, an ever-larger share of our national wealth, according to President Johnson, "will be free to meet other vital needs, both public and private."[11] Likely candidates could include, among others, rebuilding our decaying central cities, improving education, expanding the "war on poverty," and updating our industrial plant. The smaller percentage of gross national product required for national defense could also lead to tax reductions, resulting in increased private consumption and living standards.

Table 9–4 presents an estimate of the resources which could be released to support other goals if either the disarmament or the high defense alternative were implemented. The table lists the differences between the projected defense expenditures for the two alternatives, and the levels of expenditure in the 1970's if defense spending remained as in 1962 at 9.3 per cent of GNP.

Table 9–4
Reduction in Defense Expenditures Because
of Declining GNP Share Projected
for Defense, 1970 and 1975
(in millions of 1962 dollars)

	Projections for 1970	1975
1. Defense Spending at 1962 GNP Share of 9.3 per cent	$73,200	$91,200
2. Reduction in Defense Spending with Partial Disarmament Standard	27,300	52,150
3. Reduction in Defense Spending with High Defense Standard	13,650	23,650

Using the health goal as a yardstick, the decline from the 1962 GNP share for defense associated with partial disarma-

---

11. President Johnson's Message on National Defense, January 18, 1965.

ment would release expenditures equivalent to 60 per cent of the $85 billion listed for the aspiration standard for the health goal in 1975. For the high defense alternative, the reduction in defense spending would be equivalent to almost 30 per cent of the health goal's cost.

Looking at current data to assess the significance of the changes in expenditure projected for the defense goal, the defense effort is the largest single source of funds for R & D. Six of the $16 billion spent for conducting R & D in 1962 were spent for defense-related projects. All told, expenditures for programs related to national defense generated 7 million jobs in that year. Of this total, over 3 million were in private industry.[12] In terms of the Federal budget, 58 per cent of Federal administrative budget expenditures in 1962, and 55 per cent in 1964, represented spending for national defense.[13]

The war in Vietnam poses the possibility that expenditures for national defense will rise substantially in fiscal year 1967 and, perhaps, for several years thereafter. At present, there is no way of knowing what defense requirements will be in the next five or ten years. The anticipation that a decline in defense spending could release resources to reduce the backlog of unmet needs in our society will depend, in large part, on the outlook for peace and stability in the underdeveloped nations of the world. However, barring a considerable increase in international tensions, it is likely that the national security could be effectively protected in the 1970's at a diminished cost in GNP percentage terms, if not in dollars. This assumes reasonably rapid economic growth in the United States.

---

12. *Manpower Report of the President,* 1964, p. 155.
13. *Annual Report of the Council of Economic Advisers,* January, 1965, p. 258.

CHAPTER 10

Housing

I.

The nation's goal in housing is summed up in the preamble to the Housing Act of 1949 as "a decent home in a suitable living environment for every American family." In 1962, spending to build new homes and to maintain or alter already built housing amounted to $29 billion. Expenditures for our housing goal are estimated to total $62 billion in 1975.

Supplying adequate housing for Americans affects many facets of national objectives and economic activity. Spending for residential construction in 1962 and in 1963 made up a third of all domestic private investment expenditures other than for inventories. Changes in residential patterns in our metropolitan centers have created decaying central cities made up largely of the poor, the childless, and minority groups, surrounded by vast stretches of suburbs populated by middle- and upper-middle income white families. Segregation in housing reinforces segregation in education, in personal relations, and in access to community facilities.

Since World War II, rising personal incomes, and public policies encouraging urban renewal and private residential construction, have substantially reduced the amount of substandard housing in the United States. Table 10–1 summarizes this progress in housing for the 1950's as reported in the 1960 *Census of Housing*.

Table 10–1
Substandard Housing as a Share of the Housing Inventory, 1950 and 1960*

Item	1950	1960	Per cent change 1950 to 1960
1. Number of Occupied Dwelling Units (in millions)	43.0	53.0	+ 23%
2. Per cent of Total			
a. Lacking facilities[a]	27%	11%	− 16
b. Dilapidated	9	6	− 3
c. Total substandard	36	17	− 19

a. "Facilities" refers to hot and cold running water, inside flush toilets, and inside baths or showers for private use of the household.
* *Census of Housing*, 1960, NC 4, Part 1A-1.

The proportion of American families living in substandard housing units fell by more than half between 1950 and 1960. This progress has been more heavily concentrated on improvement of houses lacking facilities than on elimination of dilapidated housing.

Provision for the adequate housing Americans will require in the 1970's includes two major aspects. One is concerned with the growing number of white households earning incomes considerably above the poverty minimum. As average family incomes reach $10,000 in the mid-1970's, the members of this group will use their larger incomes to buy better housing or second homes. Public policy is likely to affect their housing choices by encouraging an ample supply of mortgage credit, and by planning land use to develop attractive communities within large metropolitan centers.

Economic growth, together with measures for encouraging low-cost mortgage credit and land-use planning, is unlikely to assure an adequate supply of housing for low-income families, and for nonwhite families. High urban land and building costs can be expected to minimize the volume of unsubsidized private construction for low and moderate income families. The significance of these barriers is underscored by President Johnson's 1965 Housing Message, proposing public rent supplements for families living in substandard housing or for families moved out of their homes by urban renewal or highway programs, and subsidies to encourage moderate-income families to purchase homes. These and similar proposals can be expected to lead to greater experimentation with different combinations of private, public, and cooperative programs for urban renewal in the next decade. They should also encourage more emphasis on the construction of low and moderate cost rental housing units.

While housing conditions improved generally for Americans in the 1950's, the changes in this period were less successful in removing the disadvantageous status of the nonwhites. These changes are described in Table 10–2.

Table 10–2
Standard and Substandard Dwelling Units, Whites and Nonwhites, 1950 and 1960*

Status of Dwelling Unit	Per Cent Distribution of Dwelling Units Occupied by			
	Whites		Nonwhites	
	1950	1960	1950	1960
Standard	68%	87%	28%	56%
Substandard	32	13	72	44

* *Our Nonwhite Population and Its Housing,* Housing and Home Finance Agency, 1963, Table 29, pp. 76-77.

In 1960, as in 1950, substandard housing was far more prevalent among nonwhites than in the overall population. By 1960, only one eighth of the whites were still living in housing characterized as substandard. Over two fifths of the nonwhites, however, were still in substandard housing. For the majority of nonwhites who were renters, the preponderance of low quality or substandard housing was not reflected in substantially lower rents. The median rental paid by whites for urban housing units in 1960 was $75. The corresponding figure for nonwhites was $61.[1] Progress in providing "a decent home in a suitable living environment" for nonwhites is likely to require both rising income levels for families in this group, and changes in social attitudes and in legislation to do away with the practices that have confined them to the slums of the central cities.

Expenditures for our goal in housing include the cost of residential construction, maintenance and repair, and additions and alterations to serve the needs of the entire population. To this is added the cost of an expanded research and development program to encourage the mass production of housing components and use of new building materials and techniques of construction.

II.

Standards of housing adequacy in a dynamic society are constantly changing with the times. When the first bathtub was installed in the White House in the nineteenth century, a public controversy was stirred by what appeared to many as an unwarranted and alien extravagance. Present standards reflect a growing social consciousness and a greater awareness of the impact of housing on emotional as well as on physical well-being. By 1975, as incomes rise, the prevailing concepts of adequacy for many groups will probably include such present-day "luxuries" as central air-conditioning.

The American Public Health Association has taken a lead in promulgating housing standards. The APHA regards the primary criterion for housing adequacy to be its influence on health. It includes as contributing to health, "safety from physical hazards, and those qualities of comfort and convenience and aesthetic satisfaction essential for emotional and social well-being." The sense of frustration caused by

1. *Our Nonwhite Population and Its Housing*, Table 32, p. 86.

living in a substandard house, the APHA observes, "may often be a more serious health menace than an insanitary condition associated -with housing."[2]

The National Association of Real Estate Boards has recommended housing standards which are consistent with the APHA criteria. They stress the importance of adequate plumbing, heating, light, air, ventilation, and sufficient space to prevent overcrowding. The Housing and Home Finance Agency and the Urban Renewal Administration also have established standards. Their concept of inadequacy refers to blighted areas rather than to poor housing alone. This area concept relates housing adequacy to land use, community facilities, property values, and social problems such as juvenile delinquency. The housing standards in the urban renewal plans are generally higher than those in the municipal building codes.

The Bureau of the Census in its decennial census of housing lists several classifications which provide a basis for establishing standards in housing. The Census criteria most commonly used in classifying housing as substandard are the concepts of dilapidated housing, and of housing lacking in plumbing facilities. The Census also considers such elements as the age of units, crowding, and the condition of heating equipment. These items frequently go together—i.e., inadequate heating equipment is concentrated in dilapidated dwellings and in those with inadequate plumbing facilities.

The Census data, as summarized in Table 10–1, indicate that some 9 million of the 53 million occupied housing units in 1960 were substandard. A third of the 9 million units were classified as dilapidated. The others lacked major plumbing facilities.

The proposals considered for eliminating substandard housing in the housing goal refer to these Census classifica-

---

2. See American Public Health Association, *Planning the Neighborhood*, 1948; *Planning the Home for Occupancy*, 1950; *Construction and Equipment of the Home*, 1951.

tions. Cost estimates for the aspiration standards include the expenditures for replacing all dilapidated units which are expected to be inhabited in 1975 and replacing or repairing major plumbing facilities where absent or deficient. The housing built for purposes other than eliminating or rehabilitating substandard housing would supply replacements for removals from the housing inventory, accommodate the increase in the number of households, and also allow for the greater housing needs of a more prosperous and mobile population, and for special groups such as the aged.

III.

The standards for housing adequacy discussed in the previous section are concerned with the qualities of houses rather than with the technology of home building or the organization of the residential construction industry. The prospects for reducing costs and improving quality in housing largely depend on changes in this technology. Improvements in the technology of homebuilding, therefore, are also an important national objective.

The use of mass production methods by large firms with elaborate research facilities is still in its initial stage in the homebuilding industry. A survey by the National Association of Home Builders several years ago indicated that three fifths of their members built 25 or fewer houses in the survey year. Only 1.5 per cent of the members built 500 or more houses.[3] Firms in the industry are usually too small to engage in risky or costly research and development efforts. Innovations are frequently barred by building codes or craft regulations which rigidly specify the types of permissible building materials or methods of construction.

The entire construction industry, including residential

3. Meyerson, Terrett, and Wheaton, *Housing, People, and Cities*, 1962, p. 105.

construction, employed some 55,000 scientists and engineers in 1960.[4] Of this total, 53,000 were engineers. While scientists and engineers in construction made up about 5 per cent of the national total, they represented less than 1 per cent of all R & D personnel.[5] Most of the research affecting residential construction is conducted outside the industry by manufacturers of building materials.

Experience since World War II points to the large merchant builder as the strategic element in furthering innovation in residential construction. The merchant builders have taken the lead in encouraging offsite manufacture and onsite assembly of housing components. They have also been the major factor in introducing everyday use of new building materials in place of the traditional wood, brick, and stone.

Innovations in residential construction include the use of plastics or other synthetics as surface coverings, for pipes, or in sandwich panels. The sandwich panels—two thin skins of surfacing material banded to the sides of a structural core— have been taken over from the aircraft industry. Aluminum has also been substituted for the traditional materials. So far, the prefabricated houses have met with less success than those which utilize prefabricated components. Prefabricated housing still accounts for less than one tenth of all residential building.[6] Other technological changes include use of a plaster gun which enables a crew to double the amount of plaster applied in a day. The homes representing innovations in design have usually been the ones in which there has been more experimentation with new materials and building techniques.

In the early 1960's, American manufacturing firms spent an average of slightly less than 2 per cent of their receipts to

---

4. Colm and Lecht, *Requirements for Scientific and Engineering Manpower in the 1970's,* Committee on Utilization of Scientific and Engineering Manpower, National Academy of Sciences, 1964, Table 2.

5. Colm and Geiger, *The Economy of the American People,* National Planning Association, 1961, Appendix Table XIV, p. 187.

6. *Housing, People, and Cities,* p. 114.

finance research and development.[7] If spending for R & D by firms in the construction industry engaged in building new homes were to reach half this rate in the 1970's, they would be spending approximately $300 million by 1975. These expenditures, together with those of the firms manufacturing building materials, would make for significant advances in home building. Part of these funds could be used to encourage new designs and use of new materials in housing, another part to standardize and improve the prefabricated components. A small percentage of the total could be spent to devise building codes better adapted to the potentialities of modern technology than the present ones. Some of these changes would probably displace employees or eliminate craft demarcations. Part of the R & D expenditures, say $5 million, could be set aside for a human relations commission to investigate the effects of innovations on the industry's work force. It would also propose measures such as retraining programs or displacement allowances to protect the interests of the employees while encouraging technological change.

IV.

The cost estimates for the housing goal assume that economic growth will increase family incomes sufficiently to enable most Americans to provide themselves with adequate housing. If the economy were to grow at 4 per cent a year over the next decade, an anticipated 30 million houses and apartment units would be built between 1960 and 1975. Of this total, 2.1 million are listed for 1970 and 2.6 million for 1975.

These estimates are based on recent and expected tendencies in the housing market. On the demand side, the projections reflect the large growth in demand anticipated for multi-family units such as apartments, for smaller houses,

---

7. *Research and Development in Industry, 1960*, National Science Foundation, 1963, p. 41.

and for rental housing. The critical age for household formation is the 20- to 30-year age group. Thirty-one million persons are expected to attain this age group by 1970—about 9 million more than in 1960. A large share of households made up of younger persons means a greater emphasis on rental houses and on apartments. The greater mobility of the American population is also likely to add to the market for rentals. Growth in the number of older persons will create a special need for small housing units. Rising income levels should expand the demand for second homes. They are predominantly small, inexpensive units in vacation areas. All told, the multi-family housing units are projected to grow from 12 per cent of the units constructed in the 1950's to 40 per cent of the total built in the next decade.

Emphasis on multi-unit structures and second homes, along with cost reductions expected from technological change, should keep building costs for the typical dwelling unit from rising. The average price per dwelling unit, excluding the site, is projected at the 1962 average value of close to $13,000. Site costs are excluded as they do not enter into the GNP.

The changes likely to result from the nation's concern with civil rights can be expected to increase the demand for housing. With greater equality in educational and employment opportunities, the incomes earned by nonwhites should move closer to the national average. As the financial and social barriers to home ownership diminish, it is reasonable to anticipate that many nonwhite families living in less than adequate rental housing in the central cities will follow the national pattern and purchase more adequate homes in the suburbs. The potential increase in demand this addition to the market for purchasing homes could represent is summed up by the data on home ownership. In the early 1960's, nonwhites owned 38 per cent of the dwelling units they occupied compared to 64 per cent for whites.[8]

In regard to the financing of purchases of homes, housing

---

8. *Our Nonwhite Population and Its Housing*, Table 24, p. 66. This addition to the market for purchasing homes would run counter to the anticipated overall growth in the national market for rental housing.

is a massive consumer of long-term investment capital. The projections for housing expenditures assume that continued availability of mortgage finance, and public policy measures to minimize the risks of mortgage lending, should prevent sizeable increases in interest rates for prospective home purchasers for the next decade.

For substandard housing, it is estimated that demolishing and replacing the dilapidated housing will cost an average of $15,000 per unit. This estimate does not ignore the fact that dilapidated housing can often be rehabilitated. However, the costs of rehabilitation tend to run high. For the housing intended for low income groups, replacement is typically cheaper than thoroughgoing rehabilitation of houses which are frequently already sufficiently deteriorated to be classified by the Census as dilapidated. Dilapidated units in rural areas and small towns may be expected to be vacated permanently as their former occupants move to the urbanized areas. Repair of housing with major plumbing defects is anticipated to cost about $2,000 per housing unit, with a wide range of costs in particular cases. In some instances, the costs of providing adequate facilities could run as high as $5,000. Where only a shower stall or hot water unit need be installed, repair costs could total less than $200.

V.

The goal of adequate housing for all American families sets up the framework for projecting the cost of our standards in the 1970's. The significance of economic growth in realizing the goal can be indicated by comparing housing expenditures and the volume of residential construction anticipated if the GNP were to grow at 4 per cent a year over the next decade with a benchmark estimate. The benchmark assumes that construction of new housing units and expenditures for housing will increase at the same rate that new households are likely to be added to the population—at 1.6 per cent a year. This is our preempted yardstick for housing.

The projections corresponding to the *status quo* benchmark and to the growing economy are listed in Table 10–3. If housing starts merely kept pace with growth in the population of households, we would be building less than a fourth more units in 1975 than in 1962. We would also be spending $7 billion more a year for housing by the mid-1970's. But GNP is expected to grow at a considerably more rapid rate than the 1.6 per cent annual increase projected for households. Housing starts and expenditures, accordingly, would also be larger. By 1975, if GNP were to grow by 4 per cent a year, starts would be two thirds greater than in 1962 and expenditures $28 billion more. As more new homes were built, and more income was available to families for maintenance and repair work, the number of occupied dwelling units which were still substandard would fall off sharply.

The 6 per cent of the housing units estimated to be substandard ten years from now would cost much less to replace or repair than the 17 per cent characterized as substandard in the early 1960's. The standard for the housing goal stipulates that all occupied housing should meet minimum standards for adequacy by 1975. Dilapidated housing is assumed to be replaced and the plumbing defects corrected over a ten-year period beginning in 1966. The overall cost of elimi-

Table 10–3
Housing Starts and Expenditures, 1962, 1970 and 1975

Item	1962	Preempted Benchmark 1970	Preempted Benchmark 1975	4 per cent GNP Growth Rate 1970	4 per cent GNP Growth Rate 1975
1. Housing Starts[a] (in thousands)	1,550	1,750	1,900	2,100	2,550
2. Housing Expenditures[b] (in millions of 1962 dollars)	$29,400	$33,200	$36,300	$46,300	$57,400
3. Substandard Housing Units as % of Total	17%[c]	—	—	8-½%	6%

a. The estimates for housing starts refer to the number of houses and apartment units for which construction has started during the year.
b. Includes spending for new residential construction, additions and alterations, and maintenance and repair.
c. Figure listed is for 1960.

nating substandard housing during this period is summarized in Table 10–4.

Table 10–4
Estimated Cost of Eliminating Substandard Housing by 1975
(in millions of 1962 dollars)

Item	Projected Expenditures
1. Cost of Replacing all Dilapidated Units, 1966–1975	$28,500
2. Cost of Providing Plumbing Facilities to all Deficient Units, 1966–1975	5,200
3. Total Expenditures to Eliminate Substandard Housing, 1966–1975	33,700
4. Expenditures in 1970[a]	3,400
5. Expenditures in 1975[a]	4,300

a. This estimate assumes that 8 per cent of the total expenditures to eliminate substandard housing are spent in the initial year, 1966, and that expenditures increase thereafter by ½ of 1 per cent each year to 1975.

The beneficiaries of the expenditures to eliminate substandard housing would be concentrated in the groups which are largely outside the living standards of middle class America—the low-income population, including a large number of Negroes, Puerto Ricans, Indians, and Spanish-speaking families in the Southwest. For the majority of the population earning incomes above the poverty minimum, their spending for housing suited to their needs is also part of the goal of providing adequate housing.

Total expenditures in the 1970's for the housing goal for all groups in the population are described in Table 10–5.

To realize the goal of making adequate housing available to all Americans by 1975, spending for housing in that year would reach an anticipated $33 billion more than in 1962. With reasonably rapid economic growth, expenditures for housing would rise moderately as a claim on GNP, from 5 to 6 per cent. As family incomes increased, spending to improve existing housing would rise more rapidly than the expenditures for new construction. Most of the increase in spending for new homes would represent private expenditures resulting from growth in average family income and in the number of families.

Table 10–5
Estimated Costs for the Goal of Adequate Housing,
1970 and 1975
(in millions of 1962 dollars)

Item	Expenditures in 1962	Projected Expenditures for Aspiration Standards in 1970	in 1975
1. New Residential Construction	$20,000	$29,600	$36,500
2. Additions and Alterations	4,400	8,500	10,700
3. Maintenance and Repair	5,000	11,600	14,500
4. Industry R & D Program	n.a.	200	300
5. Total Expenditures	29,400	49,900	62,000
6. Expenditures as % of GNP	5.3%	6.3%	6.3%

While our goal in housing is framed in terms of spending for housing units or for research, these expenditures are the means to create viable communities in an urbanized and democratic society. For this reason, the nation's concern with housing, like its concern with education or civil rights, can be expected to gain momentum in the next decade. Progress in housing affects our objectives in these areas and in many others. As we build some 2 or 2-1/2 million housing units a year in the 1970's, additional expenditures will also be required to transport the residents of these housing units to work and to shop, to give their children schooling, for police and fire protection, and for health, recreational, and cultural facilities. This spending is more likely to develop a meaningful pattern for urban living if it is pursued as part of an overall development plan for our metropolitan areas.

CHAPTER 11

Research
and
Development

I.

To add to knowledge, to improve men's lives, to meet increasing industrial needs, and to protect the nation's security, are our goals in research and development. Achieving these objectives in the next decade will mean a continuation of the "research revolution" of the past decade and its general diffusion throughout our society. Attainment of our goals in R & D would involve increasing spending for research and development from almost $17 billion in 1962 to $39 billion by 1975.

Expenditures for research and development tripled between 1953 and 1962. Spending grew at an annual rate, in constant 1962 dollars, of more than 10 per cent a year. This

pace of growth was considerably greater than the corresponding rates of increase in GNP or in its major components—
such as business investment—or government purchases of
goods and services. With R & D expenditures amounting to
3 per cent of GNP in 1962, research and development, for
the first time in our history, has become an important element in the nation's expenditures.

The growth of research and development, and its application in new technology, vitally affects all our national objectives and most segments of our society. The increase in life
expectancy at birth from an average of 54 years in 1920 to
70 years in 1960 is largely the result of medical research.[1] It
has been estimated that one fifth or more of the growth in
output between 1929 and 1957 was due to an increase in
knowledge and its application.[2] The translation of scientific
advances into new technology in agriculture has made it
possible to reduce the share of the population occupied in
producing food and agricultural raw materials from 70 per
cent of the total in 1860 to only 7 per cent a century later.[3]
Mass production of automobiles and trucks, a result of research and development efforts in the late nineteenth century,
has served as the strategic variable in creating the metropolis
and the suburb, and in transforming the United States into
a predominantly urbanized society. Changes of this order
are, of course, the end products of a complex social process.
They reflect advances in science and engineering, and changes
in government policy and business management, both of
which increase our nation's propensity to foster and apply
research.

The possibilities of creating new and radically different
technology, as in the space program, have enabled us to adopt
national objectives which could not have been conceived

1. *Statistical Abstract,* 1963, p. 59.

2. Denison, E. F., *The Sources of Economic Growth in the United States,*
Committee for Economic Development, 1962, p. 230.

3. *Federal Research and Development Programs,* Hearings, Select Committee on Government Research, U.S. House of Representatives, 1963, p. 420.

of a decade or two ago. In other areas, especially national defense, R & D has revolutionized the means for attaining our goals. Multiplication of the destructive potential of war through research, in turn, has changed the meaning of national security by increasing the urgency of world peace.

Research and development is an important factor in stimulating economic growth by inducing private expenditures for new types of plant and equipment or for additional productive facilities to manufacture new products. In 1962, according to the *McGraw-Hill Survey of Business Plans for New Plants and Equipment,* 25 per cent of the sales of the manufacturing firms included in the survey were in new products not made ten years earlier.[4] Industries which seldom participate in R & D, such as mass transit, tend to become either "sick" industries or industries characterized by high and rigid cost structures. Regional economic growth has been influenced by the tendency of firms closely linked with R & D to cluster near centers of research such as Boston or cities in southern California.

Along with the benefits of research and development are the unresolved problems they help to create. The burden of adjustment to technological change in recent years has fallen with special force on the less skilled, and particularly on nonwhites. "Muscle jobs" and positions as machine tenders, the primary sources of employment for these individuals in the past, have significantly diminished as their work has been taken over by automated and other machinery. The effects of automation on employment are difficult to disentangle from other economic and social changes which have affected manpower requirements. However, the potential long-term impact of automation on the labor force could be similar to the impact of nuclear weapons in military technology. Our goals in education, manpower retraining, area redevelopment, and in civil rights represent, in part, attempts to remedy the causes which could otherwise

---

4. *16th Annual McGraw-Hill Survey, Business Plans for New Plant and Equipment,* 1963, pp. 11–12.

create a mass of unemployed and unemployable wage earners in a technologically advanced society.

Research and development influence our international relations. Part of our public economic aid to the developing nations consists of technical assistance. American firms also supply technical assistance by participating in the planning and construction of industrial plants and social overhead facilities in the less developed countries. Research programs, such as the International Geophysical Year, in which many nations participate, offer opportunities for encouraging international cooperation. Foreign governments, and individuals and private organizations in other countries conduct R & D projects for Federal agencies. Federal obligations to foreign research performers working outside the United States amounted to $67 million in 1963.[5]

Growth in R & D, and changes in the programs and objectives involved, have transformed the organization and financing of research. They have also influenced the organization of industry. Most of this growth represents the work of research teams in large laboratories or development centers rather than of individual researchers operating on a small budget. The equipment needed for much research, high energy physics for example, is too costly for small laboratories or even for universities to acquire with their own funds. Research capability has become a critical business asset facilitating the growth of firms in the aerospace or electronics industries. The greater ability of large firms to finance risky and costly research ventures is one of the variables affecting the degree of concentration in industry.

The forces which have prompted the great increase in R & D spending have also created a mixed economy in research. The Federal Government supplies two thirds of the funds for the conduct of R & D for the entire nation, while the bulk of the research and development is carried on by industry and, to a lesser extent, by universities and

---

5. *Federal Funds for Research, Development and Other Scientific Activities, 1962, 1963, and 1964*, National Science Foundation, 1964, p. 42.

by private non-profit research organizations. With most of our public and private R & D financed by Federal funds, the pace of scientific advance, the areas of advance, and the objectives of our R & D effort have become largely the responsibility of the national government.

The revolution in research since World War II has made America a research-oriented nation. This development is mainly attributable to the role of R & D as a means for achieving national objectives in defense, atomic energy, space, and health. Science and technology, in this sense, have become a major national resource.

II.

Current expenditures for R & D in the private and public sectors indicate the scope of the mixed economy in research and development. They also underscore the role of national priorities in defense, atomic energy, and space in providing the impetus for the growth of R & D in the past decade.

The importance of the different sectors as performers of R & D and as sources of funds is summarized in Table 11–1. Table 11–1 also lists Federal expenditures for R & D plant and for scientific information activities.

While the Federal Government finances most of the R & D, private industry carries out seven tenths of it. Similarly, the research conducted by universities and non-profit organizations is very largely financed by the Federal Government. Spending for R & D has grown rapidly as a share of Federal expenditures. In fiscal year 1940, R & D, including related plant expenditures, amounted to 1 per cent of all Federal expenditures, and in fiscal year 1955, it had risen to 5 per cent. By 1962, R & D accounted for over 12 per cent of all Federal spending.[6]

Most of the massive R & D expenditures are made up of spending for development, for using existing knowledge to

---

6. Derived from *Federal Funds for Research, Development and Other Scientific Activities*, p. 27.

Table 11-1
Expenditures for R & D Activities, 1962*
(in millions of 1962 dollars)

	Source of Funds		Expenditures for Performance of Research	
Item	Amount	Per Cent	Amount	Per Cent
1. Conduct of R & D				
a. Federal Government	$10,550	66.0 %	$ 2,400	15.0%
b. Industry	5,000	31.5	11,550	72.5
c. Universities and non-profit research organizations	400	2.5	2,000	12.5
d. Total, conduct of R & D	15,950	100.0	15,950	100.0
2. Federal Expenditures for R & D Plant	750			
3. Federal Obligations for R & D Informational Activities[a]	150			
4. Total Federal Expenditures	11,450			
5. Total, R & D Expenditures	16,850			

a. The actual Federal expenditures for R & D informational activities in 1962 is not available.
* Table derived from *Federal Funds for Research, Development and other Scientific Activities*, National Science Foundation, 1964, pp. 57, 107; *Reviews of Data on Science Resources*, National Science Foundation, December, 1964, p. 5; *Annual Report of the Council of Economic Advisers*, January, 1964, p. 108.

produce new products and equipment, rather than spending for research. In the early 1960's, for example, only one tenth of the total was spent for basic research; research undertaken to increase and improve our scientific knowledge.[7] Activities connected with the Atomic Energy Commission, the Department of Defense, and NASA constituted approximately nine tenths of all Federal R & D spending in fiscal years 1962 and 1963. The distribution of Federal R & D expenditures in these two years is summarized in Table 11-2.

The largest Federal research and development expenditures, aside from the three agencies listed in Table 11-2, are those associated with health-related research. This research, including the medical research sponsored by Defense, AEC, and NASA, amounted to over 7 per cent of all Federal R &

7. *National Trends in R & D Funds, 1953–1962*, National Science Foundation, 1963, p. 3.

Table 11–2
Distribution of Federal R & D Expenditures, Fiscal Years 1962 and 1963*

Agency[a]	Per cent of Total Accounted for by Agency	
	in fiscal year 1962	in fiscal year 1963
1. Department of Defense	65.5%	58.0%
2. Atomic Energy Commission	12.5	11.5
3. NASA	12.0	19.5
4. Total, 1—3	90.0	89.0
5. All other Federal Agencies	10.0	11.0

a. Includes expenditures for performing R & D and for R & D plant.
* *Budget of the United States Government for the Fiscal Year ending June 30, 1964;* pp. 391, 392, 394, 395.

D spending in 1962 and 1963. All told, the expenditures for R & D by the other agencies, plus the health research conducted by Defense, AEC, and NASA, represented 13 per cent of total Federal R & D spending in 1962 and an estimated 12 per cent in 1963.[8]

While it is apparent that most of the nation's R & D effort is directed to security-oriented programs, distinctions between "national security" and "civilian economy" R & D constitute differences in emphasis rather than mutually exclusive classifications. Scientific and engineering advances in defense, atomic energy, and space have included programs directly or indirectly applicable to the entire economy. Jet airplanes were pioneered by the military, and defense needs played a prominent role in facilitating development of the computer. Space research has contributed new possibilities for improving weather forecasting and international communications, while the atomic energy program is concerned with power generation and the use of isotopes for medical research. R & D in space is related to national security in the sense of the United States role in world technology, and the political implications of the space program, rather than to a narrow concentration on military aspects of space. Yet,

8. *Federal Research and Development Programs,* p. 625.

allowing for the substantial overlaps between security-space and civilian economy R & D, the differences in support for the two types of research underscore the priorities in our recent research programs. They also provide a basis for anticipating possible changes in these priorities which may become significant alternatives in the 1970's.

In keeping with these priorities, firms in the industries related to defense, atomic energy, and the space program conduct most of the research done in industry. Two industries, aircraft and missiles, and electrical equipment and communications, were responsible for three fifths of all R & D funds spent by industry in 1962. Together, they received four fifths of the Federal R & D funds allotted to industry in that year.[9]

An important characteristic of industry-financed R & D is the great difference in the degree of participation. In the early 1960's, firms with R & D programs spent an average of slightly less than 2 per cent of their revenues from sales for company-financed R & D. Firms in the chemical industry, or in the production of machinery, electrical and communications equipment, and professional and scientific equipment spent 3 per cent or more of their sales revenues for R & D. However, firms in the paper industry, in foods, textiles and apparel, lumber, metals, and in the petroleum industry spent 1 per cent or less of their revenues for company-financed R & D.[10] There is also little R & D reported in residential construction and in the railroad industry or mass transit. The firms which financed very small amounts of R & D from company funds also typically utilized little or no Federal funds.

The rapid expansion of federally financed R & D in the past decade has created a similar disparity in the research function of colleges and universities. The bulk of the funds have gone to the large universities already actively engaged in research. Within the universities, the influx of Federal research grants and contracts has been overwhelmingly con-

---

9. *Research and Development in Industry, 1961,* National Science Foundation, 1964, pp. 9, 12.

10. *Research and Development in Industry,* pp. 40–44.

centrated in the physical and biological sciences. This concentration has emphasized the differences in support for research in the natural sciences as compared with the social sciences and the humanities. The availability of Government funds, according to Henry T. Heald, President of the Ford Foundation, "tend(s) to shape the content of knowledge . . . and . . . to control graduate enrollments."[11] The recent legislation to establish a national foundation for the arts and humanities constitutes the beginning of an effort to redress this imbalance.

It is probably inevitable that the growth of R & D should be predominantly supported by public sources. Increases in research expenditures beyond those supplied by the private economy are desirable since individual firms are likely to underinvest in invention and research because it is risky, and because the product can be appropriated only to a limited extent.[12] Public support for R & D has created "Big Science" and near-saturation staffing and financing of projects regarded as essential for the national interest. Beginning with the Manhattan Project in World War II, we have developed techniques for bringing about the technological changes we regard as essential and for developing the scientific information which makes the technology possible. The United States has become a major contributor to basic research as well as to applied research and development. Because the growth of R & D has been closely tied to national priorities in a limited number of areas, we have been less able, to date, to diffuse this remarkable growth so that it serves the range of needs throughout our society.

III.

Our goal for research and development presupposes the continued growth of R & D as an important objective. While public expenditures concerned with defense, space, and

---

11. *Federal Research and Development Programs,* p. 385.
12. See *The Rate and Direction of Inventive Activity,* National Bureau of Economic Research, 1962, p. 619.

atomic energy research are expected to constitute a substantial part of the R & D total in the next decade, the standards for the goal also incorporate a greater emphasis on "civilian economy" research. This includes greater provision for public support of basic research, for R & D in new fields or in national problem areas, such as oceanography and mass transportation, and for research in the social sciences. For the same reason, increases are also projected for company-financed R & D in industries which have conducted little research.

Dr. Jerome B. Wiesner, then Special Assistant to the President for Science and Technology, suggested in 1963 that the factors responsible for the heavy emphasis on security-related R & D in the past decade are likely to lose some of their urgency in the near future. Dr. Wiesner stated in testimony before the House Select Committee on Government Research that "ten years ago there was a close relationship between military-oriented R & D and civilian needs. . . . Now we are faced with . . . a general stabilization of the turbulent scientific-military revolution of the past decade. . . . Weapons research and development can no longer pace our program to the same extent, and new and possibly more conscious ways of insuring long-range scientific and technological advances are now required."[13]

Dr. J. Herbert Hollomon, Assistant Secretary of Commerce for Science and Technology, has indicated possible target areas for an expanded R & D effort in the civilian economy in testimony before the House Committee in 1963. Dr. Hollomon comments, "I do not believe . . . we are spending a sufficient amount . . . to meet major civilian . . . requirements such as urban development, such as transportation, and such as the support for the basic technology related to industry, particularly to that industry which isn't so sophisticated; that is, textiles, building, and construction."[14]

Dr. Hollomon's contention is illustrated by R & D in trans-

---

13. *Federal Research and Development Programs*, p. 259.
14. *Ibid.*, p. 303.

portation. The Federal Government has been spending $4 billion a year for highway construction and $25 million for R & D associated with highways. In the early 1960's, the railroad industry was spending a total of $7 million a year for research and development.[15] Similarly, in the critical area of urban mass transit, it is estimated that less than one million dollars a year have been spent for research and development.[16] The recommendation in the President's 1965 Transportation Message that Congress appropriate funds, estimated at $20 million, to develop a passenger train running at speeds of more than 100 miles an hour between New York, Boston, and Washington indicates a greater emphasis on R & D in mass transportation as an alternative to the near-bankruptcy of railroad passenger transportation in the northeastern megalopolis.[17]

Water pollution, to cite another instance, has become a major national problem. Pollution jeopardizes our water supply, menaces health, destroys aquatic life, and often creates a disagreeable environment. Water pollution is a direct result of rapid growth in population, especially in urban population, together with the unprecedented advances of industry in the past two decades. Detergents, synthetic chemicals, radioactive materials, along with the increase in the sheer bulk of pollutants, greatly complicate the problem of assuring good quality water. A large increase in the use of agricultural chemicals has created a similar land drainage pollution problem in rural areas. Yet, according to Congressman Robert E. Jones, chairman of the National Resources Subcommittee of the House Government Operations Committee, "we continue to rely, even in the more modern sewage treatment plants, on a method of waste treatment which is the same in principle as that used by the Egyptians, 2,000 years ago." Water pollution research, Con-

---

15. *Federal Research and Development Programs,* pp. 296, 300.

16. *Urban Transportation and Public Policy,* Institute of Public Administration, 1961, Chapter 5, p. 51.

17. *The New York Times,* March 5, 1965.

gressman Jones states, "must develop an effective new science. . . . The analytical tools and scientific knowledge which served well for the problems of the past are proving increasingly inadequate in dealing with present . . . problems."[18]

President Johnson pointed out in 1964 that cancer, heart disease, and stroke currently afflict 15 million Americans. Two thirds of all Americans now living, he observed, "will ultimately suffer or die from one of them." The Public Health Service is currently spending over a quarter of a billion dollars annually for research to find ways of combatting these diseases. But, the President notes, "much remains to be learned."[19]

Greater expenditures for research in heart disease, cancer, and stroke would probably lead to new knowledge which would add to longevity. With a much larger number of aged persons in our society, we would need to know more about techniques for adapting housing, employment and retirement practices, medical care, and recreation to take account of the special needs and the potential contribution of persons over 65.

The research revolution since World War II has been a revolution in the natural sciences and in the development of new technology. Dr. Robert D. Calkins, President of the Brookings Institution, comments that "there has been little conscious effort to strike a rational balance between the needs of the nation for research in the natural sciences and its needs for research in the social sciences."[20] In spite of large expenditures for law enforcement and for prisons, and our concern with crime in the cities, we still know comparatively little about the causes of crime and delinquency or about effective methods of rehabilitation. The growing public expenditures to combat poverty intensify the need to improve our understanding of motivations and attitudes

18. *Federal Research and Development Programs*, p. 954.

19. *Message from the President of the United States to Congress Relative to the Health of the Nation*, February 10, 1964, p. 9.

20. *Federal Research and Development Programs*, p. 911.

in getting and holding a job, in seeking or failing to seek to learn in school, or toward other races. The role of technological advances in changing national objectives in manpower policy, education, economic growth, and urbanization is itself an important area requiring research. Yet in 1962, only 4 per cent of Federal obligations for research were allotted to the social sciences, including psychology.[21]

Our foreign aid program includes technical assistance for the developing nations. It is doubtful if many of these nations can economically utilize much of the highly sophisticated and costly technology developed for advanced industrial economies. Research and development emphasizing simpler and less expensive technology, and employing indigenous materials and peoples, would yield large returns as part of our technical assistance program. There are, however, important areas where sophisticated and expensive technology is necessary to do a job effectively. An example is water desalination. Research in desalination technology, probably using nuclear power, could be a major factor in enabling the developing nations to support their rapidly growing populations by converting arid land into fertile farmland.

Expanding research and development for the civilian economy would also involve sizeable increases in basic research. For instance, molecular biology has recently cracked the biological code determining the transmission of genetic information. Further research in this area might develop better understanding of the causes of cancer, birth defects, and viral diseases. New research fields with names scarcely heard of twenty or thirty years ago, such as high energy physics, solid state physics, or plasma physics, offer promising fields for greater research efforts. Development of the general theory of relativity makes it possible to conduct new and fundamental investigation in the nature of gravitation. According to Dr. Lloyd V. Berkner, President of the Graduate

---

21. *Federal Funds for Research, Development, and Other Scientific Activities,* p. 28.

Research Center of the Southwest, support for such research is next to impossible to obtain "both because of the great probability of failure, and also because such questions are not at the moment in the main stream of science. Yet discovery here would have an enormous payoff to society."[22] Research in oceanography could yield important discoveries, leading to improved weather forecasting and increases in the world's food and mineral supply by "farming" and "mining" the oceans. Exploration of the earth's interior through deep-drilling techniques could add to knowledge about the age, origin, and composition of our planet, the evolution of life, and the age and structure of the ocean basins.

As research and development have grown, scientific information has proliferated to an extent that creates complex problems in making this information available to scientists and engineers. Since science advances by building on existing knowledge, effective use of technical information is an important phase of the research and development process. The existing mass of scientific information could be made more readily available to potential users if new and expanded facilities were created for information storage and retrieval systems geared to the growth of research and development. The Science Information Exchange of the Smithsonian Institution currently contains brief technical summaries of 60,000 active federally supported research projects. Expansion of this and similar systems to include a nationwide storing and retrieval system utilizing microfilm and data processing and retrieval technologies has become a necessity. Public expenditures to assist in financing the publication and dissemination of scientific documents and abstracts are also an integral part of a scientific information program. In turn, the utilization of our information resources could be enhanced by research into the dynamics of information use as a basis for developing more effective systems for storing and retrieving information.

---

22. *Federal Research and Development Programs*, p. 425.

I V .

Our two aspiration standards for the R & D goal reflect the forces which are likely to influence objectives and expenditures in the coming decade. One standard, the "civilian economy" alternative, assumes that relaxation of international tensions will be accompanied by partial disarmament, and that the manned lunar landing program will be stretched out to the mid-1970's. The other, the "security space" standard, is oriented toward a future in which our defense needs and international objectives will require heavy concentration on R & D related to defense, space, and atomic energy. For both alternatives, total R & D spending, public and private, is estimated to increase to over $38 billion in 1975.

To assist in assessing the changes in R & D spending listed for the two standards, it is useful to estimate the level of R & D expenditures in the 1970's if we continued to spend the same 3 per cent of GNP for R & D as in the early 1960's. This is our hypothetical preempted benchmark. If expenditures merely kept pace with GNP growth, we would be spending $30 billion for R & D in 1975. Without increasing the share of our resources devoted to research and development, we would be spending $13 billion more than in 1962.

In the more peaceful world taken for granted in the civilian economy standard, the large percentage increases in Federal R & D expenditures are for health, natural resources, basic research, and for research in the social sciences and for education. In the security space alternative, research for these purposes also increases, but more slowly. In this standard, R & D expenditures for atomic energy, defense, and space in 1975 are $7 billion greater than in the more optimistic alternative.[23] Both standards include expenditures to

---

23. In the civilian economy standard, Federal R & D spending for purposes other than atomic energy, defense, and space is projected to rise to 83 per cent of the expenditures in these three areas by 1975. In the security space standard the research in the civilian areas increases to 42 per cent of the larger security-related total by 1975.

enlarge public programs for storing and retrieving R & D information. In addition, a Federal extension service to make the findings of research available to the private economy, and especially to small businesses and the technologically less advanced industries, is projected to cost $600 million a year by the mid-1970's.[24]

Expenditures for R & D by the Federal Government for the two standards are listed in Table 11–3.

Table 11–3
Projected Federal Government Expenditures,
R & D Goal, 1970 and 1975
(in millions of 1962 dollars)

Expenditures for	Civilian Economy Standard		Security Space Standard	
	1970	1975	1970	1975
1. Defense[a]	$ 8,150	$ 7,300	$ 9,450	$10,900
2. NASA[a]	2,950	3,450	5,400	5,900
3. AEC[a]	1,750	1,700	2,350	2,650
4. Total, 1–3	12,850	12,450	17,200	19,450
5. Health	1,900	2,700	1,900	2,700
6. Natural Resources	1,900	2,900	1,900	2,900
7. Transportation	300	400	200	200
8. Agriculture	250	300	250	300
9. Increase in Basic Research	1,300	1,500	800	1,050
10. Other R & D[b]	1,700	2,600	1,000	950
11. Total R & D[c]	20,200	22,850	23,250	27,550
12. R & D Information Systems	500	600	600	700
13. R & D Business Extension Service	400	600	400	600
14. Total, Federal Programs	21,100	24,050	24,250	28,850

a. Health related research estimated at 1½% of the totals for these three agencies has been deducted since it is included under health.
b. Includes expenditures for R & D programs for the technologically less advanced industries within the United States, research in the social sciences and in education, basic research, and R & D assistance to the developing nations not included under other headings.
c. Including expenditures for the conduct of R & D and for R & D plant.

Since the mid-1950's, company-financed R & D has grown less rapidly than the Federal expenditures so that privately

24. In 1965, Congress enacted the State Technical Services Act to encourage the dissemination of scientific and technological information to private enterprises. The Act authorizes $60 million in Federal matching funds to states for this purpose over the next three years. *The New York Times*, September 15, 1965.

financed research has become a diminishing share of the total. If public R & D spending increases rapidly for national security purposes in the next decade, it is very likely that this tendency will continue. For this reason, the industry-financed R & D in the security space standard is listed at the same percentage of GNP as in the early 1960's, at 0.9 of 1 per cent.[25] If international tensions diminish, and Federal expenditures for defense-related programs grow at a reduced pace or decline, many firms with substantial research capabilities can be expected to seek opportunities to develop new markets in the private economy through greater use of company funds for research. They may also seek to apply the operations research techniques widely used in military or space research to develop new transportation technologies for metropolitan areas or new synthetic building materials for residential construction. Accordingly, the R & D financed by industry in the civilian economy standard is projected to increase more rapidly than public expenditures, rising to over half of the Federal total by 1975.

It would be unreasonable to expect the major sources of basic research, the universities and non-profit research organizations, to finance a large share of their R & D outlays from institutional funds. The pressures of increasing enrollments in universities, together with greater emphasis on undergraduate instruction, and limitations on raising endowments are likely to pose formidable barriers. R & D expenditures financed by these organizations are listed as increasing to $1.2 billion in 1975. If they were to spend about $4 from Federal Government sources for every dollar of institutional funds, universities and private non-profit research organizations would be spending an estimated $5 billion for research in 1975.

Table 11–4 lists the sources of funds for the R & D goal in the 1970's.

25. Derived from *National Trends in R & D Funds, 1953–1962,* National Science Foundation, 1963, p. 4. Company-financed expenditures for R & D, it should be added, are not reckoned as an end product in computing GNP.

Table 11-4
Estimated Public and Private Expenditures
for R & D Goal, 1970 and 1975
(in millions of 1962 dollars)

| | | PROJECTED EXPENDITURES | | | |
| | Expendi-tures in 1962 | Civilian Economy Standard | | Security Space Standard | |
Source of Funds		1970	1975	1970	1975
1. Federal Government[a]	$11,450	$21,100	$24,050	$24,250	$28,850
2. Industry	5,000	10,050	13,200	7,100	8,800
3. Universities and Non-profit Research Institutions	400	800	1,200	800	1,200
4. Total Expenditures, R & D Programs	16,850	31,950	38,450	32,150	38,850
5. R & D Expenditures as % of GNP	3.0%	4.0%	3.9%	4.1%	4.0%

a. Includes Federal expenditures for the conduct of R & D, for R & D plant, for information and retrieval systems, and for a research extension service.

While the totals listed for the two standards are very similar, Government-financed R & D is a larger part of the total in the standard stressing the impact of defense needs. The projections imply that R & D spending will grow more slowly as a percentage of GNP in the next decade than in the past ten years. However, given reasonably rapid economic growth, this moderate increase in the share of our resources used for research and development would mean an increase in R & D spending by 1975 to $22 billion more than in 1962.

The greater R & D outlays listed in the aspiration standards could not lead to corresponding scientific and technological advances unless the increases in funds were matched by a roughly parallel growth in the work force of scientists and engineers. The absence of qualified manpower has been as great an obstacle in the recent past to expanding research in many fields as the shortage of funds. This has been especially true in health research. Since four to eight years of higher education are needed to educate scientific manpower, and additional time is also needed to construct facilities for more students, the limits to expanding the supply of research personnel in the 1970's will be set by the educational facilities added in the 1960's, and by the number of students beginning their college education in the later years of this decade. There are good possibilities for economizing on the utilization of scientists and engineers by turning over many of their routine tasks to technicians. However, the net effect of rapid growth in R & D outlays, without these increases in manpower, would be to deplete college faculties and to create recurring national shortages of scientists and engineers.

Increasing R & D expenditures along the lines discussed would have many other ramifications. Research and development in the next decade is likely to involve greatly expanded use of computer and data-processing facilities. As computer technology and systems planning become more advanced and more widely used, many of the functions of middle management will be taken over by the new machines, and persons in these occupations are likely to face the prospect of loss of employment. With technological change altering labor requirements at different levels of skill and training, collective bargaining will become increasingly concerned with accommodating to these changes by protecting job rights or claims to further training, by pressing for reduced hours and longer vacations, and by advocating programs for sharing the cost reductions made possible by the new technology.

As in the past, part of the increase in our capacity to produce induced by R & D will probably be taken in the form of higher living standards, and part in the form of more leisure. Growth in R & D is a major factor in the projected increase in average family income to $10,000 a year and the anticipated decline in average weekly hours of work to 37 in 1975. If, as some observers anticipate, technological change leads to massive productivity increases in the next decade, the impact of rapidly rising productivity for employment would probably set up pressures for a more drastic reduction in work hours.

The spectacular increase in our R & D effort in the past generation owes its impetus to World War II and to the international tensions which followed this conflict. R & D related to national security can reasonably be expected to continue on a large scale in the 1970's. It can also be anticipated that R & D expenditures will be concentrated more heavily on the needs of the civilian economy. Most of these needs are related to health, to changes in industry, or to new demands created by an urbanized society. The degree to which civilian economy R & D will figure in our nation's objectives is likely to depend, in large part, on the prospects for world peace.

CHAPTER 12

Natural
Resources

I.

Progress in achieving our nation's goals depends on the availability of adequate and abundant natural resources. Expanding our resource base, without seriously increasing costs or decreasing quality, is itself an important national objective. To attain this goal, expenditures for conserving and developing natural resources are projected to triple from $6 billion in 1962 to $17 billion by 1975.

Natural resource problems loom large when crises abroad, such as wars or revolutions, threaten to cut off supplies of raw materials. The impact of these crises reinforces a tendency to identify natural resources with raw materials, especially imported minerals, and to consider resource problems in terms of absolutes—absolute shortages or absolute necessities.

The natural resources which are vital for our national

well-being include land and the products of mines and forests. They also include, with increasing importance, water and air reasonably protected against pollution. Greater leisure and mobility increase the need for outdoor recreational areas which also enhance the significance of the remaining wilderness areas. With economic advance and population growth, the national heritage of fish and wildlife is diminished by chemical pesticides and river pollution as well as by hunting and fishing. In addition, consideration of future resource requirements has to take into account not only rising levels of use in the United States, but also the use of resources in other industrial countries and in nations in the process of industrialization.

Many of the resources used in the United States, e.g., water, must be obtained domestically. Others, like coal, are preferably obtained from domestic sources because of high costs of transportation. For some materials, we are largely dependent on imports from other nations—e.g., tungsten or industrial diamonds. Still others, such as oil, may be obtained from domestic sources or from abroad, with the choice depending on prices, and on defense or balance of payments considerations. Expansion of our resource base within the United States, and encouraging the world trade which is the source for some of our raw materials and increases our options in others, both contribute to developing the nation's supply of natural resources.

Some of the facts about minerals seem to support the concern with shortages. Proven reserves of petroleum in the United States at the end of 1962 came to only ten times the annual production.[1] Consumption in the decade ahead is estimated as greater than the total proven reserves. Even more than in the past, however, research and development offer possibilities for pushing out the limits set by the availability of natural resources to economic growth and well-being. Research and development creates new resources, or

1. *Minerals Yearbook,* 1962, II, pp. 374, 382.

it devises substitutes for existing ones. Research may soon enable us to economically extract petroleum from shale rock, to utilize atomic energy in the place of fossil fuels, or to increase the world's supply of agricultural land by desalinating water. Research and development also increases the efficiency with which resources are extracted or put to use. The size of the work force in the traditional resource industries in the United States, including agriculture, was just about the same in 1960 as in 1870, some 7 million persons. But the value of their output had increased by five times.[2]

Projections for conservation and development expenditures in the 1970's reflect the changes anticipated within the resource industries and in the larger society which they serve. The use of uranium as a fuel represents an important change within the mining industry. The basic problem in relating our resources development to the needs of a wealthy and urbanized society was summed up by the Secretary of the Interior, Stewart L. Udall. He states

America today stands poised on a pinnacle of wealth and power, yet we live in a land of vanishing beauty, of increasing ugliness, of shrinking open space, and of an over-all environment that is diminished daily by pollution and noise and blight. . . . This, in brief, is the quiet conservation crisis of the 1960's.[3]

The important and costly policy decisions in the next decade are more likely to be concentrated in the areas mentioned by Secretary Udall than in the traditional areas of "critical materials." As one indicator of changing resource needs, per capita consumption of minerals increased at about 1.5 per cent a year between 1940 and 1960. In this period, per capita participation in outdoor recreation increased by 6 per cent annually.[4]

---

2. Landsberg, H., *Natural Resources for U.S. Growth,* 1964, p. 4.

3. Udall, S. L., *The Quiet Crisis,* 1963, pp. viii, 175.

4. Derived from Landsberg, Fischman, and Fisher, *Resources in America's Future,* 1963, p. 225; and Potter and Christy, *Trends in Natural Resource Commodities, 1870–1957,* 1962, p. 9.

II.

Expenditures to conserve and develop natural resources in 1962 amounted to about 1 per cent of GNP. Public spending made up three fifths of this total and private spending something less than two fifths. These expenditures supported a complex of activities concerned with minerals, timber, fish and wildlife, outdoor recreation, water use and land conservation. What the $6 billion spent for resources purchased in 1962 is summarized in Table 12–1.

Table 12–1
Public and Private Expenditures for Resources Conservation and Development, 1962
(in millions of 1962 dollars)

1. Minerals	$ 590		4. Fish and Wildlife	$ 140
Stockpiling	170		Propagation	100
Research	420		Research	40
2. Timber	420		5. Outdoor Recreation	150
Forest protection and			Land acquisition[b]	25
management	400		Improvements	125
Research	20		6. Land Conservation	850
3. Water[a]	3,700		Improvements	750
Capital outlays	1,840		Research	100
Current costs	1,800			
Research	60		7. Total Expenditures	$5,850

a. Expenditures for water refer to municipal and industrial spending for waste collection and treatment, and for storage.
b. Land acquisition costs are not reckoned as a claim on GNP.

Spending for water resources represented the largest single item in the 1962 expenditures. About $600 million was spent for minerals. Another $600 million was spent for research. Two thirds of this spending was for minerals research, primarily for atomic energy.

III.

The cost estimates for the aspiration standards are related to the prospective changes in supply and demand for major resource groups over the next decade. The standards are largely derived from the recommendations of such public bodies as the Committee on Natural Resources of the Federal Council for Science and Technology. The estimates include the cost of research and development to devise substitutes for existing resources or ways of using them more efficiently. They also include the expenditures for achieving the higher levels of resource use which can reasonably be anticipated for the larger population, higher incomes, greater urbanization, and the $1-trillion output expected in the 1970's. The projections for the standards are discussed separately for each of the major resources and they are listed in Table 12–2 in the last section of the chapter.

Minerals

The expenditures listed for minerals are for stockpiling critical materials and, to a much larger extent, for research and development. The durability and small volume of many important minerals make them good subjects for stockpiling. Domestic reserves are likely to be insufficient in the near future for bauxite and manganese. Important materials for which the domestic supply is small or nonexistent include tungsten, nickel, tin, mercury, and industrial diamonds. We import 30 per cent or more of our copper, lead, and zinc. These minerals would probably be included in the domestic strategic reserves.

The necessary stockpiling for current levels of use for most minerals was largely completed by 1961. The continuing cost of a program to meet the greater volume of use anticipated in the next decade consists of the expenditures for the annual additions to the stockpile and the maintenance charges. Assuming needs increase at the same rate as GNP, the expenditures for the growing stockpile are projected at $420 million by 1975.

Petroleum and bituminous coal are the nation's major mineral resources. Serious shortages are unlikely to develop for either of the two within the next decade. Although there appears to be a relatively short future for domestic oil production utilizing present sources and technology, in the near future imports from a world surplus market should be easy. Looking toward the more distant future, oil shale within the United States is believed to contain a greater potential than the oil-bearing formations now approaching exhaustion. There is also the possibility of converting coal into oil. Either of these sources is likely, at least initially, to raise the price of gasoline at the pump which meets current octane standards—perhaps by 50 to 100 per cent.

Reserves, proved or inferred, for bituminous coal are estimated at several centuries use. The demand for bituminous coal, lower in recent decades, is likely to resume its climb as coal again replaces the more costly petroleum or gas frequently used in generating electricity and in industrial processes requiring heat. New techniques for transmitting electricity from generating plants close to the mine or for shipping coal by pipeline can be expected to increase this demand.

The Federal Council for Science and Technology has recommended an increased emphasis on research in fossil fuels, particularly coal, and in renewable energy sources including solar and water power. Other studies indicate a similar need for research in the long-distance transmission of electricity, in the shipment of coal by pipeline, and in fuel cells. Research in fuel cells could develop a source of power for motor vehicles free of the exhaust and crankcase fumes which contribute so heavily to air pollution. However, the bulk of the Federal Government's research in the area of minerals and energy sources is in atomic energy. Public and private research has made nuclear energy a nearly economical source of power. Nuclear reactors for generating power are planned or operating in Detroit, Pittsburgh, and elsewhere. The Atomic Energy Commission has reported that spending for civilian nuclear power research reached approximately $200 million in 1962. To speed up the present pace of nuclear power development, these expenditures are projected to increase to $500 million a year by the mid-1970's. Including the civilian nuclear power research, R & D expenditures make up four fifths of the $2 billion listed for the 1970's to assure an adequate supply of minerals and energy sources for the nation's future in the next decade and beyond.

Timber

The expenditures for timber are very largely for forest protection and management. They are the expenditures which make it possible to use timber as a crop to be periodically harvested rather than as a resource to be mined once and for all. *Resources in America's Future,* a recent authoritative study of resource needs, anticipates that timber consumption will increase from the 11 billion cubic feet utilized in 1960 to 32 billion in the year 2000.[5] To sustain this level of consumption by the end of the century, increases in spending for planting trees and protecting forests estimated at $6 billion will be required in the near future. Made over the next ten years, these investments in our future timber supply would add $600 million a year in the 1970's to the $400 million now spent for forest protection and management.

Only about $20 million was spent for timber research in 1962. Yet timber research is an area where an expanded R & D effort might pay excellent dividends. Part of the gains would be in better control of pests and diseases which now consume about as much timber as man. Research and development could also increase the yield of forest land by aiding reproduction and growth, and by ascertaining the optimum time for cutting timber. In recognition of the potential returns from research, the Federal Council for Science and Technology has proposed that expenditures "should be scaled upward three to four times in the next ten years."[6] This

5. *Resources in America's Future,* p. 815. The estimates refer to the medium projections. Although the *Resources* study projects a tripling in total lumber consumption between 1960 and 2000, aggregate lumber use has remained unchanged since 1900.

6. *Research and Development in Natural Resources,* Federal Council for Science and Technology, 1963, pp. 53–54.

recommendation, together with a large backlog of research needs in forestry, is the basis for listing timber research spending as rising to $120 million by 1975.

Water

Almost half the expenditures considered for resources in the 1970's are for collecting, purifying, and storing water. The nation's water problems include assuring an adequate supply of water and, even more importantly, assuring regularity and purity of the supply. About 1,000 communities in the United States have had to restrict use of water within the past half-dozen years.[7] In the arid West, the total water now available is inadequate for the demands anticipated from metropolitan growth, irrigation agriculture, and the industries consuming large quantities of water. In all areas, but especially in the Northeast, water pollution poses a growing problem. The danger of pollution becomes acute principally in the seasons of low water flow. These seasons generally coincide with the periods of maximum water use.

Studies made for the Senate Select Committee on Water Resources have estimated the capital outlays needed to assure a high quality of water, and for storage facilities adequate for dry-season supplies plus waste dilution.[8] The "maximum" program projects expenditures for water treatment facilities in the 1954–1980 period at $54 billion and spending for storage facilities at $38 billion.[9] Capital outlays in the 1970's for this program are estimated at $3.5 billion a year. The annual costs for labor and materials, plus in-

7. Galton, L., "The World is Getting Thirstier," in *The New York Times Magazine,* September 27, 1964.

8. The most convenient single index of water pollution is the biochemical oxygen demand. This is a measure of the extent of sewage and similar wastes discharged into streams whose decay uses up the oxygen dissolved in the water.

9. See Wollman, N., *Water Resource Activities in the United States,* U.S. Senate, Select Committee on Water Resources, 1960, p. 11.

terest and depreciation, corresponding to this level of water protection and supply would probably add another $3.5 billion.

Spending for water resources research has been growing at about 10 per cent a year. Water research could lead to new techniques for storing or purifying water. It could ease the water shortage in the West by devising an economical means for desalinating water or utilizing underground wells more effectively. Today, at least 60 underdeveloped countries face water shortage problems.[10] More far-reaching projects could lessen the impact of the population explosion on the resource base of the developing nations by devising means for using nuclear power to desalinate sea water. To attain these objectives, it is proposed that water research expenditures in the next decade grow at twice their recent rate of increase. Total R & D outlays would approximate $400 million in 1975.

Fish and Wildlife

Economic advance makes for drastic losses in fish and wildlife with entire species, as in the case of the passenger pigeon, sometimes virtually exterminated. Although conservation measures have saved some species—e.g., the buffalo—more appear to be in danger today than ever before. These losses threaten to eliminate part of our nation's heritage which contributes to the quality and interests of life. Elimination of wildlife resources also constitutes a loss of food potential and raw materials for industry.

Conservation measures for the future should be expected to include more effective controls of the use of pesticides, better management of our remaining wildlife resources, and public education. Protection against forest fires and measures to diminish river pollution and water drainage also aid in preserving fish and wildlife. Fish hatcheries and game

---

10. *The New York Times Magazine*, September 27, 1964.

farms offer positive possibilities for increasing the available supply.

It is reasonable to expect that spending to encourage wild-life and fish propagation will grow at the same rate as out-door recreational activity.[11] Taking into account both the present shortages of facilities and the anticipated growth in outdoor recreational activities, total spending for fish and wildlife is listed as increasing to $580 million a year in the next decade. This includes $180 million for research.

Outdoor Recreation

Utilization of outdoor recreational facilities has been in-creasing more rapidly than the acquisition of additional acreage and accommodations. Visits to national parks in the past twelve years have risen by over 200 per cent. National park acreage has increased by 3 per cent. The Outdoor Rec-reation Resources Review Commission reported in 1960 that the demand for state park facilities was at or above capacity in from 30 to 60 per cent of the areas they had surveyed.[12] These changes, plus a similar situation in city parks, are responsible for what one authority in the field, Marion Clawson, refers to as "The Crisis in Outdoor Recreation."

Clawson's program for bridging the gap between utiliza-tion and resources calls for a massive expansion of "inter-mediate recreation areas"—intermediate between "user ori-ented" city parks and "resource oriented" national parks. An adequate rate of expansion, Clawson suggests, would require the addition of 60 million acres of park land, pri-marily in state parks, by the year 2000.[13] To have an adequate supply of land available for this kind of park development

11. Visits to parks, one index of outdoor recreational activity, have been increasing by about 8 per cent a year.

12. *Public Outdoor Recreation Areas—Acreage, Use, Potential,* Outdoor Recreation Resources Review Commission, Study Report No. 1, 1960, pp. 52–61.

13. Clawson, M., *The Crisis in Outdoor Recreation,* 1958.

in the next decade would mean acquiring 3 million acres a year in the 1968–1975 period.

Resources in America's Future anticipates a tripling of visits to national parks between 1960 and 1980.[14] Overcrowding has already diminished the natural attractiveness of many of our national parks. If we are to have sufficient park land to keep the number of visitors per acre from rising, an additional 50 million acres will be needed for national parks by 1980. Spread over a 20-year period, this amounts to 2.5 million acres a year. The 5.5 million acres to be added to state and national parks annually are projected to cost nearly $2 billion in 1975.[15]

Providing roads and camping, picnicking, and related facilities in state parks would involve expenditures increasing by 5 per cent a year merely to keep up with the anticipated growth in the number of visitors. In the national forests, in 1964, only 70,000 camp and picnic "family units" were available—about half the required number. To catch up with the existing backlogs and to allow for growth, spending for improvements and accommodations in state and national parks and forests is expected to cost approximately $700 million a year in the next decade.

About $400 million of the total listed for improvements and accommodations is for national parks and forests. The experience of the Civilian Conservation Corps in the 1930's indicates a possible route for undertaking the effort involved in the 1970's to improve and expand facilities in national parks and forests. The Civilian Conservation Corps spent $2.8 billion between 1934 and 1941. Not all of this spending was for improvements to outdoor recreational areas. Additional work in developing parks and forests was also done by the Works Progress Administration and the Public Works

---

14. *Resources in America's Future*, p. 229.

15. For the state park land, it is assumed that this land would cost $400 per acre, one third more than the average price for state park land in the mid-1950's. Since the national park acquisitions are usually in more remote areas, their per acre costs are estimated at $300.

Administration. A program similar to the CCC, the Job
Corps, was started in 1964 to offer education, training, and
an opportunity to work for unemployed and poorly educated
young people. The Economic Opportunity Act, the law which
established the Job Corps, provides that its program could
include responsibility for developing, managing, and protecting public recreational areas. The rise in wages for young
unskilled adults since the CCC experience has probably been
largely offset by increases in productivity. Accordingly, the
costs for a Job Corps effort comparable to the CCC are estimated to amount to some $3 billion. Spread over eight of
the next ten years, this breaks down to $400 million a year
—the sum projected for annual improvements in national
parks and forests in the coming decade.

Land Conservation

An expanded program of land conservation is highly desirable if we are to assure an adequate supply of usable land
in the future for farm land. The large acreages of land being
taken for cities, highways, airports, and parks would rule
out the option of creating additional productive farm land
through clearing if the present surpluses of farm output were
to disappear in a later decade. Sizeable programs are needed
to protect existing farm land from erosion and other losses
of fertility. Additional investments are likely to be required
for irrigation and for the transfer of crops from unsuitable to
productive land.

The Land and Water Policy Committee of the Department of Agriculture has estimated the cost of conserving and
developing our land resources at $44 billion by 1980.[16] Dis-
tributed between 1960 and 1980, the costs of land conservation would average over $2 billion a year in the 1970's. Most
of this spending would be done by individual farmers.

Currently we are spending about $100 million a year for

---

16. *Land and Water Resources—A Policy Guide,* U.S. Department of Agriculture, 1962, p. 61.

research in land conservation and use. Research could narrow the present great lack of knowledge about land phenomena, and their classification, mapping, and use. With an annual increase of 15 per cent in research expenditures, total spending would reach a level of $500 million a year by the mid-1970's.

IV.

The expenditures projected to develop our natural resources relate to a growing list of "needs," "demands," and areas of "catching up." This list partially reflects a deterioration of the available resources in such areas as agricultural land or wildlife. In part the needs have become more intense because a more affluent America consumes many of its resources on an unprecedented scale.

To cope with accelerating needs, the expenditures listed for the standards in 1975 are typically three times their 1962 levels. They are summarized in Table 12–2. A yardstick for assessing the cost of the changes included in the standards are the expenditures needed if per capita spending for resources conservation and development were to be maintained at the 1962 level for another decade. Maintenance of the *status quo* in per capita spending for the larger population in the mid-1970's would raise resources expenditures to $7.1 billion, or only by slightly more than 20 per cent. This yardstick estimate is our hypothetical preempted benchmark for natural resources.

Achieving the improvements in resource use considered for the natural resources goal is expected to raise spending for conservation and development by $11 billion a year in the mid-1970's. This increase includes an additional $2 billion for R & D. Measured by GNP, the costs projected for the resources goal, amount to 1.5 per cent of the gross national product in 1975, excluding the land acquisition costs, which create no claim on GNP. This represents an increase from 1 per cent in 1962.

Forecasts of exhaustion of natural resources in the United States have typically failed to materialize. In the past, these

Table 12–2
**Estimated Expenditures for Natural Resources Goal,
1970 and 1975
(in millions of 1962 dollars)**

Item	Expenditures in 1962	Projected Expenditures for Aspiration Standard in 1970	in 1975
1. Minerals	$ 590	$ 1,550	$ 2,000
Stockpiling	170	350	420
Research	420	1,200	1,580
2. Timber	420	1,070	1,120
Forest protection and management	400	1,000	1,000
Research	20	70	120
3. Water[a]	3,700	6,650	7,400
Capital outlays	1,840	3,500	3,500
Current costs	1,800	2,900	3,500
Research	60	250	400
4. Fish and Wildlife	140	380	580
Propagation	100	280	400
Research	40	100	180
5. Outdoor Recreation	150	2,500	2,650
Land acquisition[b]	25	1,950	1,950
Improvements	125	550	700
6. Land Conservation	850	2,300	2,900
Improvements	750	2,000	2,400
Research	100	300	500
7. Total Expenditures	5,850	14,450	16,650

a. Expenditures for water refer to municipal and industrial spending for waste collection and treatment, and for storage.
b. Land acquisition costs are not reckoned as a claim on GNP.

forecasts have usually concerned minerals. The resource needs in the 1970's will be different from the problems faced by earlier generations of Americans. Like spending for housing and mass transit, the largest part of the expenditures listed for the resources goal represent the cost of supplying, treating, and storing water, and developing outdoor recreation areas for an urbanized and mobile nation. Research and development, joined with greater expenditures for land and facilities, can continue to supply an adequate flow of resource commodities for changing and growing needs in the next decade. They can also help assure adequate reserves for the decades which follow.

CHAPTER 13

International
Aid

I.

The need of the developing nations of Africa, Asia, and Latin America for sustained economic growth poses one of the most complex and important problems confronting the United States. Economic and military aid to these countries is part of our goal of strengthening the United States by strengthening the community of free nations. Support for the international organizations which help preserve the peace and provide assistance to the less developed countries contributes to the same objective.

The underdeveloped countries make up some two thirds of the world's population. Their annual domestic output has been estimated by the United Nations at about three eighths of the GNP of the United States.[1] Per capita GNP

---

1. United Nations, *World Economic Survey*, 1962; Part 1, "The Developing Countries in World Trade," 1963, p. 6.

in the early 1960's for the nations which have been the major
recipients of U.S. economic aid ranged from about $80 in
India and Pakistan to over $300 for countries well on the
way to sustained economic growth such as Mexico.[2]
While much of the discussion of the underdeveloped economies is in terms of industrialization, these nations also face
difficult problems in assuring an adequate food supply. The
Food and Agriculture Organization of the UN states that
one sixth of the world's population, roughly 500 million
people, suffer from active hunger. An additional third are
exposed to malnutrition and diet deficiencies.[3] It is anticipated that the population of the developing countries will
grow by 2.5 to 3.0 per cent a year in the next decade. Minimum nutrition targets for this mushrooming population are
estimated by the FAO at 2,300 to 2,500 average calories per
person per day. The increase in food supplies needed to
realize this target in the next decade amounts to about 45
per cent in Africa and over 50 per cent in the Far East. Incomes per person would have to increase by 2 per cent a year
to enable the population to purchase the larger caloric in-
take.[4]

The developing nations are characterized by tendencies
toward social unrest and political instability. Rising levels
of aspiration accompany the shift from colonial dependency,
or semi-dependency, to national independence. Social disorganization becomes widespread, especially in the urban
centers, as traditional loyalties and mores dissolve in the
transition to an industrial society. The export of medical
technology has increased life expectancy and population.
There has been no corresponding accumulation of capital
to raise living standards. International divisions along lines
of per capita incomes are intensified by the predominance of

2. *Annual Report of the Council of Economic Advisers,* January, 1964, p.
160.

3. UNESCO, *United Nations Development Decade,* E/3613/Add. 1, 1962,
p. 10.

4. *Ibid.,* pp. 10–12.

white persons in the population of the wealthy nations, and a predominance of black-, yellow-, or brown-skinned persons in the underdeveloped areas.

The United States has attempted to assist the less developed nations to become viable societies through a complex of activities which in recent years have included supplying development capital and military aid, and providing financial support for UN operations such as the emergency peace-keeping task force on the borders of Israel. It is reasonable to expect that economic assistance, aside from serving other purposes, will also contribute to our national security. However, it is far from self-evident that economic development, by itself, will assure democratic governments or peaceful behavior in the emerging nations. But our objectives assume the probabilities are

1. that vigorous economic development is a necessary condition for the maintenance of political stability in nations surging with expectations of a better future;

2. that societies which are making satisfactory economic progress are likely to make friendlier neighbors and better members of the international community than societies which are stagnating economically.

II.

Large-scale public economic aid grows out of the American experience in helping the European countries after World War II. Between 1945 and 1948, the United States contributed almost $17 billion for relief and rehabilitation of the war-disrupted European economies. The task of reconstruction was facilitated by the Marshall Plan after 1948. The United States supplied over $11 billion for this program.

Passage of the Mutual Security Act in 1951 made for a far-reaching departure from the earlier concept of foreign assistance. The Act was based on the assumption that the Marshall Plan would speedily bring recovery to Western Europe. Hence, a shift was to be made and economic aid was to be concentrated on the developing nations. Since the communist countries were attempting to penetrate these areas, economic assistance was to be supplemented by military support.

The shift from Western Europe to Africa, Asia, and Latin America meant a change in emphasis from reconstruction to development. The support measures for Europe were intended as short-term programs. Their objective was to rapidly restore the productive capacity and trading potential of economies with a skilled labor force and abundant entrepreneurial talent. Assistance to encourage economic growth for the developing countries is a long-term process. Most of these nations require both technical and capital assistance and a host of changes in their societies to enable them to make effective use of the assistance. Their labor force is overwhelmingly agricultural. Few persons are skilled as industrial workers, technicians, or managers. The new countries lack the basic investment in roads, harbors, utilities, schools, and health facilities. Low incomes result in a level of saving which is inadequate to finance the desired development.

The military component of foreign aid consists of equipment, supplies, and services furnished to other countries, primarily in the form of grants. Korea and South Vietnam are currently the major recipients. Economic aid consists of long-term low-interest loans and grants. With the establishment of the Agency for International Development in 1961, development loans for specific projects have become the heart of the economic aid program. AID also supports technical assistance programs to establish facilities and train personnel in agriculture, education, health, and public administration. The Peace Corps, although organizationally not a part of the foreign aid program, should be considered as part of the overall aid effort because it is concerned with augmenting the skills of the host countries.

The launching of the Alliance for Progress in 1961 has been the major development in economic aid in the recent past. The purpose of the Alliance is to accelerate the annual rate of growth in Latin America to a minimum of 2-1/2 per cent per person. The Alliance is the first systematic exposition of the determination of the United States to raise living standards in an entire region. It is expected that the participating countries will require some $20 billion of external capital from the United States and other countries to achieve the Alliance's objectives by 1970. By the middle of 1964, Alliance support had helped to construct 220,000 homes, 23,000 classrooms, and 2,900 miles of road.

Another important element in the foreign aid complex is the Agricultural Trade Development and Assistance Act, commonly called Public Law 480. The essence of the law is that the Federal Government sells surplus commodities in exchange for domestic currencies of the recipient countries. Most of the currency may then be loaned back for approved projects. Public Law 480 transactions increase American exports and reduce farm surpluses. They help less developed countries by enabling them to increase their consumption of food and other agricultural products, and, in some cases, by using these commodities to pay in part for work done on development projects. Overseas sales and grants of U.S. surplus agricultural commodities under Public Law 480 in 1963 amounted to an estimated $1.5 billion.[5]

Since the end of World War II, the United States Government has expended over $90 billion in foreign assistance for postwar relief, in economic and military aid, and for investment in international financial institutions such as the International Monetary Fund. This aid includes both loans and grants. The distribution of the total is indicated in Table 13–1.

Economic assistance, including the investments in the financial institutions, has outweighed the military aid by a ratio of two to one. Four fifths of the economic aid has been

5. Derived from *The Foreign Assistance Program, Annual Report to Congress,* Agency for International Development, fiscal years 1963 and 1964.

Table 13–1
U.S. Government Net Foreign Assistance,
1945 to 1962*
(in millions of dollars)

Total Net Expenditures[a]	$91,500	
Per Cent Distribution of Major Components:		
1. Military Aid	33.8%	
to developed countries		16.6%
to developing countries		17.2
2. Economic Assistance	60.5	
to developed countries		32.5
to developing countries		28.0
3. Investments in International		
Financial Institutions	5.7	

a. Fiscal years 1945-1962.
* *Statistical Abstract*, 1963, p. 859.

in the form of grants, and one fifth, predominantly in recent years, in loans. The developing countries have received slightly more than half of the military aid, and slightly less than half of the direct economic assistance. Economic and military aid to the developing countries has exceeded $40 billion. By 1963, total U.S. assistance to all nations since 1945 had risen to $96.7 billion.[6]

By region, Asia has been the largest beneficiary of American assistance for the developing nations. Ten countries have accounted for about 60 per cent of all the economic aid, and 70 per cent of the military assistance extended since World War II to nations outside of Western Europe and Japan. They are Korea, Nationalist China, the Philippines, Vietnam, India, Pakistan, Israel, Turkey, Greece, and Brazil.[7]

As a claim on resources, U.S. Government assistance to the developing nations amounted to about four fifths of 1 per cent of GNP in 1962. In the past few years, this assistance has been declining. The aid extended to the developing

6. *Statistical Abstract*, 1964, p. 857.
7. *The United States Balance of Payments—Perspectives and Policies*, Joint Economic Committee, Congress of the United States, 1963, p. 68.

nations in 1962 and aid commitments in fiscal year 1964 are described in Table 13–2.

Table 13–2
U.S. Government Assistance to Developing Nations, 1962 and 1964*
(in millions of dollars)

Item	Net Assistance in 1962		Commitments in Fiscal 1964	
	Amount	Per cent of Total	Amount	Per cent of Total
Military Assistance	$1,260	27%	$1,120	33%
Economic Aid[a]	3,380	73	2,275	67
Total	4,640	100	3,395	100
Expenditures as % of GNP	0.8%		0.6%	

a. Includes contributions to international financial organizations of over $100 million.
* Estimate for 1962 is derived from *Statistical Abstract*, 1963, pp. 861-863. Figures for 1964 are from *Annual Report for Fiscal Year 1964*, Agency for Intrnational Development, pp. 3, 37-38.

The Council of Economic Advisers estimates that the governments of the industrial nations contributed about $6-1/2 billion to the developing countries for economic assistance in 1962.[8] The U.S. contribution was about 55 per cent of the world total. In addition, the net flow of private capital to the underdeveloped nations was approximately $2 billion. U.S. participation in providing private capital was considerably lower, probably about 25 per cent of the total.

III.

Private capital supplied massive funds for economic development in the non-industrialized areas of the world in the century before the 1930's. Until World War I, private capital was usually most successful in stimulating growth when it was accompanied by a large migration of population from the

8. "Economic assistance" in this estimate consists of government grants, public loans of more than five years' duration, and contributions from official sources to multilateral agencies for use on behalf of the less developed countries. See *Annual Report of the Council of Economic Advisers,* January, 1964, p. 157.

European nation providing the capital. The pre-war export of capital reflected the industrial supremacy of Europe, and, aside from the United States, the role of the capital-receiving nations as agricultural and raw materials sources. The success of these ventures was made possible by a world money market based on stable, freely convertible currencies tied to the international gold standard.

It was only after World War I that the United States emerged as a leading international creditor. With the depression of the 1930's, international private lending in the United States came to a halt. After 1945, the outflow of private capital resumed. Unlike the European capital exports before 1914, American private investment abroad has been predominantly direct investment.

American private capital outflows after World War II have gone largely to the industrially advanced nations. The value of all U.S. private direct investment abroad in 1963 was approximately $40 billion. Of this total, about $12 billion represented investments in the underdeveloped countries, primarily in Latin America.[9] U.S. direct investments in Canada in recent years have exceeded all the investments in the developing nations.

The modest role of private capital in the total flow of U.S. funds to the developing nations is summarized, for 1962, in Table 13-3.

The low share of private capital in this total can be partially attributed to unsettled political and social conditions in many of the developing nations. Fears of expropriation, or discriminatory taxation, or blocked withdrawals of earnings make foreign capital shy. High rates of return in the advanced countries have served as a barrier to risky ventures in the non-industrialized areas. Limited domestic markets and inadequate facilities in transportation and utilities have also discouraged investment.

---

9. *Survey of Current Business*, August, 1964, p. 10. The figures cited refer to the book value of direct investments.

Table 13–3
U.S. Government Economic Aid and Private Capital Flow to the Developing Nations, 1962*
(in millions of dollars)

Item	Amount	Per cent of Total
1. Private Capital Outflow[a]	$ 550	14%
2. Public Net Economic Assistance	3,380	86
3. Total	3,930	100
4. Total as % of GNP		0.7%

a. This total has fluctuated considerably from year to year. The corresponding total in 1961 was $1,040 million.
* Source of estimate for private capital outflow: The United States Balance of Payments—Perspective and Policies, Joint Economic Committee, Congress of the United States, 1963, p. 28.

Foreign private investments in the developing countries in the past often established beachheads of modern technology and economic efficiency surrounded by general backwardness. In the dual economies which resulted, the private capital was concentrated in the industries serving world markets and primarily in the extractive and raw materials industries. As recently as 1963, some 95 per cent of the U.S. private direct investment in the Middle East represented investment in the petroleum industry. As economic growth proceeds, foreign investment becomes more generally diffused throughout the economy. In Latin America, to cite another 1963 illustration, over 40 per cent of our direct investments were in manufacturing, public utilities, and trade.[10]

IV.

Part of the task of building a community of nations is carried on by a network of international organizations. The United Nations and its affiliates are the leading examples. These organizations are concerned with world peace and international or regional cooperation. They also provide technical assistance to help bridge the gap between the in-

10. *Survey of Current Business,* August, 1964, p. 10.

dustrial and the non-industrial societies. American contributions to the international organizations add to the resources for aiding the developing nations.

Each of the member nations of the United Nations is assessed an agreed-upon share of its budget. Voluntary contributions by the member nations support a number of special programs sponsored by the UN. They include the UN Children's Fund and the Relief and Works Agency for the Palestine Refugees. Private groups in the United States, such as CARE or certain church groups, have provided assistance for similar programs outside of UN channels. U.S. support has also helped finance NATO and regional organizations including the Pan American Union. The United States contribution of $200 million represented half of the total assessments for international non-financial organizations in 1963.[11]

In addition to these non-financial organizations, the United States contributes to five international financial organizations. They include the International Monetary Fund, the International Bank for Reconstruction and Development, and the Inter-American Development Bank. The financial institutions contribute to economic growth in the new nations by making loans on "hard" or "soft" terms for development or economic stabilization projects. They offer a partial substitute for the private lending activities and world-wide money markets of pre-World War I days. In the four years after 1961, the multi-national financial institutions increased their capital assistance to the developing nations by 50 per cent.[12]

With the addition of U.S. contributions to international organizations to the government-to-government economic and military assistance, total U.S. public international aid amounted to $4.9 billion in 1962. Taking into account the $550 million private capital flow from the United States to

---

11. *Statistical Abstract*, 1963, p. 942.
12. President's Foreign Aid Message to Congress, January 14, 1965.

the developing nations, public and private international aid together reached $5.4 billion.

V.

While population, food needs, and expectations have been rising rapidly in the less developed nations, their ability to finance economic growth through international trade has not kept pace with these changes. A decline in the ability of the underdeveloped countries to purchase the imports they need with foreign exchange earned from the sale of exports has increased their dependence on loans and grants from abroad as a source of funds for development.

The changes in the status of the non-industrialized nations in world markets are summarized by the experience from 1950 to 1960 described in Table 13–4.

Table 13–4
Selected Foreign Trade Data, Less Developed Nations, 1950 and 1960*

	Less Developed Nations		Changes from 1950 to 1960	
	1950	1960	All Nations	Less Developed Nations
1. Average Annual Rate of Growth in[a]				
a. Exports			6.4%	3.6%
b. Imports			6.4	4.6
2. Average Unit Price of[c]				
a. Exports	100	101		
b. Imports	100	110		
3. Per Cent of Total World Trade[b]	30.0%	20.4%		

a. Growth pertains to the volume of exports and imports measured in dollars.
b. Per cent of world trade in current prices.
c. Figures cited are indices of unit prices.
* Derived from *World Economic Survey, 1962, Part 1,* United Nations, 1963, pp. 1–3.

The volume of imports and exports of the developing countries in the 1950's grew more slowly than the world total. Imports, however, grew more rapidly than the ability to finance imports through sales of goods and services on world markets. The average price of their exports scarcely rose between 1950 and 1960. The prices of the goods they purchased abroad increased by an average of one tenth. The net effect of the lagging growth of trade and the worsening terms of trade was to reduce the underdeveloped nations' share of world trade by one third in a decade. While export prices for the underdeveloped nations have risen since 1962, the fundamental imbalance remains.

The deterioration of the trading status of the non-industrialized areas has offset part of the economic aid from the advanced countries. For the ten-year period after 1950, the UN estimates that this loss was equivalent to about one third of the total receipts of long-term capital and public grants received by these countries in the same period.[13]

In 1962, the United Nations projected the probable external capital needs of the developing nations in 1970. The projection was prepared in connection with the UN's Decade of Development Program. As a target growth rate for the program, the national income of the less developed countries was assumed to grow at 5 per cent a year by 1970. Realization of the target growth would increase per capita incomes by 2 per cent a year if population grew at an average annual rate of 3 per cent. It would also enable the underdeveloped countries to modernize their agricultural economies and to acquire the schools, transportation networks, public utilities, and health facilities they so sorely need.

The UN has estimated the external capital needs for the Decade of Development targets from the perspective of the constraints set by foreign trade. After allowing for the impact of measures for increasing the exports and reducing the imports of the developing nations, the funds required from external sources to accomplish the desired growth in national income are projected at $14 billion in 1970.[14] This capital

---

13. *World Economic Survey, 1962*, Part 1, p. 114.

14. Derived from *World Economic Survey, 1962*, Part 1, United Nations, pp. 6–7. The UN estimate assumes that the gap is reduced by $4 billion through international policy measures increasing the exports and diminishing the im-

could be raised, according to the UN General Assembly, if the advanced industrial nations would increase their flow of private and public capital to the less developed countries from the 0.7 of 1 per cent they contributed in 1961 to a level of 1 per cent.[15]

V I .

International aid has continued as a feature of national policy through postwar changes in administration and in public opinion. Widespread support for increasing the private capital flow to the developing nations has been frustrated by a limited absorptive capacity for private capital and an unfavorable investment climate in many of these nations. Acceptance of public economic aid as a general goal has gone hand in hand with considerable differences in opinion over the amounts of assistance, the types of assistance, or the desirable duration of the assistance program. The choices in the next decade are likely to reflect the extent to which growth in private foreign investment can diminish dependence on public economic aid.

Part of the controversy over government-to-government economic aid grows out of popular fatigue with a long-term program lacking the dramatic results of the Marshall Plan in Europe. Another part stems from doubts that foreign aid has brought about the internal stability in the developing nations it was expected to achieve. Some Americans question the wisdom of supplying capital to enable other countries to expand the public sectors of their economies or to assist nations whose foreign policies may sometimes be at odds with our own. Others believe that the aid burden has not been fairly distributed among the advanced industrial countries. The impact of the aid program on the U.S. balance of

ports of the developing nations. *Ibid.*, p. 9. We have preferred to regard this $4 billion residual as part of the capital requirements of the developing nations.

15. *Ibid.*, p. 119. The concept of national income to which these percentages refer is the "gross domestic product."

payments has aroused concern. Private foreign investment, on the other hand, frequently meets with obstacles created by an absence of facilities, or lack of domestic markets, or by persistent inflation, intense nationalism, and political instability.

Our standards in international aid relate to these tendencies in public thinking. They consist of two alternatives. Both accept the UN Decade of Development target of one per cent of national income as an appropriate yardstick for the public and private capital flow from the United States to the developing nations. One standard anticipates a diminishing role for public funds in supplying development capital. The increases in the capital flow in this standard are all private funds. The other stresses continued reliance on government-to-government aid with private investment rising gradually to one third of the total. Economic and political changes in the nations utilizing the capital are likely to inhibit or facilitate emphasis on either of the two alternatives.

Pressures for growth, it is anticipated, will encourage the underdeveloped countries to expand their development planning programs and adopt techniques for more effectively utilizing the capital which is made available. The external capital these nations will require is projected to increase from $14 billion in 1970 to $17 billion in 1975. The capital which would be supplied from the United States for the two standards in 1975 is described in Table 13–5.

Table 13–5
Estimated Capital Flow from the United States
to the Developing Nations, 1975
(in millions of 1962 dollars)

Component	Total in 1962	PROJECTION FOR 1975 Private Aid Standard	PROJECTION FOR 1975 Public Aid Standard
1. Private Capital Outflow	$ 550	$6,350	$3,250
2. Public Loans and Grants	3,380	3,400	6,500
3. Total	3,930	9,750	9,750

Increasing private investment is in keeping with the spirit of the Act for International Development. The Act states that "American private enterprise can play a vital role in fostering the growth of the less developed countries. . . . Where ordinary business justifications do not exist, government incentives or protections will be provided." To implement the intent of the Act, the convertibility of earnings from direct investments abroad may be insured, and the investments are guaranteed against losses due to expropriation, war, or insurrection. By the middle of 1964, $1.4 billion of American investments in 61 nations were guaranteed against one or more of these risks.[16] These guarantees should increase the flow of private U.S. capital to the developing nations in the next decade.

Those who advocate a shift to private foreign investment point out that one of the objectives of public economic aid is to make the recipient nations self-sustaining. Nationalist China, Greece, and Israel have already achieved annual rates of GNP growth in the 6 to 10 per cent range for over a decade.[17] Their need for U.S. public assistance is likely to cease shortly. As other nations approach self-sustaining growth, they can be expected to have limited needs for further government-to-government economic assistance. The cumulative effects of growth should enable these nations to create the facilities and the domestic markets for attracting private foreign capital serving national as well as world markets.

The establishment of regional "common markets," as in Central America, would also help enlarge internal markets and attract domestic and foreign private capital. Regional or continental mass markets could be a strategic element, as they have been in the United States and Western Europe, in making it possible to take advantage of the economies of large-scale production inherent in modern

16. *Foreign Assistance Program,* fiscal year 1964, p. 10.
17. *Annual Report of the Council of Economic Advisers,* January, 1964, p. 160.

technology. The capital requirements for an efficient regional steel plant, for example, could provide an important outlet for U.S. private investment.

A shift to private foreign investment in the emerging nations takes it for granted that the intense nationalism and political instability characterizing many of the new countries will lessen. Rising per capita incomes created by economic growth, it is assumed, will change the political climate and weaken the incentives which encourage the resort to discriminatory measures against foreign enterprises. Similarly, growth in output and political stability should diminish resistance to measures for controlling the persistent inflationary tendencies which hedge investment with great uncertainty.

Advocates of government-to-government economic aid are less optimistic about the prospects for creating a favorable investment climate or self-sustaining growth in the developing nations. They anticipate that the primary uses for the external capital will be in areas usually financed by public funds—roads, harbors, school and health facilities, and basic utilities. Rapid population growth is also expected to accentuate the importance of the projects which typically utilize public capital. If rates of population increase reach the 2.5 or 3 per cent a year projected for the end of the decade, the race to provide minimum facilities for a rapidly growing population will intensify existing needs for social overhead capital and create new ones. To supply food for an ever-increasing population, large sums of capital will be required to reclaim land and to build dams, irrigation systems, and country-to-city roads. As in the United States, these projects are financed very largely by public capital.

Many of the emerging nations are still largely traditional societies whose production and consumption patterns are largely those of self-sufficient households. As the Council of Economic Advisers points out in its 1964 *Report*, their primary need in breaking loose from economic stagnation is for technical assistance—"for teachers and technicians to build skills and institutions basic to economic growth."[18] This assistance is typically supported by public funds.

Remnants of tribalism and feudalism are important in many of the new countries. Creation of unified national societies with opportunities for independent farmers, middle class persons, and wage earners is likely to involve far-reaching social changes. The political instability associated with rapid social change intensifies difficulties in accumulating domestic capital or in attracting foreign private investment. In these circumstances, it is reasonable to anticipate that external capital for the take-off to self-sustaining growth will be largely made up of public funds.

While the proportion of private and public funds in the flow of capital from the United States to the developing nations in the 1970's cannot be predicted in advance, it is apparent that both types of capital serve the same ultimate objectives. Either private or public capital can serve as a dynamic force for transmitting technological advance or developing professional and technical skills in nations just beginning to emerge as industrial societies. Rising incomes in these countries from either source would increase the demand for imports from the United States. With time and growth, they might follow the example of Japan where, since 1950, American imports have tripled.

VII.

Support for international organizations is also part of our goal of strengthening the community of free nations. While these organizations benefit all countries, they are in a strategic position to make far-reaching contributions to the modernization of the developing nations. The new countries will require the assistance of FAO, WHO, or UNESCO in establishing adequate educational systems, agricultural research

---

18. *Annual Report of the Council of Economic Advisers,* January, 1964, p. 152.

and extension centers, health centers, water supplies, and administrative and statistical services. The international organizations are likely to enlarge their support of world-wide research and development programs. Their resources and findings would be available to nations unable to finance large-scale R & D programs of their own. International research programs in water desalination, or oceanography, or in peaceful uses of atomic energy could assist the underdeveloped countries in coping with the explosive population growth which has offset so much of their increase in production.

By 1975, U.S. support for the international non-financial organizations is projected at $1.5 billion a year. Half of this total represents support for a permanent UN Peace Force.

The number of independent nations with their own armed forces has increased markedly since 1945. As nuclear and missiles technology becomes more widely diffused and less expensive, more nations, probably including many now characterized as underdeveloped, are likely to acquire means for producing missiles or nuclear weapons. The existence of a UN Peace Force could help preserve the peace by making it apparent that resort to military force would invite countermeasures limiting the use of force. To the extent that the Peace Force succeeded, it could facilitate economic growth in the developing nations by releasing resources otherwise required for national defense to be used as development capital. The scope of a UN Peace Force, and its effectiveness, is likely to depend on the level of international tensions and the overall support for the UN by the nations of the world in the next decade.

VIII.

The cost of the standards for our international aid goal include expenditures by the United States Government and by U.S. private sources for the complex of activities intended to facilitate the growth of less developed nations as economically viable and stable members of the world community in the coming decade. To assess the magnitudes involved in the cost estimates for our objectives, it is useful to indicate the cost of continuing the programs which are least involved in the current controversies. They are the contributions to the international non-financial organizations, military aid, and the "Food for Peace" program. Together they yield an estimated level of spending of $3.1 billion a year for minimum programs in the 1970's. This package is the basis for our hypothetical preempted yardstick for the international aid goal in the next 10 years.

The expenditures for the international aid goal are summarized in Table 13–6.

Table 13–6
Estimated Expenditures for International Aid Goal,
1970 and 1975
(in millions of 1962 dollars)

Item	Expenditures in 1962	PROJECTED EXPENDITURES FOR			
		Private Aid Standard		Public Aid Standard	
		1970	1975	1970	1975
1. Capital Supply to Developing Nations					
a. Private	$ 550	$4,400	$6,350	$1,950	$3,250
b. Public	3,380	3,400	3,400	5,850	6,500
c. Total	3,930	7,800	9,750	7,800	9,750
2. Military Aid	1,260	1,000	1,000	1,000	1,000
3. Support for International Non-financial Organizations	220	1,000	1,500	1,000	1,500
4. Total International Aid	5,410	9,800	12,250	9,800	12,250
5. Expenditures as % of GNP	1.0%	1.25%	1.25%	1.25%	1.25%

Enlarging the role of the UN and attaining the Decade of Development target would raise the cost of international aid in 1975 to over $12 billion, or $7 billion more than in 1962. Measured by GNP, the projections for overall public and private international aid expenditures would amount to 1.25 per cent of the U.S. gross national product in the 1970's.

Our estimates for public economic assistance could be subject to downward revision if the industrializing nations were able to finance a larger-than-anticipated share of their economic growth from earnings in world trade. Easing of tariff barriers in the advanced nations, a larger volume of exports, and higher prices for their exports are probably necessary if the underdeveloped countries are to finance more of the development programs through international trade. Rising national incomes in the industrial nations could contribute to the same result as higher incomes lead the industrial nations to increase their imports from the less developed countries. On the other side of the ledger of future possibilities, more aid is likely to be required if population growth exceeds even the expected high levels, or if threats of external aggression compel some of the new countries, such as India, to divert more of their resources to military preparedness.

For all these possibilities, economic development abroad can be expected to influence national objectives at home. The impact on our educational system will probably involve greater emphasis at all levels of the curriculum on Asia, Africa, and Latin America. Colleges and universities are likely to be educating teachers, researchers, engineers, business managers, and public administrators to export American technology and administrative techniques to the industrializing nations. New transportation modes produced in the United States, such as hydrofoils, should prove attractive to nations possessing inland waterways or protected seacoasts but lacking the capital for establishing costly highway or railroad networks. Experience gained in renewing American cities could help urban renewal in Calcutta or Cairo. This interchange would be a two-way process as the findings of medical research in tropical diseases or amoebic dysentery abroad became available in the United States, or as the knowledge acquired in building dams or in water-use planning in Asia or North Africa influenced similar projects throughout the world.

The aspirations propelling efforts to modernize and raise per capita incomes in the formerly colonial areas are very similar to the aspirations which motivated growth in the United States. Without substantial external aid, the capital which is accumulated is likely to be extracted through forced savings created by restrictions on consumption. China today, and the Soviet Union in the Stalin era, are the classic examples of this pattern of industralization. The accumulation of capital is more likely to encourage democracy if large-scale capital imports make it possible for the developing nations to simultaneously raise living standards and add to productive capacity. Since the democratic alternative is so much in the interest of the United States, its means—supplying capital and supporting international organizations—can be expected to continue as an important national objective in the 1970's.

CHAPTER 14

Space

I.

Our goal in the space program is to advance our knowledge of life, of the earth, the sun, and other planets, and to apply this knowledge toward increasing man's control over his environment. This goal was symbolized by the late President Kennedy in 1961 when he announced our intention of "landing a man on the moon and returning him safely to earth." We interpret this to mean that embarking on a sustained space research and development program has become an important national objective. Expenditures for our goals in space are estimated to range as high as $9-1/2 billion in 1975.

Congress, in enacting the National Aeronautics and Space Act in 1958, spelled out the nation's space objectives as including, among others,

1. The expansion of knowledge of phenomena in the atmosphere and in space.

2. The development of vehicles capable of carrying equipment, instruments, and living organisms through space.

3. The preservation of the role of the United States as a leader in space sciences and technology.

4. Cooperation with other nations in space research and in the peaceful application of its results.

5. The making available of discoveries affecting national defense to the defense agencies.

To implement our national policy that "activities in space should be devoted to peaceful purposes for the benefit of all mankind," the Act specifies that the space program should be directed by a civilian agency, the National Aeronautics and Space Administration. NASA exercises control of virtually all space research and development activities other than those primarily associated with defense.

The space program is the outstanding instance of the planning of research to develop a new science and a new technology wholly beyond the capabilities of existing knowledge. It is also the largest and most costly research and development program in history. The total costs for APOLLO, the manned lunar landing project, are estimated at $20 billion or more. By comparison, the cost of the Manhattan Project for developing the atomic bomb during World War II was approximately $2 billion.

The space effort holds promise of contributing to scientific knowledge and technological advance in many segments of our society. It should greatly expand our knowledge about the universe and the earth. Space research is creating a new field of study: space science—an amalgam of astronomy, biology, the atmospheric sciences and geophysics. This science will undoubtedly become an important part of scientific and engineering education. It is also likely to influence man's view of himself and of his position in the universe. To achieve our space objectives, we have created a new technology with its particular "hardware" of space vehicles. The "spin-off" effects of space research include the use of equipment and material introduced in connection with the space program for improved weather forecasting; for new techniques of reconnaissance; and for quick, reliable, and inexpensive international communications. The technology developed or advanced by the space programs emphasizing miniaturization and self-correcting systems should prove adaptable, with further research, to a great many other uses, possibly including artificial replacements for worn out or defective human organs.

Since space is an area without national claims to ownership, it offers a fertile field for international cooperation. Many nations, including the United States, have joined the World Meteorological Organization to further the development of a world-wide weather forecasting system. Satellite surveillance techniques are also likely to increase the prospects for arriving at arms reduction agreements by augmenting the possibilities for enforcing them. Surveillance satellites may be used to detect the presence of nuclear weapons or missile launching sites. In this way, they reduce the need for onsite ground or conventional over-flight inspections.

The space program, together with the development of long-range missiles, has transformed the aircraft industry into a new and unique enterprise, the aerospace industry. This industry is the largest privately owned aggregation of technical manpower and research facilities in the world. It employs 2-1/2 times as many professional workers in R & D as the next largest private employer, the electronics industry, which itself includes many aerospace establishments.[1] Aerospace firms produce the bulk of their output for one customer, the U.S. Government. NASA purchases from these firms in 1965 are estimated at over $4 billion.[2] This output very largely represents research and development intended to lead to the production of a single prototype, or a small number, of rockets or rocket subsystems, rather than the mass production typical of other large industries. The space and missile programs have converted the aerospace firms from

---

1. Miller, Thomas G., *Strategies for Survival in the Aerospace Industry,* Arthur D. Little, Inc., 1964, p. 12.
2. *Ibid.,* p. 21.

airframe manufacturers into centers of invention with research capabilities potentially applicable to many areas of
our society.

II.

The space program has become popularly identified with
Project APOLLO, the manned lunar landing. However, in
fiscal year 1964, the lunar landing project accounted for less
than half of all space expenditures. In the past five or six
years, the space effort has grown into a comprehensive program of research, development, and application involving
NASA, the Department of Defense, the Atomic Energy Commission, the Weather Bureau, and the National Science
Foundation. Private enterprise is now represented by the
Communications Satellite Corporation, COMSAT, established to develop the application of satellite systems for a
global telecommunications network.

In 1959, NASA spent $150 million. Total space expendi-
tures by all agencies in 1962 exceeded $3 billion and they
rose to $5 billion in 1963. The breakdown of this spending
is summarized in Table 14-1.

A brief survey of current activities indicates the complex
of activities included in the space effort. Aside from the
manned lunar landing, NASA conducts basic research in
the space sciences. Studies of the earth, the planets, and the
space environment are conducted by sending up manned and
unmanned spacecraft carrying scientific equipment, cameras,
or infrared and other sensors. As part of this research, one
MARINER satellite has approached within 22,000 miles of
Venus, and in 1964 another started on its way toward Mars
on a photographic mission. The space sciences program is
largely made up of activities which, aside from their contribution to the moon landing project, also contribute to
our store of fundamental knowledge in many scientific fields.

NASA's developmental research and technology program
is devoted to advancing the "state of the art" in space tech-

Table 14-1
Space Program Expenditures, 1962 and 1963
(in millions of dollars)*

		Expenditures	
Agency		1962[a]	1963[a]
1. NASA		$1,900	$3,355
	a. Manned space flight	1,100	2,190
	b. Basic space sciences	435	575
	c. Developmental research and application	365	590
2. Department of Defense		1,220	1,485
3. Atomic Energy Commission		155	200
4. Weather Bureau		7	12
5. National Science Foundation		1	2
6. Total		3,283	5,054

a. Calendar year estimates obtained by averaging the fiscal years which include half of each calendar year.
* Source: The Budget of the United States Government for Fiscal Year 1964; Report, National Aeronautics and Space Council, 1965, pp. 157-158.

nology. It includes research in space vehicle structures, propulsion, and guidance and control systems. The end result of this program is to advance our understanding of the engineering principles underlying space technology and to apply the knowledge acquired in the design of operational launch systems for spacecraft. NASA is also concerned with the application of space technology in meteorology, communications, and navigation. After NASA has developed satellite systems for these purposes, they are turned over to such agencies as the Weather Bureau for operational use. NASA, for example, was responsible for developing the highly successful TIROS weather satellite and the more advanced NIMBUS experimental meteorological satellite system.

The Department of Defense is the second largest participant in the space program. Military space research expenditures in 1964 amounted to about one fourth of all military R & D spending.[3] Our interest in the military aspects of the space program is primarily defensive. It is summed up by

3. Report, National Aeronautics and Space Council, p. 41.

the statement of Roswell Gilpatric, then Deputy Secretary of Defense, that "an arms race in space will not contribute to our security."[4]

About half the present defense effort in space relates to applications in navigation, communications, and surveillance. This includes Project VELA, a satellite launched in 1963 for detecting nuclear tests. The Air Force's photographic surveillance satellites are other examples. The Defense Department has also cooperated with NASA in projects designed to develop techniques for the orbital rendezvous and docking of spacecraft, and to study the effects on astronauts of prolonged presence in space.

The Atomic Energy Commission's principal role in space has involved the development of nuclear reactors for propulsion and onboard sources of power for spacecraft. The first operational civilian application of space technology—the meteorological satellites—has been administered by the Weather Bureau. By the last part of 1964, the TIROS meteorological satellites had sent back some 400,000 photographs and they had helped to identify and track 25 hurricanes and 45 typhoons.[5]

One measure of the possible gains from improved weather forecasting by the use of satellites was suggested by President Johnson in 1963. The President, then Chairman of the National Aeronautics and Space Council, estimated the annual savings if we could predict weather accurately only five days in advance as follows

$2½	billion in agriculture
3	billion in water resources
100	million in surface transportation
75	million in retail marketing
45	million in the lumber industry

These savings, President Johnson observed, "are just for

4. Quoted in Diamond, Edwin, *The Rise and Fall of the Space Age*, 1964, p. 116.

5. *Report,* National Aeronautics and Space Council, p. 22.

the United States. Worldwide benefits would be many times as great."[6]

COMSAT's first commercial satellite, EARLY BIRD, was launched in 1965. It has a capacity of 240 two-way voice channels. The channels can be used for telephone or telegraphic messages or to transmit television programs from one continent to another. These communications satellites should introduce new possibilities for high-speed data transmission on a global basis by linking data signals from a computer in one area with a receiving computer in another. The arrangements for COMSAT envision an international investment program with shares in the "space segment" owned by individuals or governments in different user countries. Agreement was reached with 19 countries in 1964 on the preliminary arrangements for a global communications system. The agreement establishes the principle that a single commercial system should be set up to provide world-wide coverage open to all nations on a non-discriminatory basis.

Aside from global telecommunications, cooperative international projects have been especially important in the orbiting of small satellites to gather scientific information in the space immediately surrounding the earth. By 1964, eleven countries were participating in the cooperative launchings of sounding rockets, and 40 different nations had been involved in special projects in support of our weather satellite programs.

There is no exchange of funds between NASA and foreign cooperating agencies in these projects. The cost to NASA of the parts of its experimental programs involved in the international cooperation are reduced to the extent that facilities, equipment, and manpower are provided by the agencies of the cooperating countries. The joint international endeavors have also served to stimulate purchases by space agencies abroad from firms in the U.S. aerospace and electronics industries.

6. Quoted in *Astronautics and Space Engineering*, April, 1963, p. 25.

III.

There is general agreement in the United States that a sustained space research program is an important and continuing national objective. However, there is widespread disagreement concerning the pace at which the program should be pursued. The differences largely center on the gains anticipated from landing a man on the moon by 1970. They also reflect a concern that a rapidly expanding space program may divert a substantial share of the nation's research expenditures and resources from other purposes to this one area.

In part, the differences arise because our goals in space include scientific and technical objectives, and they also include considerations of defense, international prestige, and our role as a contender for world leadership in space technology. Some of the annual costs of an accelerated space effort represent a premium we are paying for the political objectives of the space program. And, the magnitude of the premium we are willing to pay is affected by a variable beyond our control—the scope and degree of success of the other large national space effort, the Soviet program.

It is not possible to isolate the cost of the individual objectives in the space program since the pursuit of any one objective affects the likelihood of achieving the others. Dr. Lloyd V. Berkner, President of the Graduate Research Center of the Southwest, comments, "it is impossible to unravel the complex interrelations between science-in-space, the civil and military objectives, and the political goals. . . . Each part of the package has strong reflections and interactions with the others—we cannot avoid commitment to the whole package. The only control available to us is the rate at which we can proceed."[7]

Some persons, including scientists who stress the scientific

---

7. Berkner, L. V., "Space Medicine from the Perspective of Space Geophysics," address, Aerospace Medical Association, Los Angeles, California, April 29, 1963.

objectives of the program, question the wisdom of the 1970 lunar deadline. They contend that much of the scientific knowledge to be gained from an accelerated program to land a man on the moon could also be realized, and at a lesser cost, by the use of instrumented landings. A manned landing, they contend, should take place at a later date, when the potentialities of the instrumented landings have been fully exploited.

This point of view was summed up by *The New York Times* in an editorial commending the successful accomplishment of the RANGER 7 lunar photographic mission. The *Times* concluded from the mission's success that "the potentiality for obtaining so much more information . . . from unmanned instrument-carrying rockets strengthens the case for abandoning the arbitrary 1970 deadline . . . and substituting a schedule permitting orderly progress toward a manned voyage to the moon without hazards or costs dictated only by the desire to achieve this objective under maximum draft."[8]

On the other side of the controversy, scientists who favor the early manned landing point out that the technical advantages of an early human landing become decisive as the lunar program progresses. To quote Drs. Jastrow and Newell, two space scientists, "When more difficult experiments are attempted . . . the trained human observer brings to the supervision of these experiments the ability to deal with unforeseen difficulties and to respond to unanticipated opportunities. The automatic instrument in this advanced stage . . . must be designed . . . at a heavy price in reliability and cost of development, to achieve even a crude imitation of human sophistication and flexibility." And, according to Jastrow and Newell, "The pace of the program must be set not by the measured patterns of scientific research, but by

8. "Triumph for *Ranger 7*," editorial, *The New York Times*, August 2, 1964, Section IV, p. 8.

the urgencies of the response to the national challenge."[9]

In part, the divergences in opinion reflect a concern that an accelerating space program may concentrate such a large share of the nation's research effort in one particular area as to diminish the research resources available in other areas, such as mass transport or control of air and water pollution. Measured by the GNP yardstick, the costs of the space program are minor, about 1 per cent of gross national product in the mid-1960's. However, expenditures by NASA in the 1964 fiscal year represented over one fourth of all Federal spending for the conduct of research and development. They were almost triple the amount of all Federal support for R & D in that year for areas other than space, defense, or atomic energy.[10] The number of scientists and engineers employed in NASA-sponsored projects increased from 15,000 in 1960 to an estimated 43,500 in 1963.[11] There is some apprehension that continued rapid expansion in the technical manpower demands for space could reduce the supply of scientists and engineers for colleges and universities attempting to enlarge faculties to cope with sharply rising enrollments.

The controversies over the appropriate level of the space effort primarily grow out of differences in the emphasis placed on the scientific and political objectives in our space program. They also involve differences in the priorities attached to space in relation to other national objectives that also have claims on our research resources. While these differences cannot be resolved within the scope of the present study, the alternative standards listed for the space goal relate to the conflicting tendencies in informed opinion.

9. Jastrow, Robert and Newell, Homer E., "Why Land on the Moon," *Atlantic Monthly,* August, 1963, pp. 43, 45.

10. Derived from *The Budget of the United States Government for Fiscal Year 1966,* pp. 444, 445.

11. "Requirements for Scientists and Engineers," report submitted by NASA to the Subcommittee on Employment and Manpower, Committee on Labor and Public Welfare, U.S. Senate, November, 1963.

I V .

Our standards for the space program project different levels of effort in the 1970's, reflecting differences in the assumed pace of the program. The "peak level" standard anticipates that the manned lunar landing will be accomplished by 1970, and will be followed by a program of exploration of the moon and large-scale preparations for a manned flight to Mars between 1980 and 2000. The "slow-pace" standard projects an emphasis on instrumented landings on the moon for another decade, with the human visit taking place in the mid-1970's. All told, space expenditures for the slow-pace alternative are estimated at $5 billion a year in the 1970's. They are projected to rise to over $9 billion for the peak level effort in 1975.

Estimates of the cost of the space effort five or ten years from now are, of necessity, rough orders of magnitude. Costs in the 1970's are likely to be affected by changes in space technology which introduce new types of equipment, or by economies which reduce unit costs as equipment is produced on a larger scale and with more experience. Discoveries before the lunar landing occurs, similar to the discovery of the Van Allen radiation belt in the early 1960's, will probably influence the direction of the future space effort, its potential applications, and the equipment systems best suited for particular missions.

James E. Webb, NASA Administrator, has stated in response to a Congressional inquiry about possible expenditures by NASA in 1970, that "there is an ongoing level of research and development that I believe should run at something like one and a half billion dollars a year, maybe a little more."[12]

The expenditures for ongoing R & D take into account the cost of the basic sciences program, the advanced research and technology studies, and new practical applications com-

12. Quoted from *Hearings on the Fiscal Year 1965 NASA Authorization*, Committee on Science and Astronautics, U.S. House of Representatives, 1964, p. 2833.

parable to the TIROS meteorological satellite. These programs would build up a fund of scientific information, supply us with useful applications, and provide concepts and equipment to enable us in the future to do the things in space we may decide to pursue. By 1975, the ongoing R & D expenditures are projected to increase to $2 billion in both standards.

If the present plans for the manned lunar landing are carried out on schedule, the major expenditures for the program will have been made by 1968. Maintaining a level of effort comparable to the APOLLO peak would mean beginning large additional projects in the late 1960's. Possible candidates have been suggested by Dr. George E. Mueller, NASA Associate Administrator for Manned Space Flight, in testimony before the House Science and Astronautics Committee. Dr. Mueller lists as potential candidates a project for exploring the moon, the development of an earth-orbiting laboratory, a space station orbiting 200 to 500 miles away from earth as a stepping stone for more advanced operations, and flights to other planets in our solar system.[13]

Dr. Mueller's suggestions indicate possibilities for the space program which could well maintain the peak level pace after APOLLO in the 1970's. We interpret a flight to other planets as involving a manned landing on Mars in the decade or two after 1980. A Mars landing is the logical next step to follow a lunar landing in 1969 to 1970. At intervals of about two years from 1969 to 1973, the earth will make a succession of favorable approaches to Mars. A study panel convened by the National Academy of Sciences in 1965 recommended that a substantial effort should be undertaken to exploit these favorable opportunities. "We believe it entirely reasonable," the panel of scientists reported, "that Mars is inhabited with living organisms and that life independently originated there."[14] Aside from testing this hypothesis, flights to Mars could greatly increase

13. *Hearings on the Fiscal Year 1965 NASA Authorization*, p. 447.
14. *Biology and the Exploration of Mars*, Space Sciences Board, National Academy of Sciences, 1965, p. 6.

our understanding of the origins of life on earth and the origins of the solar system. The Mars flight would probably include the earth-orbiting laboratory project as an intermediate phase.

The order of magnitude for the total cost of the Mars program through the initial manned landing has been estimated as in the neighborhood of $100 billion.[15] In the mid-1960's, the program would include fly-bys of small space craft in the vicinity of Mars—similar to the recent flights. Before 1971, according to the National Academy panel, it should be possible to place a 200-pound space vehicle in orbit around Mars. In 1971 or 1973, an unmanned Automated Biological Laboratory would be landed. Assuming, perhaps conservatively, that the initial human landing occurs in the year 2000, expenditures for the Mars flight are projected to average $3 billion a year.

A full-scale program of human exploration of the moon is also likely to follow the early manned landings. This project could include construction of permanent and semipermanent installations, construction of a lunar astronomical observatory, expeditions to map the moon's surface, studies of the effects of life on the moon on living organisms, and forays to gather samples of lunar materials for chemical and physical analysis. Expenditures for exploring the moon are estimated to rise to $1 billion by 1975.[16]

The slow-pace alternative anticipates a decade or more of instrumented landings on the moon preceding the first human visit or a large-scale Mars program. Ths would place the manned landing in the mid-1970's, about 1976 or 1977. If it were decided to slow down the pace of the APOLLO program, commitments of funds and plans for "tooling up" made in advance would prevent expenditures from falling substantially for a few years after the decision had been reached. But, by 1975 the cost of a stretched out lunar land-

15. *The Rise and Fall of the Space Age,* p. 3.

16. It has been suggested that the total cost for the lunar exploration program could amount to as much as the APOLLO Project, about $20 billion. See *The Wall Street Journal,* July 23, 1964.

ing program added to the ongoing R & D yields an estimated
level of spending by NASA of about the same dimensions
as in 1963—$3-1/2 billion. In addition to the activities conducted by NASA, other
organizations will be contributing important advances to-
ward realizing our space goals in the next decade. The
Atomic Energy Commission is likely to expand its research
as it progresses in developing onboard nuclear reactors to
include reactors for large spacecraft. Because of their high
power-to-weight characteristics, nuclear rockets would probably be utilized for a manned Mars landing. The Weather
Bureau plans to use improved TIROS satellites to provide
cloud coverage of the earth at least once a day on a continuing basis. They will be joined by an expanded NIMBUS
system, a series of advanced meteorological observatories in
space. Both satellites will be integrated with APT, the Automatic Picture Transmission System, to yield a steady flow
of photographic information for world-wide weather forecasting. The National Science Foundation can be expected
to undertake additional programs similar to STRATO-
SCOPE II, a project to study infrared radiation from other
planets by lifting a 36-inch, 6,800-pound telescope by bal-
loon to altitudes near 80,000 feet. COMSAT's global telecommunications network should be fully operational well
before 1970. General Telephone and Electronics, one of the
carriers participating in the COMSAT program, foresees
annual system revenues of $250 million by 1970.[17]

It is reasonable to anticipate that as space research advances, the military space program will become a larger part
of total defense spending for R & D. In the slow-pace alternative, military research expenditures, including space, are
related to the level of defense spending which is regarded as
consistent with partial disarmament, following the lines of
Stage I of the U.S. disarmament proposals at Geneva in
1962.[18] The totals for this alternative project sizeable ex-

17. *Fortune Magazine*, June, 1962.
18. For a discussion of defense expenditures assuming partial disarmament,
see Chapter 9.

penditures for monitoring and surveillance satellites. In the peak standard, military R & D is expected to be considerably larger to allow for projects to test and develop the defensive applications of the new technology. An operational Satellite Inspector system illustrates these possibilities. The Satellite Inspector is a manned spacecraft which would inspect, repair, disarm, or destroy orbiting objects in space.

The costs of the two standards for the space goal are summarized in Table 14–2. The slow-pace alternative is essentially a projection of the cost of extending our commitment for an ongoing civilian and military R & D program, plus a minimum commitment to the manned lunar landing. Accordingly, the expenditures for this standard also serve as our hypothetical preempted benchmark estimate of the cost of extending the current level of the space program for another decade.

Table 14–2
Estimated Expenditures for the Space Goal, 1970 and 1975
(in millions of 1962 dollars)

| | | PROJECTED EXPENDITURES | | | |
| | Expenditures in | Peak Level Standard | | Slow-pace Standard | |
Agency	1962	1970	1975	1970	1975
1. NASA	$1,900	$5,500	$6,000	$3,000	$3,500
a. Manned lunar landing	1,100	300	—	1,500	1,500
b. Exploration of the moon	—	700	1,000	—	—
c. Project Mars	—	3,000	3,000	—	—
d. Basic space sciences	435	750	1,000	750	1,000
e. Developmental research and applications	365	750	1,000	750	1,000
2. Department of Defense	1,220	2,400	3,000	2,020	1,870
3. Atomic Energy Commission	155	200	250	180	230
4. Weather Bureau	7	35	35	35	35
5. National Science Foundation	1	5	5	5	5
6. COMSAT	a	60	60	60	60
7. International Space Cooperation[b]	a	(100)	(150)	(100)	(150)
8. Total	3,283	8,200	9,350	5,300	5,700

a. Not available.
b. The expenditures for international cooperation are also part of the estimates listed for NASA and the Weather Bureau.

Spending for our space objectives in the peak level standard in 1975 is projected to almost triple the 1962 expenditures. The reduced emphasis on manned space flight and the lesser military space effort in the alternative standard would hold the increase in expenditures to about 80 per cent. As a claim on resources, spending for the space goal in the 1970's is not expected to exceed the 1965 proportion—about 1 per cent of GNP.

The space effort involves the incurring of large expenditures in the present or near future for benefits at a more remote future date which, at best, can be very imperfectly foreseen. It is reasonable to anticipate far-reaching gains in knowledge and in the enlargement of human opportunities on earth from exploration of the moon and the planets. As with the terrestrial voyages of discovery in earlier centuries, the unanticipated consequences are likely to exceed in importance those which can be anticipated in advance. In these circumstances, we cannot meaningfully estimate the monetary value of the benefits resulting from the program or compute cost-benefit ratios for different packages of space activities. The expenditures projected for the space goal are fundamentally investments in increasing human knowledge with the expectation that such investments are likely to yield a large tangible and intangible return.

CHAPTER 15

Agriculture

I.

Our goal in agriculture is to produce food and fiber effectively and to enable the farm population to participate more adequately in the American standard of living. This means developing a prosperous and stable agricultural economy in a society in which the rural segment has become a sharply diminishing share of the total. Expenditures by the Federal Department of Agriculture exceeded $7 billion in 1962. Spending for our goals in agriculture in the next decade is projected to range between 5 and 9 billion dollars a year.

For much of the world, including the Soviet Union and most of the developing nations, the significant problems in agriculture are those arising out of low farm productivity and shortages of food and raw materials. The agricultural problem in the United States centers on the problem of surplus—a surplus of crop output and of people in agriculture. The applications of scientific advance which have transformed American industry have had even more strik-

ing effects in agriculture. In 1860, the output of one farm
worker could provide for himself and four other persons.
In 1940, one farmer could supply about 9 others, and by
1960 he could provide for over 25.[1]

This vigorous growth in farm productivity affords us a
nutritious and varied diet at relatively low cost in terms
of take-home pay. In periods of rapid expansion of the
non-agricultural economy, workers released from agriculture provide a reserve labor force which helps to prevent
bottlenecks from developing elsewhere in the economy.
Rapidly expanding farm output also makes it possible to
supply surplus commodities without charge to needy families and school children in the United States, and to provide
other nations with food to cushion the effects of natural
disasters and to foster economic development.

However, the benefits which rising agricultural productivity have made available to our nation generally have not
been accompanied by greater economic opportunity for most
farmers and farm laborers. The share of civilian employment accounted for by agriculture has declined from 17
per cent of the total in 1940 to 7 per cent in 1962.[2] Farm
income has shrunk from an annual average of $16 billion
in 1947–49 to $13 billion in 1962. Income per person for
the farm population was approximately 60 per cent of the
non-farm average in this same year; $1,430 in agriculture
compared to $2,440 for the non-farm population.[3] With
low incomes prompting many small farmers to leave agriculture, 1.3 million commercial farms disappeared between
1950 and 1959.[4]

The 1964 *Manpower Report of the President* estimates
that farm employment will fall to 4.5 per cent of civilian
employment by 1975.[5] For many of the young people in

---

1. *Agriculture and Economic Growth*, U.S. Department of Agriculture, 1962.
2. *Manpower Report of the President*, 1964, pp. 199, 244.
3. *Fact Book of U.S. Agriculture*, 1963, USDA, p. 101.
4. Derived from *U.S. Census of Agriculture*, 1950 and 1959.
5. *Manpower Report of the President*, 1964, p. 244.

rural areas, the prospects for future employment will depend on opportunities to obtain employment in fields other than agriculture. The prerequisite to large-scale migration out of agriculture, to quote a recent report by the National Planning Association, is "the maintenance of a strong and vigorous economy with expanding opportunities for employment."[6]

Unlike the firms in industries made up of a small number of large corporations, or wage earners enrolled in unions, farmers lack the market power to protect their incomes by influencing the prices of the commodities they sell. Farmers have turned to the Federal Government to achieve this objective through acreage allotments, price supports, land retirement, and surplus disposal measures.

II.

Rapid growth of productivity and of output in agriculture, coupled with much slower growth in consumer spending for farm products, constitutes the basic dynamism behind the problems of agricultural surplus and low incomes. Attempts to cope with these problems by expanding consumption or limiting production and market supply have formed the strategic ingredients in public agricultural policy since the 1920's.

Between 1948 and 1962, output per worker in agriculture increased by an average of 4.7 per cent a year. This compared with an annual increase of 3 per cent in manufacturing and 2.4 per cent for the whole economy.[7] The production of agricultural raw materials, after allowing for price changes, grew at a rate of 2.4 per cent a year in the 1950–1960 decade. Consumption of agricultural raw ma-

6. "Farm Operator Career Adjustments and Farm Policies," *A Statement by the National Planning Association Agriculture Committee on National Policy,* 1964, p. 2.

7. *National Economic Projections Series,* 1963, National Planning Association, p. I–23.

terials in the United States rose annually by only 1.2 per cent.[8] Consumers' expenditures for food in this period grew by about two thirds the percentage increase in total personal consumption expenditures.[9] Much of the growth in consumer spending for food, however, is attributable to the greater costs of marketing foods to consumers and to the demand for more elaborate processing services (e.g., frozen foods). Less than one fifth of family take-home pay has been spent for food, and this proportion has declined.[10] While exports amounting to $5 billion in 1963 helped to expand markets for farm output, crop production has continued to outrun demand in foreign and domestic markets.

The technological changes which have made this rising output possible have increased the capital requirements for an efficient farm. They have also drastically reduced the labor requirements. The capital invested in the average farm in 1940 was $6,000. By 1962, the corresponding figure, in current dollars, was $47,000.[11] Much of the increase in capital investment has been used to mechanize farm operations. Grain combines and cornpicking machines, for example, were five to seven times as numerous in 1960 as in 1940. The mechanical picker has replaced human labor in harvesting cotton. Materials handling has been mechanized by the use of farm grain elevators or automatic poultry feeders. These and similar changes have reduced the share of labor inputs in agricultural production by half from 1940 to 1960.[12]

Technological advance has tended to create a dual farm economy. Production and earning capacity have become

---

8. *Statistical Abstract*, 1964, p. 704.

9. *Annual Report of the Council of Economic Advisers*, January, 1965, p. 201.

10. President Johnson's Budget Message to Congress on Agriculture, April 5, 1965.

11. *Fact Book of U.S. Agriculture*, 1963, p. 6.

12. Fox, Ruttan, and Witt, *Farming, Farmers, and Markets for Farm Goods*, Committee for Economic Development, 1962, pp. 28–29, 35.

concentrated in the minority of farms with the capital, the skill, and the land to take advantage of new opportunities. Commercial farms with annual sales of $10,000 and over made up less than one third of all commercial farms in 1959. However, they were responsible for seven tenths of all sales of farm products. More than one fourth of all commercial farms had annual sales of less than $5,000. These farms accounted for one tenth of the sales of farm output.[13] Farm operator families on the farms with sales of more than $10,000 earned an annual average income of almost $10,000 including off-farm income. The corresponding family income for operators of the farms with sales of less than $5,000 was $3,450. Over two fifths of this income represented earnings from non-agricultural work.

While the main problems facing farm operators have been low income, unstable income, and underemployment, farm laborers earn lower incomes, and their occupation involves substantial seasonal work and unemployment. The median annual money earnings of male farm laborers in 1962 were $1,350—one of the lowest earnings figures reported for any occupation. Their unemployment rate, 9 per cent in 1963, was two thirds greater than in non-agricultural industries. Nearly one tenth of hired farm workers, according to a recent Department of Labor survey, reported that their "chief activity" during the year was unemployment.[14] Farm workers are excluded from coverage in most of the social legislation enacted since the 1930's. They do not benefit from such measures as unemployment compensation, Federal minimum wage laws, or workmen's compensation for occupational accidents or disease.

Farmers and farm laborers have been moving to urban centers and to non-farm employment since our nation was founded. The persons moving have been primarily young adults. In states such as West Virginia or Mississippi, some 50 per cent of the rural youth who were 10 to 17 years old

---

13. Derived from *Food and Agriculture,* p. 50.
14. *Manpower Report,* 1964, pp. 86, 88.

in 1950 had moved away from the rural areas of their state by 1960.[15] Migration of young adults has left the rural areas with a high proportion of their population under 18, or 65 and over. The individuals in these age groups are largely dependents who earn little income. However, meeting their minimum needs requires large state and local expenditures for education and social welfare.

The ability of the farm population to continue shifting to non-agricultural work in the next decade is likely to be limited, even in a growing economy, by rising educational and skill requirements in the occupations for which employment is expanding. The average number of years of schooling completed by farmers in 1964 was less than 9, compared to 12 years for persons in all occupation.[16] Rural high schools have typically paid little attention to vocational training for the mass of young people who must migrate to urban areas if they are to obtain employment. "Low producing farmers and inefficient farmers," according to the National Planning Association's report, "form perhaps the largest group of vocationally misfitted individuals in the nation."[17] Increasing opportunities for non-agricultural jobs will require an imaginative and large-scale effort in education and vocational training in the rural areas, and special consideration of rural needs in the nationwide programs for retraining and area or regional redevelopment.

III.

Expenditures for national objectives in agriculture have been primarily devoted to activities for improving farmers' income by encouraging the consumption of crop output or

15. *Ibid.*, pp. 80, 82.

16. This estimate refers to the median number of years of school completed by persons in the employed civilian labor force in March, 1964. More precisely, the figure for individuals in all occupational groups was 12.2 years, and the corresponding figure for farmers, farm managers, and farm laborers was 8.7 years. *Manpower Report*, 1965, p. 227.

17. "Farm Operator Career Adjustments and Farm Policies," National Planning Association, 1964, p. 3.

by limiting market supply. They have also included spending for programs of general benefit, such as research, technical assistance, or marketing services. Some of the expenditures for new programs in area redevelopment or manpower retraining also help to attain our goals in agriculture. Government programs which serve to increase the consumption of farm output—e.g., Food for Peace or the School Lunch Plan—contribute, in turn, to our national objectives in international aid, education, and social welfare.

The programs for directly or indirectly raising farm income, or for general support, or for encouraging the movement of farmers to non-agricultural employment, are financed by the Federal Government and very largely conducted by the Department of Agriculture.

Expenditures for 1962 are summarized in Table 15–1.

Table 15–1
U.S. Government Expenditures
in Support of Agriculture, 1962
(in millions of dollars)*

Program	Expenditures in 1962
1. To Limit Market Supply	$2,900
a. Price supports	1,300
b. Production adjustments	1,600
2. To Encourage Consumption	2,650
a. Foreign assistance programs	1,900
b. Export subsidies	250
c. School lunch, special milk programs	300
d. Perishable foods program	200
3. To Encourage Shifts Out of Agriculture	a
4. Research, Technical Assistance, Marketing Services	1,100
5. Farm Credit and Insurance	550
6. Total Expenditures	7,200

a. Includes expenditures for manpower retraining and area redevelopment estimated at less than $50 million.
* Derived from The Budget of the United States Government for Fiscal Year 1964 and various reports of the Department of Agriculture.

Much of the rapid increase in farm productivity is attributable to the research and technical assistance conducted by the Government. The Agricultural Research Service conducts studies in nutrition, industrial use of crops, development of improved crop strains or animal breeds, and eradication of plant and animal diseases. The findings of this research are disseminated to individual farmers through the Agricultural Extension Service. The Soil Conservation Service helps to apply new technology for keeping farm land and water resources permanently productive. Similarly, the Federal Government supplies credit and crop insurance on favorable terms to farmers.

The Government is obliged by law to protect farmers' incomes by supporting the prices of certain agricultural commodities such as wheat, cotton, or feed grains. The Commodity Credit Corporation, a public corporation, loans producers a sum equal to the support price of the commodity taking as collateral the output covered by the loan. If the market price fails to rise enough to prompt the farmer to redeem his loan, he can forfeit his collateral and keep the loan. To qualify for the price support assistance, a farmer must usually adhere to acreage allotments. Other measures taken in the recent past to reduce the amount of land planted in particular crops include the Conservation Reserve Program which rents land from farmers for 3 to 10 year periods and plants it in trees or grass. In return for transferring acreage to conservation uses, farmers producing wheat and feed grains have received both a higher support price, and a payment equal to about half the value of the normal production of the idled land.

The Government also carries out a variety of activities to expand the consumption of farm products in the United States and abroad. The Food for Peace program, Public Law 480, is an important form of economic aid to the developing nations. Exporters sell the supported commodities to the participating nations and payment is made in the country's own currency. The U.S. Government then pays the exporter in dollars and uses the local currency as a source of loan funds to promote economic development in the recipient country.

Export sales of suported commodities in dollar markets are also subsidized. Within the United States, the Government encourages consumption of the farm surplus through such forms of welfare assistance as the school lunch program or the Food Stamp Plan. Unsupported commodities, usually perishables, are acquired by the Government to offset temporary market gluts, and given to hospitals, schools, and other public institutions.

In addition to these measures specifically concerned with agriculture, the Federal Government has recently embarked on economywide programs which should encourage the employment of farmers and farm laborers outside of agriculture. Over 500 rural counties have qualified for assistance in the area redevelopment program.[18] In 1963, about 5 per cent of the persons enrolled in retraining courses sponsored by the manpower development and training administration were farmers or farm laborers.[19] The Vocational Education Act of 1963 and the Smaller Communities Program of the United States Employment Service are also intended, in part, to encourage the shift to non-agricultural employment.

The measures for encouraging mobility out of agriculture are, as yet, too new and too limited in scope to indicate more than significant possibilities for the future. The activities concerned with the supply-consumption balance have kept farm incomes and prices higher than they would otherwise have been since the Korean War. A recent study by economists at the Iowa and Oklahoma State Universities concludes that removing the controls from grain production would reduce net farm income from the $13.3 billion it constituted in 1962 to $7.6 billion in 1967.[20]

18. Levitan, S., *Federal Aid to Depressed Areas*, 1963, Ch. 3.

19. *Manpower Report*, 1964, p. 92.

20. See "A National Farm Program for Feed Grains and Wheat," *A Statement by the NPA Agriculture Committee on National Policy*, National Planning Association, 1964, p. 4.

IV.

Our goal in commercial agriculture is in keeping with President Johnson's basic policy objective that programs for the rural economy should develop an "opportunity for the efficient family farmer to earn parity of income from farming operations."[21] This we interpret to mean the objective of raising average family income for these farmers to a close approximation of family income levels in the non-agricultural economy in the next decade.

Five routes have been widely considered in the recent past for achieving this objective. Specifically, they are

1. Crop price supports and acreage allotments much as they existed in the early 1960's.

2. Direct control of farm output through quantity quotas —when feasible—rather than acreage allotments.

3. A greatly expanded land retirement program.

4. The Brannan Plan for direct support of farm income through public subsidies coupled with free market prices for agricultural commodities.

5. Expanding the consumption of American farm products abroad on a massive scale to ease the food deficits in the underdeveloped countries.

Cost estimates are presented for the first three alternatives. They are the options which relate to an economic environment in which public programs for influencing the supply of farm commodities, to quote the President again, "are the primary instrument which the farmer and the national economy use to cushion the force of the 'output revolution' " in agriculture.[22] To indicate the problems and the potentialities, the three alternatives are discussed as if they were independent measures. In practice, aspects of each would probably be combined into a unified program with greater or lesser emphasis on particular proposals.

---

21. Budget Message to Congress on Agriculture, April 5, 1965.
22. *Ibid.*

The costs for each of the supply alternatives represent the expenditures each would require to eliminate the surplus farm output in the next decade. The size of the surplus can be estimated by projecting the production and utilization of farm products to 1975. It is reasonable to anticipate that the productivity increases and the trends in consumption of farm products in the past decade will continue for the next ten years. Similarly, programs such as the conservation reserve plan would be part of all three alternatives. Food for Peace and research assistance to agriculture are likely to remain as national policy. While no great overall changes are expected in farm prices, because of technological improvements resulting in lower costs, income goals for farmers will probably be achieved with somewhat lower prices for some commodities.

The estimates of production, utilization, and surplus are in Table 15–2.

Table 15–2
Estimated Production and Utilization
of Farm Products, 1970 and 1975*
(in millions of 1962 dollars)[a]

Item	Estimated Production 1970	1975	Estimated Utilization[b] 1970	1975	Estimated Surplus 1970	1975
1. Crops	$25,650	$28,400	$23,500	$25,700	$2,150	$2,700
2. Livestock	22,000	24,550	22,000	24,550	0	0
3. Surplus as % of Production						
a. Crops					8.4%	9.5%
b. Livestock					—	—

a. Adjusted for a 10-per cent decrease in feed prices.
b. Includes estimated consumption of farm products resulting from public programs such as Food for Peace, School Lunch Plan, etc.
* The projections assume that *per capita* use of farm crop products will decrease by 5 per cent between 1960 and 1975, with livestock consumption increasing by 5 per cent, and per capita utilization of nonfood farm products falling by almost 25 per cent. Initial projections of production and utilization balances under constant prices showed a surplus for crops and a deficit for livestock. A deficit for livestock is unrealistic because no controls are assumed for the livestock sector and a balance would be achieved in this sector at higher livestock prices. But it may not be very realistic to assume that livestock prices would be allowed to rise very much unless production costs rose. Here, we anticipate that feed prices would be allowed to decline by about 10 per cent so that livestock production would probably expand sufficiently to match projected consumption.

As in the past decade, the surplus in the 1970's is expected to be one of crop output. The three routes for eliminating the surplus are discussed briefly below.

Price Supports

The Government, in the price support proposal, in effect purchases the surplus, paying one dollar for each dollar of excess supply taken off the market. To restrict the size of the surplus, price supports would be supplemented by acreage allotments to individual farmers and by the Conservation Reserve Program. The Government would also incur costs for storing the surplus crops, for shipping the commodities to storage points and to subsequent users, and for interest on the funds tied up in the stored products. These carrying charges amounted to almost $1 billion a year in the early 1960's. The projected costs for the price support program are listed in Table 15–3.

Table 15–3
Estimated Expenditures for Price Support Alternative, 1970 and 1975
(in millions of 1962 dollars)[a]

Item	Projected Expenditures 1970	1975
1. Cost of Loans to Absorb Surplus	$2,150	$2,700
2. Storage, Transportation, and Interest	1,100	1,400
3. Conservation Reserve Program	350	350
4. Cost of Price Supports Program	3,600	4,450

a. Adjusted for 10-per cent decrease in feed prices.

The cost of implementing the price support program is estimated to amount to almost $4.5 billion a year by 1975. Without a more effective form of output control than acreage allotments, price supports are likely to defeat their purpose by encouraging an ever increasing production per acre to be turned over to the Government and added to the surplus. The next alternative considered, direct control of output, would eliminate the problem of surplus at its source.

Output Control

The first step in setting up an output control program would be a review of production history to establish a nationwide production base for each crop and an individual production base for each farmer. In advance of the year's planting, the administering agency would estimate the quantity of each crop which would clear the market at the desired price, generally an approximation of the present support price. This total would be distributed by issuing marketing certificates to individual farmers indicating their quotas for the year in terms of quantity of product. A penalty tax would be levied on farmers who marketed in excess of the quota.

Output control would be far less expensive for the Government than price supports since no public payments to farmers and no carrying cost for the inventory of surplus output would be incurred. Assuming the administrative costs amounted to $150 million a year, and the Conservation Reserve Program were continued, total expenditures would amount to $500 million in 1975. The gains in farm income, under this alternative, would be financed through the market by raising prices to consumers.

Land Retirement

Direct control of output probably has too many resemblances to the cartel techniques of other nations to win widespread acceptance in the United States. Land retirement offers a third alternative for reducing the supply of crop output. It is essentially a combination of income supports for farmers and conservation measures. The Acreage and Conservation Reserve Program of the recent past are instances of the land retirement approach.

Two difficulties which plagued the earlier programs are likely to influence future land retirement plans. Not enough land was retired to put a significant dent in crop production; farmers receiving rental payments to retire part of their crop land increased the intensity of cultivation of the remaining land. To offset these difficulties, an effective land retirement program would involve the retirement of entire farms or of all the crop land on a farm. This would generally be done by leases running from three to ten years. Since there is a serious shortage of land for outdoor recreational areas, part of this land could be purchased by the Government, together with other land, for conversion to recreational uses.

The surplus projected for 1975 amounts to about 10 per cent of crop output. Because much of the acreage taken out of production would be land of less than average productivity, it would probably be necessary to retire 13 or 14 per cent of the crop acreage to reduce output by 10 per cent. This is estimated to require the retirement of 53 million acres of land in 1975. Purchasing 3 million acres annually, leasing the remainder, and continuing the Conservation Reserve Program is expected to cost $2.5 billion a year in the mid-1970's.[23]

If the farms on the land taken out of cultivation averaged 200 acres, approximately 250,000 farms would be withdrawn from production in 1975. The families living on these farms could utilize their income from leasing land to acquire additional education and training, or to finance their migration to other areas and to nearby cities. The rental would

---

23. Total crop acreage is projected to remain at 355 million acres as in 1960. Since leasing or purchasing whole farms would involve acquiring some land that was not used for crops, it is assumed that one acre of other land is acquired for every ten acres of crop land. Leasing 50 million acres at roughly 60 per cent of the expected gross returns in the 1970's, or $32 an acre, and purchasing 3 million acres at an expected price of $183 per acre is the basis for our estimate. The Conservation Reserve program would continue as an auxiliary measure costing $350 million.

also enable many older farmers, now eking out an existence on poor land, to retire.

The alternatives considered for eliminating the crop surplus make it apparent that our society has options in selecting programs for achieving national objectives in agriculture. The alternative which is likely to be most effective and least costly—output control—would also introduce maximum government intervention in the farm economy. The plan which entails the least direct government influence on farm inputs or outputs—price supports—is also the least effective and most costly of the three. Output control and land retirement could create a serious loss of employment for farm laborers. Land retirement is the proposal with the broadest scope, since it would finance the movement of farmers out of agriculture as well as reduce excess production.

By 1970, alternatives to the supply-oriented options may include proposals similar to the Brannan Plan, or far-reaching programs for expanding the utilization of American farm products in the developing nations. Two thirds of the world's population, according to a Department of Agriculture report in 1964, live in countries with nutritionally inadequate average diets. The deficit is very largely concentrated in the underdeveloped nations. The report estimates that a world food deficit valued at $6.8 billion will still exist in 1970.[24] Supplying American farm products to ease the food deficits abroad would absorb much, if not most, of the crop surplus in the United States. The arrangements could take the form of international agreements, perhaps sponsored by the United Nations, for making the farm surpluses in advanced nations available at low cost to developing nations with chronic shortages of food and agricultural raw materials. "Commercial agriculture in the United States and Canada," according to *Goals for Americans*, "eventually will be compelled to adopt extremely strict

---

24. *The World Food Budget, 1970*, USDA, 1964, p. iii.

controls if it cannot find better ways of making its surpluses useful to the world."[25]

V.

To eliminate the crop surplus, the alternatives for reducing market supply would be concentrated in the part of the agricultural economy which produces most of the output—the larger commercial farms. The operators of these farms could be expected to receive the bulk of the direct benefits from price supports, or output control, and, to a lesser extent and more subject to policy considerations, from land retirement.

Our basic objective for the marginal farmers and the low-income and unemployed farm laborers is summed up in the statement by the National Planning Association's Agriculture Committee that "in the long run the best way to combat low-income farming and rural poverty is to attract youth who have poor opportunities in farming into nonfarming occupations."[26] For the low-income farmers and farm laborers who remain in agriculture, the problems are part of the nationwide problem of poverty. It is reasonable to expect that the remedies for rural poverty will be similar to those proposed for other low-income groups—raising productivity through more widespread educational and training opportunities, liberalized social insurance benefits or inclusion in social insurance coverage, or the family allowances discussed in connection with goals in social welfare (see Chapter 5).

The U.S. Department of Labor estimates that employment in agriculture will decline from 5.2 million in 1962 to 3.9 million by 1975.[27] The number of persons in the farm labor

25. Soth, L. K., "Farm Policies for the Sixties," in *Goals for Americans,* The American Assembly, 1960, p. 221.

26. *Farm Operator Career Adjustments and Farm Policies,* National Planning Association, 1964, p. 1.

27. *Manpower Report,* 1964, pp. 197, 224.

force who must find jobs elsewhere in this span of time will be greater than the anticipated 1.3 million decrease in employment. Because of population growth, and the presence of a large pool of unemployed and underemployed farmers and farm laborers in the mid-1960's, probably double the 1.3 million figure, or about 2-1/2 million non-agricultural jobs will be needed to absorb the surplus farm labor between 1962 and 1975. This amounts to an average of 200,000 additional jobs a year.

The possibilities for devising programs to facilitate these transfers out of agriculture are illustrated by the manpower retraining and area redevelopment programs (see Chapters 16 and 17). Taking into account both public and private expenditures, it would require an estimated redevelopment program outlay of $225 million a year to create 25,000 additional non-agricultural jobs for farmers and farm laborers through area redevelopment.[28] Retraining 2 per cent of the rural labor force a year, or double the percentage in the national objective for the retraining goal, would qualify an additional 80,000 farmers and farm laborers annually for jobs as mechanics, home appliance repairmen, or in other occupations with good employment prospects. Subsistence and instructional allowances for this retraining can be expected to amount to $175 million. For an expenditure of $400 million in 1970 and 1975 for the two programs, slightly more than 100,000 persons a year would be assisted in making the shift out of agriculture.

Payments to farm families from the land retirement program might encourage another 40,000 to 50,000 persons to transfer annually to other employment. The importance of a high level of activity in the non-agricultural economy for all

---

28. This estimate refers to capital outlays for the redevelopment program. Average capital outlay per job is listed to be $15,000. However, for every 100 jobs created directly by redevelopment, 65 jobs are assumed to be indirectly created as a result of the greater spending brought about by the program. This reduces the anticipated area redevelopment program outlay for each job created to $9,000.

of these measures is demonstrated by the experience of the 1950's. In the recession periods of the decade, the migration out of agriculture fell to less than 3 per cent of the farm population. In the peaks of economic activity, the migration rate rose to a level of 5 to 8 per cent.[29]

Migration of the marginal farmers and farm laborers out of agriculture, together with the three alternatives considered for eliminating the surplus crop output, would raise the income of families remaining in agriculture. We cannot know in advance how many persons will shift to non-agricultural employment in the next decade. However, if the population of commercial farm families were reduced from the 2.4 million reported in the last agricultural census in 1959 to 1.3 or 1.4 million by 1975, the average income of commercial farm families is projected to rise to an estimated $11,000 a year by the mid-1970's. This is approximately the same income projected for non-farm families, not counting individuals living by themselves as statistical "families." There would be increases in income of a similar magnitude for the greatly diminished number of farm laborers.

VI.

The cost estimates for our goals in agriculture are listed in Table 15–4.

Expenditures for our goals in agriculture are projected to range between $5 billion and $9 billion a year in the 1970's. Since the estimates including output control represent a minimum level of spending for national objectives in the rural economy, they also constitute our hypothetical pre-empted benchmark projection of the minimum cost of continuing the agricultural programs in the coming decade.

The dollar totals listed indicate that expenditures in support of agriculture are likely to constitute a declining claim on GNP in the next ten years. Even for the alternative in-

---

29. *Farming, Farmers, and Markets for Farm Goods,* p. 100.

cluding price supports, the only one listing larger spending in 1975 than in 1962, expenditures would decline from the 1.3 per cent of GNP the agricultural programs represented in 1962 to 0.9 per cent by the mid-1970's. Among all 16 goals, spending for the aspiration standards is projected to fall as a percentage of GNP for only two—agriculture and national defense. This prospective change is a symptom of the diminishing role of agriculture in an industrial and urban economy.

While the estimates for agriculture include expenditures for a variety of measures extending from rural area redevelopment to price supports, they are an incomplete representation of the overall expenditures required to cope with the problems of the rural economy. Per capita expenditures and performance in education, health, and social welfare in the

Table 15–4
Estimated Expenditures for Agricultural Goal, 1970 and 1975
(in millions of 1962 dollars)[a]

| | | PROJECTED EXPENDITURES FOR ALTERNATIVE INCLUDING | | | | | |
| | Expenditures in | Price Supports | | Land Retirement | | Output Control | |
Program	1962	1970	1975	1970	1975	1970	1975
1. To Limit Market Supply	$2,900	$3,600	$4,450	$2,200	$2,550	$ 500	$ 500
2. To Encourage Consumption	2,650	2,650	2,650	2,650	2,650	2,650[b]	2,650[b]
3. To Encourage Shifts Out of Agriculture	—	400	400	400	400	400	400
4. Research, Technical Assistance, Marketing Services	1,100	1,100	1,100	1,100	1,100	1,100	1,100
5. Farm Credit and Insurance	550	550	550	550	550	550	550
6. Total Expenditures	7,200	8,300	9,150	6,900	7,250	5,200	5,200
7. Expenditures as % of GNP	1.3%	1.1%	0.9%	0.9%	0.7%	0.7%	0.5%

a. Adjusted for a 10-per cent decrease in feed prices.
b. While programs for encouraging consumption need not be part of an output control program, they are included because measures such as Food for Peace also figure as part of other goals such as international aid.

rural areas generally lag behind national levels. Creating parity of opportunity for farmers, farm laborers, and their families would also involve expenditures to eliminate these differentials. The costs of achieving this kind of parity are included in the expenditures discussed in connection with the relevant goals (see Chapters 5, 6, and 7).

Technological change has transformed the small family farmer into a commercial farm operator requiring sizeable capital resources and specialized skills to survive. It has sharply reduced the total number of farmers needed to produce the nation's food and agricultural raw materials. "The momentum of the current technical revolution [in agriculture] is such," according to a recent study by two agricultural economists, V. W. Ruttan and J. C. Callahan, "that it is reasonable to expect the production of 1975 farm output requirements with little or no rise in total inputs."[30] In particular, fewer farm inputs will probably represent human resources. Our goal in agriculture is concerned with reversing the tendency for this decline to be translated into poverty, unemployment, and lack of opportunity in agriculture.

---

30. Ruttan and Callahan, "Resource Inputs and Growth: Comparisons between Agriculture and Forestry." *Forest Science*, March, 1962, p. 68.

CHAPTER 16

Manpower
Retraining

I.

Retraining to equip the unemployed with skills that are in demand in a rapidly changing labor market is a strategic national objective for combatting unemployment and poverty. Recognition of the potential for developing human resources through retraining has led Congress to enact the Manpower Development and Training Act of 1962. Experience with retraining is little more than a few years old, and expenditures in 1962 and 1963 have averaged approximately $100 million a year. Expenditures for achieving our goals in retraining and for basic literacy education for the unemployed are projected to increase to $2.9 billion in 1975.

The need for retraining and for improved vocational training exists at many different levels of the labor force. Recent scientific and technical advances have made much of the professional education of the older generation of engineers obsolete. Developments associated with electronic data processing and computers have outmoded much of the traditional recordkeeping work done by clerks in banks and corporate offices. They are also likely to outmode many of the functions performed in the past by individuals in middle management. The nation's commitment to massive R & D expenditures has created a demand for large numbers of sub-professional technicians which is only partially satisfied by the existing vocational education system. Training and retraining programs to assist individuals in a variety of occupations to adapt to changing labor market requirements can be expected to involve many institutions including university centers for continuation education, corporation training programs, high schools, post-high school technical institutes, and community colleges.

The retraining associated with the Manpower Development and Training Act is intended for "blue collar" or clerical workers who are unemployed. Coupled with remedial education, it also aids individuals who are presently unemployable because of lack of literacy and experience with the world of work along with an absence of job skills. Effective programs for converting the unskilled unemployed—the social dynamite of our central cities—into productive wage earners will require coordination of the community's resources for training, education, and social service in order to reach individuals currently at the margin of society.

Since World War II, economic changes affecting some industries and areas have reduced employment opportunities for workers without regard to skill. Rising productivity in agriculture has diminished the labor force employed in this sector of the economy from 8 million persons in 1949 to under 5 million in 1964.[1] Workers in declining industries, such as the railroads or coal mining, are confronted with curtailed opportunities to use skills which are often peculiar to their industry. Unemployment has consistently exceeded

---

1. *Manpower Report of the President,* 1965, p. 200.

the national average in areas bypassed by economic advance;
i.e., Appalachia.

Unemployment, however, has been concentrated in occupations with few skill requirements. The significance of skill
level in relation to unemployment is summarized in Table
16–1.

Table 16–1
Unemployment by Occupational Skill Levels, 1960 and 1964*

	Per cent of Workers Unemployed	
Occupational Group	1960	1964
1. Entire Civilian Labor Force	5.6%	5.2%
2. Professional and Technical Occupations	1.7	1.7
3. Skilled Craftsmen	5.3	4.2
4. Semi-skilled Operatives	8.0	6.5
5. Laborers[a]	12.5	10.6

a. Except farm and mine.
* Manpower Report, 1965, p. 207.

Older workers, nonwhites, and very young wage earners
are the groups of individuals most heavily subjected to unemployment. They are also the groups characterized by low
levels of skill and education. Older workers tend to be employed in occupations, industries, and areas which are declining. Having once lost their jobs, their lack of the skills
currently in demand often leads to prolonged periods of
unemployment or to withdrawal from the labor force by
early retirement. Negroes are frequently barred from employment because of inadequate training and education as
well as by discrimination. Young workers in the 14 to 19 age
group are largely, but not exclusively, school dropouts. Nonwhites in this age group probably have the highest rate of
joblessness of any group in the nation. Their unemployment
rate of 26 per cent in 1964 was double the figure for white
teenagers.[2]

2. Manpower Report, 1965, p. 197.

As the pace of technological change accelerates, there is an increasing likelihood that individuals who already possess job skills will need to learn two or more occupations during their working life. According to one authority, Dr. James E. Russell of the National Education Association, "In vocational training we are facing a situation where we cannot tell whether a given form of training will carry a man as much as 10 years in time."[3] For these individuals, and for persons without job skills, retraining offers an opportunity to enter productive employment without disastrously prolonged or repeated spells of unemployment.

Training and education are obviously related, and lack of either is a severe occupational handicap. They differ in their objectives and in the implications of the absence of each for manpower policy. Training is the first phase of the learning process by which a person acquires a particular occupational skill. Education conveys information, concepts, techniques, and habits of thinking which are useful in many pursuits. A sufficient educational basis is essential for an adequate occupational adjustment, including the absorption of training. In higher education, where occupational perspectives are directed at professional, technical, and managerial positions, preparation for specific occupations includes a large amount of general education. Training in the retraining programs is at the sub-collegiate level. These programs have typically offered courses lasting less than a year and oriented toward a specific occupation for which job vacancies exist.

Retraining programs, or improved training generally, are only a partial solution for unemployment. One obvious cause of unemployment is an insufficient growth in demand for goods and services. If GNP were to grow, as in the 1950's, at about 3 per cent a year, unemployment by 1975 would be expected to reach 10 per cent of the labor force or more.[4]

---

3. *Hearings*, Subcommittee on Employment and Manpower, U.S. Senate, 1963, Part 6, p. 2009.

4. *National Economic Projections to 1974*, National Planning Association, 1964, p. 28.

Retraining in this situation is likely to lead to employment for a few selected individuals in the minority of growth occupations, and to newly acquired unutilized skills for others. The remedies for unemployment caused by inadequate growth in demand are to be sought in monetary and fiscal policies for increasing effective demand. Unemployment may also be caused by rigidities in the structure of labor markets—arbitrary age limits in hiring, retirement plans tending to discourage new hirings, racial discrimination, unrealistic hiring specifications by employers, or an unwillingness to relocate by employees. While Government policy must deal with these causes, training would be of little use in combatting them.

In a growing economy, retraining makes for more rapid growth. It also helps to check inflation. Bottlenecks in industries, which would otherwise arise because of a shortage of skilled labor, are prevented from materializing. Employment of the formerly unemployed workers adds to output, and the feedback effects as they spend their incomes increases the national income by several times the amount of their wages and salaries. As job opportunties expand, expenditures for public assistance and unemployment compensation decline and applications for early retirement diminish. These tangible economic gains add to the social and psychological benefits of being gainfully employed.

Part of the utility of training lies in its potential for supplying skills which are in demand. Training also provides credentials of entrance-level proficiency in particular jobs to persons who may otherwise be unable to demonstrate their fitness for an opening. In this event, to quote Nils Kellgren, a member of the Swedish Parliament and an authority on labor market policies, "training means . . . placing a label on a person. With this label, he is invited to the working life and is accepted."[5] By training an unem-

---

5. Kellgren, N., "An Active Labor Market Policy," *Memorandum to the Secretary*, U.S. Department of Labor, 1963, p. 61.

ployed person to the level needed to demonstrate qualifications to enter a job, he gains occupational mobility and a job, and the employer's demands for labor are met.

Retraining, as in the Manpower Development and Training Act (MDTA), holds out both a promise and a danger. The promise is that of restoring occupational purpose, productivity, and income to persons otherwise excluded from economic opportunity. The danger is that too much may be expected from a program with a limited purpose without recognition of the condition which is necessary for its success—a dynamic economy.

II.

The public programs concerned with retraining the unemployed are the Area Redevelopment Act (ARA) of 1961 and the Manpower Development and Training Act of 1962. Both laws require a reasonable expectation of employment in the occupation for which the person is to be trained. Both favor the selection of trainees who are unemployed.[6]

The training programs authorized under the Area Redevelopment Act in 1962 have been largely pilot projects confined to redevelopment areas. Unlike the ARA retraining, MDTA programs may be conducted in all parts of the country without regard to their status as redevelopment or depressed areas. Since the future programs are likely to follow the MDTA pattern, the experience with this program and its objectives supplies the basis for the standards in our retraining goal.

The overall objective of MDTA is to enable selected unemployed persons to undertake short-term training by providing facilities, instruction, and subsistence allowances for

---

6. More recently, the nationwide concern with the heavy unemployment rate among high school dropouts has led, in the Economic Opportunity Act of 1964, to establishment of two additional work-training programs for young people—the Job Corps and the Neighborhood Youth Corps. The two programs are outside the MDTA framework.

the trainees. The U.S. Employment Service selects the trainees, verifies the need for training in a particular occupation, and places persons in jobs after the training is completed. Instructors, equipment, and course curricula are generally obtained by utilizing the resources of the local vocational educational system. On-the-job training under MDTA utilizes space, equipment, and instructional materials supplied by employers. Only about 6 per cent of the first 100,000 MDTA trainees were enrolled in on-the-job training programs.[7]

The average length of training in the first fifteen months of the MDTA program was 23 weeks. The subsistence allowances paid trainees typically amounted to $35 a week.[8] Special subsistence and transportation allowances are authorized for persons training at a place beyond normal commuting distance. Expenditures in the first year of the MDTA program, and for ARA retraining in fiscal year 1963, are summarized in Table 16–2.

Table 16–2
Vocational Retraining Under the ARA and MDTA, Fiscal Year 1963
(dollar amounts are in 1962 dollars)

Item	ARA	MDTA[a]
1. Number of Trainees	13,700	71,400
2. Total Expenditures (in million dollars)	$7.0	$87.0
3. Average Expenditure per Trainee[b]	550	1,220
a. For instruction	247	575
b. For allowances	303	645

a. Covers period mid-August 1962 to August 31, 1963.
b. These expenditures do not include administrative costs, which amounted to approximately $300 per trainee for MDTA trainees and $150 for ARA trainees.

Expenditures for retraining in both of these programs have been small. However, by the end of 1964 training projects

7. Levitan, S., *Federal Manpower Policies and Programs to Combat Unemployment*, The W. E. Upjohn Institute for Employment Research, 1964, p. 24.
8. *Ibid.*, p. 16.

had been approved for almost 360,000 persons. Three fourths of the trainees who had completed their courses by mid-1964 had been placed in jobs within four months after finishing training, four fifths of them in jobs related to their training.[9] In the few years in which the program has been in operation, retraining has demonstrated its potential for developing skills needed by employers and for contributing to the increase in the economy's output.

The initial programs have tended to be selective in the occupations trained for and in the persons chosen for training. About half the trainees in the first year were preparing for five occupational fields—clerical, machine operators, practical nurses or nurses aides, automobile mechanics and repair, and welding.[10] Poorly educated and older workers were underrepresented among the trainees. To broaden the scope of the program, Congress amended the law in 1963 and reduced eligibility requirements. In addition, a basic literacy education program extending up to 20 weeks was added to the vocational training. In the 1965 Manpower Act, Congress raised the maximum training period from one to two years in order to enable MDTA to prepare workers in technical occupations requiring more extensive training.

In 1964, the Senate Subcommittee on Employment and Manpower summarized its study of retraining by observing that "years of neglect accompanied by rapid change have created a backlog of the untrained, the poorly educated, and those with obsolete skills."[11] It was apparent to the Committee that the educational system, including adult and technical education, would continue to be responsible for basic skill acquisition. Most of the training in specific jobs skills, the Committee recognized, would be furnished by private employers. The purpose of MDTA, according to the Com-

9. *Manpower Report*, 1965, p. 128.

10. Levitan, p. 17.

11. "Toward Full Employment: Proposals for a Comprehensive Employment and Manpower Policy in the United States," *Report*, Subcommittee on Employment and Manpower, U.S. Senate, 1964.

mittee, was to concentrate specialized resources on the difficult manpower problems bypassed by the more general
programs.

III.

Experience with manpower retraining in the United States
has been too limited for a consensus to emerge regarding the
appropriate number of trainees or the types of training
needed. The 85,000 persons enrolled in retraining under
ARA or MDTA auspices in fiscal year 1962–63 made up 1/8
of 1 per cent of the civilian labor force. This total reflects
the initial experience with a new program rather than an
indication of objectives.

In its budget request for 1965, the Administration submitted plans to retrain approximately 275,000 persons a
year, or 3/8 of 1 per cent of the labor force.[12] This proportion is a more adequate representation of present targets for
the scope of retraining than the 1962–1963 experience. Accordingly, it constitutes the basis for our hypothetical preempted benchmark in retraining, the yardstick for estimating
the cost of continuing the *status quo* for another decade.

At the 1964 unemployment rate of slightly over 5 per cent
of the labor force, the Administration's budget proposal
would provide retraining for one out of every 13 or 14 of
the unemployed each year. As the full effects of technological change and the impact of large numbers of younger
persons seeking jobs make themselves evident, it is likely
that our objectives in retraining will be expanded further.

The experience of Sweden offers a guidepost for assessing
the magnitudes involved in an extended training program
in the United States for the 1970's. Nils Kellgren, the Swedish labor market expert who served as a research consultant

---

12. Actual appropriations by Congress for retraining in fiscal 1965 were
about three fourths of the sum requested by the Administration. The number of trainees therefore was limited to approximately 200,000 rather than
the expected 275,000.

for the U.S. Secretary of Labor in the early 1960's, has suggested that "the Swedish experience shows . . . there is an annual total training need of 1 percentage of the labor force."[13]

Sweden boasts one of the most succesful records of all the democratic nations in maintaining full employment and in devising manpower policies to serve national needs. Sweden has been moving resolutely toward the 1 per cent goal. In 1962, about 0.6 of 1 per cent of the Swedish labor force received retraining. Plans for 1963 involve programs for some 25,000 trainees, or 0.7 of 1 per cent of the work force.[14]

The civilian labor force in the United States is expected to grow to 83 million persons in 1970 and to 91 million by 1975. Accepting the 1 per cent standard as a reasonable objective for the United States in the coming decade would mean increasing the employability of 800,000 or 900,000 unemployed individuals a year through retraining in the 1970's. If unemployment declined to 4 per cent of the labor force, a widely held target rate in the early 1960's, one fourth of the unemployed would be equipped with new job skills each year. At the 1964 rate of 5 per cent, the corresponding ratio would be one fifth.

Retraining on this massive scale is more likely to be successful if the allowances are sufficient to enable the trainees to continue their non-deferrable expenditures for food, rent, and medical expenses while in training. These expenditures could probably be covered if the allowances were half the typical loss of wages for the unemployed in each state.[15] To provide realistic up-to-date training in automated processes and in complex machine and repair techniques, instructional costs per trainee are also likely to increase—an increase estimated at half. Larger expenditures for research would also be necessary to devise more effective techniques for

13. *An Active Labor Market Policy*, p. 61.

14. *Ibid.*, p. 63.

15. Like productivity per worker, the subsistence allowances are assumed to increase by 3 per cent a year.

teaching and motivating unskilled and semiliterate unemployed adults. The techniques developed in the course of
this research and instruction, in turn, could help transform
the outmoded vocational education offered by many school
systems, and they could be adopted by employers in their
company training programs.

IV.

For the hard core unemployed and unemployables who
lack both job skills and basic literacy, training, by itself, is
not enough and is likely to constitute an uncompleted dead
end. The need for adapting programs such as retraining to
the special problems and the culture of the hard core is
underscored by a survey, sponsored by MDTA, of unemployed unskilled Negroes in a training course in Norfolk,
Virginia.

The survey notes that "the older males are steadily displaced from muscle jobs by automation and rationalized
ways of doing things. . . . The young men . . . cannot get
the crucial first job."[16] Yet the individuals surveyed had almost unanimously rejected the initial invitation to apply
for training. Subsistence allowances averaging $27 a week
discouraged unemployed workers with families. There was
great difficulty in identifying and establishing contact with
potential applicants since, to these individuals, "word that
someone is tracing them means a grim guess as to whether it
is a bill collector or one of the many arms of the law." Before
social service assistance was added to the program, personal
and family troubles prompted many of the trainees to become training dropouts—to leave before the course was completed. Trainees who finished the course began to find work
after they had learned to read and write.

Programs offering training for well-qualified applicants,
the MDTA study points out, "in fact ignore the most dis-

---

16. *The New York Times,* May 24, 1963, I., pp. 1, 40.

advantaged, service the most . . . promising and increase the gap . . . between those at the top and those at the bottom of the barrel of the lower class." The authors conclude that the needs of the unskilled unemployed require a multidimensional program combining training, literacy education, and social service assistance. These findings encouraged Congress to amend MDTA in 1963 by authorizing basic literacy education for the unemployed.

If half the trainees in the work loads projected for the 1-per cent target in the 1970's were unskilled semiliterate workers selected for the combined program, over 400,000 persons a year would be receiving basic education prior to entering vocational training, and social service aid along with both programs. Costs per student for literacy education and social service assistance would probably be less than for job training because the basic education course is typically shorter, and less equipment and facilities are required.

The costs estimated for the aspiration standard for the retraining goal, including the special programs for the unskilled, are listed in Table 16–3 (see page 318). The table also indicates the hypothetical preempted benchmark expenditures for continuing the retraining targets of the mid-1960's for the next ten years.

Total spending for the retraining goal is estimated to rise to $2.9 billion by 1975. This is almost $2.5 billion more than the cost of continuing the level of training envisaged by the Administration in the mid-1960's for another decade. Measured by GNP, the cost of introducing the greater labor market flexibility and the second chance opportunities represented by retraining are small—less than 1/3 of 1 per cent of GNP.

Retraining offers an opportunity to reduce unemployment and increase productivity by developing the talents of individuals. In this sense, retraining is an extension of the educational system in one of the areas where the schools have adapted least to the changes in our society—in vocational education. It also constitutes an alternative to reliev-

Table 16–3
Estimated Expenditures for Retraining Goal,
1970 and 1975
(in 1962 dollars)

Item	Projected Expenditures 1970	Projected Expenditures 1975
1. Retraining		
a. Average expenditures per trainee	$2,030	$2,200
for instruction	865	865
for allowances	1,165	1,335
b. Total expenditures (in millions)	1,690	2,000
2. Special Programs for the Unskilled		
a. Average expenditures per trainee	1,630	1,760
for literacy instruction	500	500
for social service aid	200	200
for allowances	930	1,060
b. Total expenditures (in millions)	685	800
3. Manpower Research Program (in millions)	50	60
4. Total Expenditures for Retraining Goal[a] (in millions)	2,425	2,860
5. Preempted Benchmark Expenditures (in millions)	390	420

a. These expenditures exclude administrative costs which are estimated to add about 20 per cent to the cost of the retraining goal.

ing poverty and joblessness through public welfare assistance and unemployment compensation. The greatest difficulty and challenge in retraining lies in reaching the hard core unskilled unemployed. Successful retraining presupposes an environment of vigorous economic growth with a sufficiently large volume of job openings to absorb the graduates of the program.

CHAPTER 17

Area
Redevelopment

I.

Area redevelopment is a program for preserving the nation's economic and human capital. Our goal for the depressed areas is to reduce substantially the concentrations of unemployment and underemployment which characterize the pockets of poverty in the United States by creating 100,000 jobs a year through redevelopment in the next decade. Achieving this objective is projected to require the mobilization of public and private, and national and local resources amounting to $1 billion annually in the 1970's.

The objective of redevelopment is to change the alternatives available to the inhabitants of the depressed areas and to their communities. Redevelopment offers an alternative to the continued exodus of the population to other areas. For many of the individuals who remain, the program creates possibilities for full-time work rather than part-time and poorly paid jobs, public assistance, or retirement on small pensions. For the depressed communities, redevelopment renews aspirations along with finances. Plans for education or other community services, discarded earlier as too costly for impoverished local governments, become realistic options for implementation as local finances revive. Translating these possibilities into reality is likely to require area redevelopment, programs for regional development, and national policies for encouraging economic growth.

The depressed areas are often former centers of prosperity which have lost their economic base. Scranton, Pennsylvania, suffering from cutbacks in anthracite coal mining, is an instance. Others—the southeastern rural depressed areas for example—have never developed an economic base capable of yielding a standard of living comparable to that of the rest of the United States. The distinguishing characteristics of these areas are their unemployment and underemployment, low per capita incomes, and a less-than-average percentage of the adult population in the labor force.

The economic profile which defined areas as "depressed" is summarized in Table 17-1. The table compares the redevelopment areas with the entire United States.

Declining employment opportunties set in motion a downward spiral of depression. As young people leave for work elsewhere, old persons and school-age children come to make up a disproportionate part of the area's population. Individuals in these age groups require community services for education and welfare, but they can contribute little to community revenues. Shrinking business activity and employment lead to diminished property values and a reduced tax base. Local units of government soon discover they lack the means to finance their needs for education and public assistance. As public revenues fall, local governments lose their ability to borrow long-term funds for improvements in roads, water systems, or sewage treatment plants to attract new industries. The former well-paying industrial or mining jobs are replaced by low-paying unstable jobs with marginal firms attracted by the large pool of unemployed persons in the area. A low level of community services and a work force with an overrepresentation of older and poorly educated individuals make more substantial firms reluctant to establish plants in these areas.[1]

Table 17–1
Economic Profiles, Redevelopment Areas and
the Entire United States, Selected Recent Years*

Item	Redevelopment Areas	Entire United States
1. Unemployment Rate, 1960	7.4%[a]	5.1%
2. Per Cent Change in Employment, 1950–1960	— 10.4%[b]	11.8%
3. Per Cent of Adult Population in Labor Force, 1960[c]	51.5%	55.3%
4. Net Migration, 1950–1960	— 10.9%	2.0%
5. Per Cent of Housing Units Listed as Substandard, 1960	30.0%[b]	17.0%
6. Average Value of Farm Lands and Buildings, 1959	$15,350[d]	$34.800
7. Per Capita Income, 1959	$ 1,500	$ 1,850
8. Local Government Revenues per Inhabitant, 1957	$ 113[b]	$ 142

a. All urban redevelopment areas.
b. Based on 30 urban redevelopment areas.
c. "Population" refers to total population 14 years of age or older.
d. Based on 34 rural areas.
e. See Chapter 10, Table 10-1.
* Levitan, S., *Federal Aid to Depressed Areas*, 1964, Tables 3-5, 3-7, 3-9, 3-11, 3-15, 3-17. 3-17.

Economic and social reasons have combined to prompt the decision to encourage redevelopment. Most, if not all, of the areas have some resource or economic advantage capable of being profitably exploited. These resources may include

1. According to a recent study sponsored by ARA, almost 40 per cent of the population in the urban redevelopment areas had a grade school education or less, compared with 27 per cent in the areas not designated as redevelopment areas. Forty per cent of the population in urban redevelopment areas were 55 or older, compared to 33 per cent in the non-redevelopment areas. Mueller, E., Barth, N., and Ladd, W., *Migration Into and Out of Depressed Areas*, Area Redevelopment Administration, U.S. Department of Commerce, 1964, Charts 5 and 6.

the skills of their inhabitants, advantages of location, natural resources, or potential tourist attractions. The depressed areas are made up of established communities with functioning governments, civic organizations, and churches. Extensive social capital has been invested in more prosperous periods in local roads, utilities, and other public facilities.

For their inhabitants, the areas constitute a link with familial traditions and personal associations which are often not uprooted without serious social loss. Many of the roots of American folk-culture and much of our nation's history lie in what are now redevelopment areas. They include the Kentucky mountain people with their folk music and Elizabethan speech, and the culture and handicrafts of the Indians still living on reservations.

Outmigration from the depressed areas can probably not be stopped, nor would it be desirable to halt the movement of the labor force to centers of expanding economic opportunity. Redevelopment proceeds on the assumption that the outmigration can frequently be reduced, if not reversed, by utilizing the actual or potential resources of these areas to promote the development of new or more productive job opportunities. What the area programs attempt to offer is an alternative to the choice of moving to boom towns or continuing to live in ghost towns.

II.

Since the Area Dedevelopment Act became law as recently as 1961, experience with the program has been brief. Appropriations have been modest and especially so in relation to the large number of areas which have been designated for redevelopment. While the scope of the redevelopment program has been changed by legislation passed by Congress in 1965, the experience gained in the early and middle 1960's can be expected to influence our objectives in redevelopment for the next decade.

Approximately 1,000 counties have been listed as redevelopment areas. This is about a third of all U.S. counties. At the end of 1962, they included 17 per cent of the civilian labor force. However, the redevelopment areas accounted for 27.5 per cent of the nation's unemployed.[2] In addition, all Indian reservations and parts of U.S. overseas possessions have been declared eligible for redevelopment assistance.

The criterion for designation as a redevelopment area is the presence of substantial and persistent unemployment or underemployment. For urban areas, this means an unemployment rate averaging 6 per cent or more in the year preceding listing; and at least 50 per cent higher than the national average for three of the preceding four years. Since economic decline in rural areas shows up in low income and underemployment, these factors, among others, are taken into account in place of unemployment rates in designating rural counties as redevelopment areas.

Redevelopment assistance is essentially seed money. It is available in the form of public loans for private industrial and commercial projects, and in loans and grants for public facilities. A striking feature of the program is the premium placed on local initiative and community participation. Before an application for a loan or grant is considered, the community applying must organize a local committee to draw up an "Overall Economic Development Program"— a balance sheet of the community's assets and liabilities which also maps out a plan of action for redeveloping the community.

ARA loans for industrial and commercial projects may run as high as 65 per cent of the cost of site acquisition, factory construction costs, and the cost of machinery and equipment. Amortization periods typically run for 25 years and the usual interest charge has been 4 per cent. Investment in motels and hotels has been the largest single outlet for the commercial loans in the first two years of the program. The

---

2. "Economic Growth in American Communities," *Annual Report,* Area Redevelopment Administration, 1963, p. 5.

greatest number of loans has been in the lumber and wood products industry, while the greatest number of jobs have been created in food processing.

Most of the grants and loans for public projects have been used to develop basic utilities and transport facilities to attract new industries. They include improvement in water systems, access roads, railroad spurs, or airport and harbor facilities. These projects are frequently undertaken in connection with the establishment of an industrial park. Other public projects involve developing local recreational and tourist attractions or research centers. A wood use demonstration center in Harlem, Kentucky has been constructed with ARA assistance, and a marine science research center at Yaquina Bay, Oregon. In addition to the public redevelopment projects, ARA also administers the Accelerated Public Works Program intended to create temporary jobs for the unemployed.[3]

Aside from supplying funds, ARA offers technical assistance to remove the technical knowledge gaps which often block local economic growth. Marketing and resource surveys, site planning for new plants, or feasibility studies for new products are frequently a preliminary to determining the types of projects with good prospects for success. In addition, ARA sponsors "Operation Second Chance"—a retraining program for unemployed workers in depressed areas.

Redevelopment expenditures authorized by ARA in its first two years of operations are summarized in Table 17–2. The table also lists an estimate of the private, state, and local government contributions to these projects.

Approved ARA loans and grants in fiscal 1962–63 were $130 million. Including the private and public expenditures from other sources, total investment associated with the re-

---

3. By the end of 1964, the total Federal expenditures obligated under the Accelerated Public Works Program amounted to almost $850 million, or about triple the corresponding amount for area redevelopment. *Manpower Report of the President,* 1965, p. 173.

Table 17–2
ARA Expenditures Authorizations and Other Expenditures Associated with ARA Projects, May 1, 1961 to December 31, 1963* (in millions of 1962 dollars)

Item	Amount
1. ARA Loans for Industrial and Commercial Facilities	$111
2. ARA Loans and Grants for Public Facilities	82
3. Technical Assistance Aid	8
4. Retraining Program	14
5. Total ARA Expenditures	215
6. Private and State-Local Public Investment in ARA Projects[a]	400
7. Total Public and Private Expenditures for Area Redevelopment	615

a. Estimate.
* Source for items 1-4, Levitan, p. 255.

development projects in that year is estimated at $350 million.

The ARA has stated that its financial assistance through the end of 1963 had directly created 60,000 jobs.[4] Some additional employment is expected to be indirectly created in the firms supplying or servicing the new facilities. If every 100 jobs created by ARA projects prompted the addition of 33 other jobs, the total number of jobs created by redevelopment would be approximately 80,000. On an annual basis, and allowing for the initial delay in implementing a new program, the additional jobs attributable directly or indirectly to area redevelopment activities average 40,000 a year.

III.

Experience with the ARA program is the basis for our standard in area redevelopment. The ARA experience also suggests possibilities for more far-reaching objectives; i.e., regional development.

4. Form ARA-55, ARA Approved Projects, December 31, 1963.

Area redevelopment is a program with a limited purpose. Its objective is to reduce unemployment in the depressed areas to approximately the national rate and to overcome underemployment in rural areas. ARA has estimated that in 1962 it would have been necessary to create an additional 600,000 jobs in the depressed areas to achieve this objective.[5] At the economy-wide unemployment rate of 5.6 per cent of the labor force in that year, some 650,000 persons would still have remained unemployed in these areas after reducing their unemployment to national levels. This suggests that meaningful area redevelopment must be accompanied by programs for maintaining a low level of unemployment in the economy generally.

We do not know which areas will be depressed a decade from now or by how much their loss in employment opportunities will slow down or accelerate. Technological changes or regional shifts in the location of industry will probably help restore the economies of some areas now on the redevelopment list. The Interstate Commerce Commission reported in 1962, for example, that two private firms were planning to build a $100-million pipeline to transport coal from West Virginia to the East Coast.[6] New candidates for redevelopment assistance may spring up in areas where tobacco is grown or manufactured or in centers of aircraft or armaments production. Similarly, the rate at which young people leave the depressed areas could change sharply depending on the pull of economic opportunities elsewhere.

The magnitudes involved in restoring the redevelopment areas to the national level of prosperity can be assessed in terms of the cost of creating 100,000 additional jobs a year. Average investment per job varies widely from industry to industry, ranging, for manufacturing industries, from about $5,000 in the apparel industry to $100,000 in the petroleum

---

5. *Annual Report*, ARA, 1963, p. 1. Reducing unemployment in the depressed areas to the national rate would also reduce the national rate.

6. *Annual Report*, Interstate Commerce Commission, 1962, p. 123.

industry. Senator Paul H. Douglas has suggested that the average capital investment required to create an additional job in the private economy is about $15,000.[7] This sum allows for investment in working capital and inventories, along with outlays for plant, equipment, and site acquisition. The $15,000 figure is projected as the average cost of creating a new job in the redevelopment program in the next decade.

The private and public spending we are likely to need for creating the additional 100,000 jobs is estimated in Table 17–3 (see page 328). In addition to the job investment costs, the total includes $40 million for expanding the technical assistance program to encourage long-range redevelopment planning on an area and multi-county basis. The costs of the package show the impact of slow and rapid economic growth on the redevelopment program.

The 100,000-job package is estimated to cost $200 million more if the economy is growing slowly than in the more favorable environment of rapid growth. The difference is due to the greater impact of the redevelopment expenditures in indirectly creating other jobs in the more rapidly growing economy. This impact is represented by the job multiplier. The multiplier of 0.65 has been derived by ARA from estimates by the U.S. Chamber of Commerce.[8] The ability of local government and private individuals to participate in financing redevelopment can also be expected to increase with local and national prosperity.

The 100,000-job package supplies a basis for revising estimates of redevelopment expenditures upward or downward as the unemployment in the depressed areas expands or contracts. If the additional jobs needed to restore the redevelop-

---

7. Levitan, p. 101. This estimate was made in 1956. Since that time the capital investment per job has increased considerably. However, the $15,000 figure has not been revised because redevelopment loans would presumably emphasize projects requiring less capital per worker than the national average.

8. *Annual Report,* ARA, 1963, p. 5.

ment areas to the mainstream of national prosperity are at the same level in the early 1970's as in the past few years, creating 100,000 additional jobs each year should eliminate the excess unemployment and underemployment in about ten years. This allows for the initial level of unemployment and for a modest increase in the size of the labor force. The near-billion outlay projected as the annual cost of the job package, under conditions of favorable economic growth, therefore represents the cost of our standard for the area redevelopment goal in the next decade.

Continuing the present level of redevelopment expenditures in the 1970's would create less than half the 100,000 additional jobs a year listed for our standard. Allowing for

Table 17–3
Estimated Redevelopment Expenditures,
100,000 New Jobs Standard,
1970 and 1975
(in 1962 dollars)

Item	IN SLOW GROWTH ECONOMY 1970 and 1975[a]	IN RAPID GROWTH ECONOMY 1970 and 1975[b]
1. Jobs Created Directly in Redevelopment Projects	75,000	60,600
2. Job Multiplier	.33	.65
3. Jobs Created Indirectly Because of Redevelopment	25,000	39,400
4. Average Investment Per Job	$15,000	$15,000
5. Total Investment for Jobs Created Directly	$1,125,000,000	$909,000,000
6. ARA Investment Expenditures		
a. Per cent of total	50%	40%
b. Amount	$562,500,000	$364,000,000
7. Private and State-Local Government Investments in ARA Projects		
a. Per cent of total	50%	60%
b. Amount	$ 562,500,000	$545,000,000
8. Technical Assistance Aid	$ 40,000,000	$ 40,000,000
9. Total Redevelopment Expenditures	$1,165,000,000	$949,000,000

a. Assumes GNP growing at 2.8% annually.
b. Assumes GNP growing at 4.1% annually.

a modest increase in redevelopment expenditures because of anticipated labor force growth, extending the *status quo* to 1975, the basis for our hypothetical preempted benchmark, would involve an annual outlay of $400 million to $450 million.

IV.

It is apparent that the prospects for area redevelopment are more favorable and less costly if the economy is growing at a vigorous rate. It is also apparent that the redevelopment program is sufficiently new to be experimental and to merge readily with other programs for encouraging growth.

Single counties, the basic planning unit in the original redevelopment legislation, seldom constitute economic entities. An effective program for many of the depressed areas typically depends on the development of an adequate base of facilities and industries in the surrounding region. Resources could be used most effectively in many instances by encouraging the growth of a city which is itself not a depressed labor market, in order to create job opportunities for the inhabitants of nearby areas with heavy concentrations of unemployment. Recognizing that single counties "are often not capable of individual growth," President Johnson proposed in 1965 that redevelopment assistance in the future concentrate on multi-county projects.[9] To encourage this change in focus, the President recommended that special bonus grants and loans be made available to encourage the organization of multi-county economic development districts.

County and multi-county redevelopment is also likely to be joined with new programs for regional development. President Johnson, and President Kennedy before him, called for a broad rehabilitation program for one depressed region—Appalachia. Appalachia covers parts of the territory of ten states. The unemployment rate in the region

---

9. *The New York Times,* March 26, 1965.

varies from two to four times the national average. Two hundred and sixty of the 340 counties in Appalachia are depressed areas eligible for ARA assistance.[10] Other candidates for regional redevelopment include the Upper Michigan Peninsula and the Ozarks region. In addition, some southern states are still emerging from their earlier status as an underdeveloped enclave within the national economy.

The regional effort would be concerned with developing the infrastructure of facilities serving an entire region. Since firms are much more likely to move into an area possessing adequate transportation, pure and abundant water, and inexpensive power, provision of the facilities to encourage private investment is the basic ingredient in regional redevelopment. Of the $1.1-billion total authorized in the Appalachian Regional Development Act of 1965, $840 million would be authorized for highway construction over a five-year period. The remaining $250 million would be spent over two years for land improvement and erosion control, timber development, restoration of mining areas, construction of health facilities, and water resource surveys. Future possibilities in regional development could include region-wide power networks or river valley development, regional control of water pollution, or the establishment of major research centers serving a region.

Expenditures for the regional programs are expected to be more costly than those for area redevelopment in the same localities. Estimates of the cost of a ten-year program for Appalachia indicate expenditures in the neighborhood of $5 billion, or $500 million a year.[11] If the equivalent of two of the Appalachia programs can be taken to represent spending for regional development in the 1970's, total redevelopment spending in the next decade will range closer to $2

---

10. *Appalachia, A Report by the President's Appalachian Commission*, 1964, p. 54. Two hundred and fifty-four of these 260 counties were already participating in the ARA program according to the Commission's report.

11. Release, Office of the President, The White House, March 9, 1965.

billion a year than the billion dollars projected as the cost of the 100,000-job standard.

While the expenditure estimates for area and regional redevelopment refer largely to facilities and natural resources, large-scale expenditures to develop human resources are also an integral part of redevelopment. The areas lacking highway and power facilities are typically the areas with substandard school systems, inadequate health and social work services, and a labor force with obsolete job skills. Since expenditures for human resources development are discussed in detail in connection with other goals, they are not estimated separately for the depressed areas.[12]

Measured by the yardstick of GNP, the expenditures projected for area redevelopment are small. The cost of our standard for the redevelopment goal in 1975 is a fraction of 1 per cent of the anticipated GNP. These expenditures are significant because of their objective, and as a symptom of an emerging national consensus. The core of this consensus is a conviction that the concentrations of poverty and unemployment in the United States can be substantially reduced, or largely eliminated, by private and public planning in the coming decade.

---

12. For a discussion of the estimates for these other goals see Chapters 5, 6, 7, and 16.

Double
Counting
and
Transfers

The gross expenditures listed for the individual goals in 1970 and 1975 overstate their total cost because they include elements of double counting and items representing transfer payments and transfers of assets. To arrive at an estimate of the net cost of the goals expressed in terms of the national income and product accounts, it is necessary first to eliminate the double counting and the transfers from the projections.

Double counting and transfers are present in the gross totals for the following reasons:

1. Part of the costs of some goals are also included as part of the cost of other goals.
2. Part of the expenditures for some goals are made up of spending for intermediate products whose value is included in the value of end products reckoned in the cost of other goals.
3. The costs of some goals, e.g., social welfare, include transfer payments which add to spending for other goals, e.g., consumer expenditures.
4. The expenditures for the purchase of land in some goals constitute a transfer of assets rather than the purchase of current output.

The $85 billion projected as the cost of the health goal in 1975, for example, includes over $55 billion of personal consumption expenditures for health and medical care. The R & D conducted by private firms, which is financed from company funds rather than by Government contracts, makes up more than one fifth of the $39-billion total projected as the cost of the R & D goal in 1975. This R & D is treated as an intermediate product in the national income accounts. It would presumably be counted twice if both the company-financed R & D and the cost of the output of the firms conducting the R & D were included in the estimates for the goals. The $92 billion listed for the social welfare goal includes transfer payments from Government to private individuals amounting to $75 billion. While these transfers do not represent income payments for participating in current production, they add to personal income and, accordingly, to the spending for goods and services in the consumer expenditures goal. The purchases of land for parks and recreational areas in the natural resources goal are also eliminated, although no double counting is present. Expenditures for the purchase of land are not considered as contributing to GNP since they do not represent payments for the purchase of current output. However, spending for improvements to land is included in the expenditures for current output.

The gross expenditures for several goals were arrived at by transferring expenditures included in the estimates for other goals. For example, the public research and development expenditures for the goals in agriculture, defense, health, natural resources, space, and transportation were transferred to the R & D goal, and they became part of the expenditure estimates for the R & D goal. These transfers represent double counting and they are eliminated in the goal from which they have been transferred in preparing the net cost estimates.

In eliminating the double counting created by overlapping items included in more than one goal, it is necessary to recognize the implicit element in much of this duplication. This is illustrated by the personal consumption expenditures for health and medical care. These expenditures are included in both the health and the consumer expenditures goals. In adjusting the estimates for the consumer expenditures goal to take account of the $55 billion estimate of personal consumption expenditures for health and medical care included in the health goal, it is necessary to reduce the $55 billion by the personal consumption expenditures for health and medical care which are already implicitly present in the projections for the consumer expenditures goal. In 1962, consumer spending for health and medical care amounted to 6.2 per cent of all consumer expenditures. Aside from the consequences of pursuing the health goal, changes in the distribution of consumer spending over the next decade are expected to increase this percentage to 6.65 per cent, or to $40 billion, in 1975. This amount of spending for health and medical care is, therefore, implicitly present in the expenditures for the consumer expenditures goal in 1975. The overlapping expenditures, which are not implicitly present in the estimate for the consumer expenditures goal, are the difference between the $40 billion and the $55 billion projection of personal consumption expenditures in the health goal, or $15 billion. Accordingly, $15 billion is added to the consumer expenditures goal in eliminating the overlap between the two goals. The entire $55 billion is subtracted from the health goal.

The methods used to eliminate the double counting can be illustrated by the expenditures for the health goal in 1975. They are described in Table A–1.

After elimination of the double counting and the transfers, the sixteen goals lose their separate identities. They become parts of the four sectors of the national income accounts. The spending listed for the consumer expenditures goal, including the amounts added from other goals, becomes the personal consumption sector. Expenditures for the private plant and equipment goal, and private spending for residential construction and additions and alterations in the housing goal, together with an allowance for changes in business inventories of slightly less than 1 per cent of GNP, become the gross private domestic investment sector. The net exports sector is derived from estimates in NPA's *National Economic Projections to 1974*. These estimates have been adjusted to take into account the effects of expenditures in the international aid and transportation goals on gross exports. The Government sector includes all public expenditures for goods and services remaining in the net cost estimates for the individual goals, plus an allowance for Government functions, e.g., police and fire protection, which do not figure in any of the goals. The amounts estimated are derived from the 1962 and 1963 expenditures for these functions. All told, the allowance for 1975 amounts to 14 per cent of total Government purchases in the hypothetical GNP corresponding to full realization of the goals.

· The sectoral distribution of the hypothetical GNP which would correspond to full achievement of the goals in 1975 is described in Table A–2, together with the actual distribution of GNP in 1962.

The distribution of the hypothetical 1975 GNP between

public and private sectors of the economy is primarily an extrapolation of the present distribution of public and private purchases of goods and services in each of the areas designated as goals. It does not represent a judgment concerning the most desirable, or the most efficient, distribution,

Table A–1
Derivation of the Net Expenditures
for the Health Goal, 1975
(in millions of 1962 dollars)

Item	1975 Estimate	Disposition
1. Gross Expenditures	$85,400	Divided into overlapping expenditures and net expenditures for health.
2. Overlaps with other goals	62,700	Subtracted from health goal total. Added to other goals which include health expenditures if these expenditures are not already present in the costs listed for these goals.
a. Personal consumption expenditures for health and medical care	55,600	$40,400 implicitly included in consumer expenditures projection. Remaining $15,200 added to total for consumer expenditures goal.
b. Research and development	4,300 [a]	Included in preparing estimates for R & D goal.
c. Private medical facilities construction	2,800	Included in preparing estimates for private plant and equipment goal.
3. Net Expenditures for Health Goal	22,700	Added to Government sector of national income accounts.
a. Public expenditures for health and medical services	16,600	
b. Public medical facilities construction	4,800	
c. Other public expenditures	1,300 [b]	

a. These represent expenditures for R & D originating in Government, private firms, universities, and non-profit research organizations. The Government expenditures for health R & D are transferred and added to the estimates for the R & D goal. The R & D expenditures by universities, non-profit research organizations, and firms are already implicitly included in the projections for the R & D goal.

b. The "other" item is largely made up of medical benefits under workmen's compensation and temporary disability insurance.

Table A–2
Distribution of GNP by Sector, 1962 GNP,
and Projected Hypothetical GNP for Goals, 1975
(in billions of 1962 dollars)

Sector	1962 Purchases of Goods and Services	Per Cent of Total	PROJECTED 1975 Purchases of Goods and Services	Per Cent of Total
1. Personal Consumption	$356.8	64.1%	$659.6	58.6%
2. Gross Private Domestic Investment	79.1	14.2	205.2	18.2
3. Net Exports	4.0	0.7	7.8	0.7
4. Government	116.3	20.9	253.9	22.5
5. Total (GNP)	556.2	100.0	1,126.5	100.0

since alternative public-private combinations are frequently possible, and the optimum combination is itself an important subject for research. The growth in the percentage of the total represented by public expenditures is largely due to the substantial increases in spending projected for several goals for which public expenditures are the predominant element, e.g., education. The larger Government expenditures for medical research and construction of medical facilities in the health goal also figures in this growth.

The utilization of the nation's resources to produce goods and services can be classified in various ways. The national income and product accounting system is the most widely used and the most extensively developed. In this context, it indicates the income originating in each industry in utilizing resources to produce the economy's current output; and, furthermore, it distributes this output by end-use categories. The input-output matrix developed by the U.S. Department of Commerce constitutes a more detailed classification of the nation's use of resources in terms of interindustry transactions.[1] It includes, correspondingly, a more detailed list of the industrial origin of the end-use categories.

1. See Goldman, Marimont, and Vaccara, "The Interindustry Structure of the United States," *Survey of Current Business*, November, 1964.

The goals approach offers the possibility for an additional point of departure which classifies the nation's use of resources in terms of the economic, political, and social purposes for which the resources are used. This approach is still in its infancy. However, all these approaches represent ways of investigating the utilization of resources which are consistent with one another.

Dollar
Cost
of Our
National
Goals

**Statement by the National Planning Association's
Committee on America's Goals and Resources**

This is the first study prepared by the NPA Center for
Priority Analysis and reviewed by the National Committee
on America's Goals and Resources. It is the purpose of the

Center to provide information for those who wish or have to take a position with respect to American goals and priorities among them. Goals are understood here in their broad definition which includes objectives pursued both by public and private endeavor. However, they are dealt with in a narrower sense. The great intangible goals and values are always kept in mind but are not analyzed in full in these studies. Instead, the studies are directly concerned with those aspects of the goals which make a claim on the productive use of resources.

Our study of national goals takes it for granted that there is a general consensus in the United States concerning major national objectives in health, education, social welfare, standards of living, development of resources, urban renewal and rapid transit, space exploration, and so on. Within this consensus there are considerable differences of opinion regarding the speed with which particular goals should be achieved, the programs for achieving them, or the priority to be given some goals in relation to others.

The present first study was designed to estimate the costs in dollar terms of the various national goals in the next decade. For the list of goals to be studied, the report of President Eisenhower's Commission on National Goals was taken as a point of departure. Goals had to be translated into quantifiable targets—specifying what is to be accomplished within a given period.

Many groups and agencies, public and private, are concerned with particular individual goals. Teachers' associations publicize needs in education; the Department of Health, Education, and Welfare estimates the cost of our objectives in health; the Corps of Engineers makes cost-benefit analyses of proposed public construction projects. The NPA project is designed to add perspective on our goals as a system of competing, and sometimes supporting claims on resources.

For each goal two estimates were prepared of the costs involved. The first merely takes account of the rise in population and other demographic factors, assuming no improvement in the services. Thus, outlays would remain constant, for instance, in education per pupil or in health per capita of population. Second, alternative estimates were prepared for our "aspiration goals" which allow for an improvement in the quality and costs of performance, based on recommendations made by experts about desirable standards for each of the goals. For both sets of estimates the total costs for the various goals were then added up, making allowance for some double counting which results, for example, from the fact that consumer expenditures include personal outlays for medical services and education which are also included in estimates for the goals of health and education.

Adding up only the increased outlays required for an expanded population, we obtain a total substantially below what the American economy, assuming a reasonable rate of economic growth, can achieve. Thus, there is no question that in addition to taking care of a growing population we can afford to make improvements in our performance related both to international and national objectives.

However, if we should attempt to accomplish within a decade or so even the aspiration goals presently conceived—all the desired improvements for all our goals—the claims on resources would substantially exceed the resources likely to become available during this period. The present study comes to the conclusion that it would be possible to achieve these aspiration goals only if our potential and actual production of goods and services grew more than 5.5 per cent per year steadily over a 10-year period. In our opinion it is not feasible to attain a steady rate of growth of that dimension. It would require forced draft growth and imply controls in peacetime which would violate traditional freedom of action, one of our intangible goals.* Assuming a 4-per cent

---

* *David Riesman:* Indicative planning such as the French appear to have used and which exists in the United States in inchoate and informal fashion in certain areas, may indeed violate our traditional ideology of freedom of action (but less our practice). It may be necessary to work along this line in

average rate of growth over the decade, which is believed compatible with our economic and social institutions, it would appear that full pursuit of all goals would imply a claim in excess of our resources as high as $150 billion, or about 15 per cent of available resources.

At a time when many people are worried about what to do with our productive resources in a "society of abundance," this is a significant conclusion.

The members of the Committee have reviewed the assumptions made for each goal. They found that the standards of accomplishment set for each goal reflect what most Americans probably would recognize as desirable objectives. Also, the assumed increase in the availability of resources appears plausible. Therefore, the Committee accepts the broad conclusions of the study, although not every member necessarily subscribes to all aspects of the report.

This study should be regarded, however, as only a first step in a series of studies. Estimates of the dollar costs of national objectives in areas such as health or education or transportation tell us very little about their feasibility. If we attempted to pursue all the goals simultaneously, in all probability bottlenecks would occur in specific resources, such as highly trained manpower, long before many other resources had been fully utilized. Therefore, a study has already been initiated which will translate the dollar estimates into manpower requirements. Also, bottlenecks with respect to other resources—e.g., water—may arise and require remedial action.

The value of this summary report lies in the overviews, with perception of the inner workings, of what we now choose to call the American Enterprise. By analyzing the total system in terms of the increments of gross national product, we not only ascribe greater significance to this index of our national

---

order to minimize unemployment, to provide for the inevitable growth of our ambitions for ourselves, and to rechannel resources from defense into other public areas.

economic well-being, but, for the first time, challenge our ability to synthesize a meaningful picture or model of what the politician is fond of describing as the American Way of Life.

While the primary purpose of this compendium is to afford the decision maker, both public and private, with the perspective and with basic information necessary for setting up a schedule of expenditures according to ascribed priority values, the potentials, when implemented by further studies, go beyond this limited objective. The gross national product becomes a device for budgeting our goals in terms of total resources. It suggests the feasibility of analyzing the interactions involved in the pursuit of several goals by techniques which have proved of inestimable value in the study of complex systems. Operations research and its translation into a dynamic plan through systems engineering, as now applied to military and corporate operations, are proven tools. The kind of information out of which such studies are evolved is presented, though only in an initial stage, in the "costing" of the American goals.

The fact that the costs of goals exceed the available resources leads to an important general conclusion, namely, that in any specific period of time not all goals can be pursued to the same full extent. This means that choices—priority decisions—have to be made. In our pluralistic society these priority decisions are being made by a large number of individuals and organizations within and without the Government. No central agency and no research effort can make these decisions for the people. However, in order to make a prudent decision or to take a meaningful position we need some guidelines spelling out what our objectives are likely to cost, and we need more information on how the pursuit of one goal supports other goals or competes for the same kind of resources with other goals. We need information on the extent to which pursuit of goals only absorbs resources or also adds to their development. We need more knowledge about the kind of information needed for the decision makers, and we need more detailed analysis on the goals and their interrelationship.

The present study is only the first, but significant, step in the direction of providing needed information. It does not yet permit conclusions about desirable priority packages; that is, combinations of goals which are in balance with available resources and internally consistent. The value of the study lies in the fact that it undertakes a bold foray into an uncharted land. We recommend the publication of the study and trust it will stimulate a wide debate which should be of value in the guidance of the subsequent steps in priority analysis.

MEMBERS OF THE COMMITTEE
SIGNING THE STATEMENT

Chairman
EARL P. STEVENSON
Consultant,
Arthur D. Little, Inc.

Members
FRANK ALTSCHUL
Director, General American
Investors Company

J. A. BEIRNE
President, Communications
Workers of America, AFL-CIO

GILBERT H. CLEE
Director, McKinsey and Company

ABRAM T. COLLIER
Senior Vice President and
General Counsel, John Hancock
Mutual Life Insurance Company

JOSEPH L. FISHER
President, Resources for
the Future

ERWIN N. GRISWOLD
Dean, Harvard University
Law School

LUTHER H. GULICK
Chairman of the Board,
The Institute of Public
Administration

LELAND HAZARD
Director-Consultant, Pittsburgh
Plate Glass Company

HARLOW J. HENEMAN
General Partner, Cresap,
McCormick and Paget

CHRISTIAN A. HERTER
The Special Representative
for Trade Negotiations

KENNETT W. HINKS
Ivy, Virginia

HUDSON HOAGLAND
Executive Director, Worcester
Foundation for Experimental
Biology

HOWARD E. ISHAM
Boca Raton, Florida

JOHN A. JOHNSON
Vice President, International
Communications Satellite
Corporation

J. E. JONSSON
Chairman, Texas Instruments
Incorporated

JOSEPH D. KEENAN
International Secretary,
International Brotherhood of
Electrical Workers, AFL-CIO

MERVIN J. KELLY
Short Hills, New Jersey

MAX F. MILLIKAN
Center for International Studies,
Massachusetts Institute of
Technology

ARTHUR H. PHILLIPS
General Counsel,
Cabot Corporation

* DAVID RIESMAN
Harvard University

ELMO ROPER
Elmo Roper and Associates

GLENN T. SEABORG
Chairman, Atomic Energy
Commission

---

* See footnote to Statement.

STUART F. SILLOWAY
President, Investors
Diversified Services, Inc.

SHERROD E. SKINNER
Detroit, Michigan

H. CHRISTIAN SONNE
New York, New York

LAUREN K. SOTH
Editor of the Editorial Pages,
Des Moines Register and Tribune

R. B. STEINMETZ
President, Anaconda Wire and
Cable Company

JAMES A. SUFFRIDGE
International President,
Retail Clerks International
Association, AFL-CIO

GEORGE W. TAYLOR
Wharton School of
Finance and Commerce,
University of Pennsylvania

ARNOLD S. ZANDER
International President Emeritus,
American Federation of State,
County, and Municipal
Employees, AFL-CIO

Index

Employment Service, U.S., 294, 312
(see also Manpower Development and Training Act)
Europe (see also Marshall Plan, International aid)
manpower skills in and economic
aid to, 252
Europe, communist, 188–89
Exports, U.S., 253, 265 (see also International aid)
agricultural, 267, 287, 289, 292–94

Family allowance program; see So-
cial welfare goal
Federal Aviation Agency, 166–67,
167n, 172, 172n
Federal Council for Science and
Technology, 34, 239–41
Federal government expenditures, 23
Fein, Rashi, vi
Feldman, J., 130, 130n
Fiscal and monetary policy, 6–11, 73,
310
goals, national, and, 342, 342n, 343
inflation and, 66, 133
interest rates and, 67
mortgage credit and insurance and,
136, 203–204, 211
Fischman, Leonard L., vi, 163n,
237n, 241n, 245n
Fisher, Joseph L., 163n, 237n, 241n,
245n, 346
Food deficit, world, 300
Food for Peace; see Agriculture, In-
ternational aid
Ford, Henry, 54
Ford Foundation, 223
Forest Science, 305n
Forgash, M., 172, 172n
Fortune Magazine, 283n
Fort Worth, Texas, 29, 87
Fox, K. A., 289n, 303n
France, 181–82, 342n

Galbraith, J. K., 70, 70n
Galton, L., 242n
Geiger, T., 19n, 208n
General Telephone and Electronics

Corporation, COMSAT and, 283
Geneva Disarmament Conference,
1962, 189, 283
Germany, 52, 108
Gillogly, David K., vi
Gilpatric, Roswell, 274–75, 275n
Goldman, M. R., 338n
Gordon, M. S., 108n, 109n
Graduate Research Center of the
Southwest, the, 227–28, 277
Great Britain, 46, 177, 181–82
Greece, 254, 263
Grier, Eunice and George, 91n
Griswold, Erwin N., 346
"Gross Domestic Product," 261, 261n
Gross National Product (GNP), U.S.;
(see also Economic growth)
actual, 20–21, 27t, 32, 50
distribution of, by sector, 20, 336–
38, 338t
growth rate, 6–12, 27, 27n, 28, 28n,
29, 40, 41t, 43, 50–51, 80, 101,
143, 216, 309
projected growth rates, 19, 69t, 72,
74, 76t, 78, 120, 122, 209, 211–12,
239, 242–43, 328t
land acquisition and, 334–35
projected deficit for full realization
of goals, 18–19, 21, 42, 43t, 44–
45, 50
projected disposable GNP, 41, 42t,
44
projected expenditures for family
allowances and, 65t
projected expenditures for residential construction and, 211–12,
212t
projected GNP, 27, 27t, 28, 30, 32–
33, 40–41, 57, 80, 239
projected increase in, 40–41, 41t,
44, 44n
GNP and national goals, actual and
projected expenditures as per
cent of
agriculture, 303–304, 304t
area redevelopment, 331
consumer expenditures, 69t
defense, national, 199, 199t, 200,
200t, 201